DIFFERENTIAL STRUCTURE AND AGRICULTURE: ESSAYS ON DUALISTIC GROWTH

To Professor Rosovsky

謹呈

大川一司

DIFFERENTIAL STRUCTURE AND AGRICULTURE: ESSAYS ON DUALISTIC GROWTH

BY

KAZUSHI OHKAWA

ECONOMIC RESEARCH SERIES
NO. 13
THE INSTITUTE OF ECONOMIC RESEARCH
HITOTSUBASHI UNIVERSITY

KINOKUNIYA BOOKSTORE CO., LTD.
Tokyo, Japan

Printed by
Kato Bummeisha Printing Co., Ltd.
Tokyo, Japan

PREFACE

Out of the papers and notes written over the last sixteen years, those dealing with "dualistic growth" (itself discussed in the Introduction) are selected for this volume. Since they were originally published in a wide variety of journals and books, and five only in Japanese, their publication in this volume will make them more accessible and useful particularly for foreign readers. Most of them are by-products of a quantitative analysis of the modern economic growth of Japan and not necessarily based on adequately organized empirical evidence; rather they are essays on selected themes. Some, if not much, duplication is unavoidable; in retrospect, the direction of thought can be seen to shift between certain papers. Hopefully, the reader will not be troubled unduly.

The term "differential structure" was first used in a paper written in 1959 (contained in Part I), translated from the original "Keisha kōzō" which had been defined and developed in previous articles in Japanese. This usage was concerned with a static aspect of the problem. Later, in collaboration with Professor Henry Rosovsky, Harvard University, the same term has been used, referring to the historical and dynamic aspect of the problem.[1] Most of the essays of Part I, however, contain a little about the dynamic aspect of this notion.

The problem of growth phases is dealt with from the specific aspect of labor supplies particularly in the essays contained in Part II, but no attempt is made to develop a comprehensive analysis of growth phases in any of the essays.

Agriculture is representative of the traditional sector, and most of the essays contained in Parts III and IV deal with the problem of agriculture in relation to the dualistic growth of the Japanese economy. However, no paper gives an overall description of the historical process of agricultral development of Japan in this volume.[2] Some of them discuss agricultural problem in Asian perspective, but no attempt is made to develop a general theory of agricultural development in any of the essays.[3]

Only stylistic changes have been made in some of the papers originally published in English, but revisions are made in others as noted in the footnotes to the papers. In making an English version of the papers originally written in Japanese, revisions, additions and ommisions are made in consideration of foreign readers. In so doing, I am indebted much to the valuable comments made by Professor E. Sidney Crawcour, the Australian National University and Professor Bernard Key, University of Western Australia.

Most of the researches underlying these papers and notes were carried out at the Institute of Economic Research, Hitotsubashi University, from which I am going to retire. I am most grateful

[1] K. Ohkawa and H. Rosovsky, "Postwar Japanese Growth in Historical Perspective: A Second Look" in L. Klein and K. Ohkawa eds., *Economic Growth: The Japanese Experience Since the Meiji Era*, The Economic Growth Center, Yale University, 1968.

[2] See K. Ohkawa, "Phases of Agricultural Development and Economic Growth" in K. Ohkawa, B.F. Johnston, and H. Kaneda eds., *Agriculture and Economic Growth: Japan's Experience*, University of Tokyo Press and Princeton University Press, 1969.

[3] See Yujiro Hayami and Vernon W. Ruttan, *Agricultural Development: An International Perspective*, The Johns Hopkins Press, 1971.

to the collaboration and assistance which all the members of the Institute have rendered me. Lastly, thanks are due to various publishers, as noted in the footnotes to each essay, for permission to reprint the various works here.

Tokyo,
March 1972

Kazushi Ohkawa

CONTENTS

CONTENTS

CONTENTS

INTRODUCTION:

DUALISTIC GROWTH AND

ECONOMIC BACKWARDNESS

Historical Setting

In studying Japan's experience since the Meiji Restoration of 1868, I have followed the concept *Modern Economic Growth*, built by Simon Kuznets. In so doing, I have stressed the particular importance of structural changes from both analytical and historical points of view.[1]

The purpose of this article is to make a further step towards understanding the process of modern economic growth as a problem of growth with dualistic structure. Dualistic structure is here a historical concept. I would like to propose a notion *dualistic growth* in this sense. The conventional use of the term dual structure or dualism refers to co-existence of modern and traditional enterprises and does not rightly raise the problem of the historical process of structural change without which modern economic growth cannot take place.

[1] K. Ohkawa, *Nihon keizai bunseki—Seichō to kōzo* (Analysis of Japanese Economy—Growth and Structure), Shunjū sha, Tokyo, 1962. K. Ohkawa and H. Rosovsky, "A Century of Japanese Economic Growth" in *The State and Economic Enterprise in Japan*, edited by W.W. Lockwood, Princeton University Press, 1965.

An English version, with revisions, of the first part of "Kindai keizai seichō to kōzōhenka", Ikkyō Ronsō *Vol.* 55, *No.* 1, *January* 1966 (*pp.* 36–52).

Let us begin with a widely-recognized proposition that the pattern of modern economic growth is strongly influenced by the historical heritage which each country had from the pre-modern epoch at the initial stage and hence it differs from one country to another. While recognizing this, it is of course possible to stress the importance of common factors which can be seen through the experience of various countries. In the light of Japanese experience, however, an over-generalization particularly based on the Western experience, in my view, may not be fruitful. What we learn from the historical heritage is the basic fact that modern economic growth was accompanied by strong persistence of pre-modern or traditional elements. The mechanism of growth seems to be best understood through recognizing interactions between the modern elements and tradional elements in the process of which the former came to predominate over the latter. In this sense, modern economic growth is not a single, homogeneous process but a process of changes in dualistic structure. Such a historical process I would like to call *dualistic growth*.

What is the modern element? What is the traditional element? Without answering these questions, the notion of dualistic growth cannot be substantiated. This is too big a problem to be discussed fully here and we have to confine ourselves to the aspects which are relevant to our present discussion.

A rapid rise of GNP; high rates of population growth accompanied by a sustained rise in real income per capita; high rates of transformation of the industrial structure; and the presence of international contacts—all these phenomena distinguish modern economic growth from its predecessor. Among the basic factors which enable these phenomena to emerge, I would like to mention particularly two factors—the application of modern scientific thought and technology to various industries (following again S. Kuznets' criteria), and the social pattern of human behavior

2

and institution which makes it possible to carry out technological progress of the modern type. These can be called the modern elements. A slow rate of technological progress based on the accumulation of local human experience; the social pattern of human behavior and the type of institutions which correspond to it—these can be called the traditional elements.

Even for such a simplified proposition, two comments are needed. First, the modern elements thus defined can be applied in general both for capitalistic and socialistic development. In particular, for Japan's case it is applied to the capitalistic development since the Meiji Restoration. Second, the premodern elements do not necessarily mean merely the so-called "feudalistc" ones but pertain to all the initial conditions given to the society at the time of inaugurating modern economic growth.

The relation between the modern and traditional elements manifests itself in the process of implementing technological progress through making various combinations of capital and labor. Concerning the capital, the pattern of searching for profits and concerning the labor, the pattern of supplying labor input—these two constitute the core of the problem in the case of capitalistic development. Depending upon the various relationships which may take place between the two, both the speed and type of technological progress will be determined. On the other hand, possibilities of applying scientific knowledge will affect the relation between capital and labor. Thus we have a complex mechanism, which also pertains to changes in the institutional setting. The total mechanism of modern growth in this sense is of course beyond our interpretation and what we are concerned with here is the role played in it by the traditional elements. Given the initial conditions and a self-sustaining process of growth of the modern elements, the traditional elements would necessarily go through a process of dissolving overtime. However, the two cannot be mechanically divided.

Rather, the interaction between the two deserves particular attention.

The process of growth of the modern elements manifests itself in the size and speed of capital accumulation, which is in turn influenced by the role played by the traditional elements. The traditional elements do not disappear abruptly immediately after the inauguration of modern economic growth. Instead, they will continue to exist and even expand during modern economic growth in response to its impact. Only after a long historical process of capitalistic development will the traditional elements virtually disappear. Therefore, it is important to raise the question of the function to be performed by traditional technology and human behavior during the process of modern economic growth.

The idea came from observing the Japanese experience and at present I have no intention to apply this thesis of dualistic growth to other countries. This does not imply, however, that Japan's case is special or that dualistic growth is peculiar to Japan. A similar pattern will take place in a weaker or stronger form in any other country if the given conditions are similar.[2]

In this respect, two points are relevant to our thesis; one is economic backwardness and the other Asian elements. To begin with the former, my proposition is that other things being equal the later the time of inaugurating modern economic growth the stronger the characteristics of dualistic growth will be. Economic backwardness will intensify the problems associated with the gap between the newly introduced modern industrial technologies and organizations on the one hand and traditional institutions and patterns of human behavior on the other. The thesis of borrowed technology is relevant here, but is interpreted in a

---

[2] In this respect it is interesting to see the East-European experience. N. Georgescu-Roegen, "Economic Theory and Agrarian Economics," in *Agriculture in Economic Development*, edited by C.K. Eicher and L.W. Witt, McGraw Hill, 1964.

broader sense than usual.[3] It goes without saying that the possibility of borrowing technologies from advanced countries is one of the essential factors for accelerating rate of growth of economically backward countries. In view of the prevalence of traditional elements, the modern technologies can be adopted in only a very limited portion of the economy at the initial phase and thus a differential rate of growth of productivity in the modern and traditional sectors will be an inevitable result for the subsequent years if remarkable improvements may not take place in the production of traditional sectors.

The other point which concerns the Asiatic elements is a controversial issue, which cannot be dealt with fully here. What is particularly relevant to the present discussion is the distinction which has often been made between Eastern and Western characteristics. It is generally recognized that Eastern society has historically developed production technologies and the social patterns of human behavior different from those of the West. Undoubtedly, the initial conditions given for the inauguration of modern economic growth must have been different. This is the more understandable in view of the limited contacts between East and West before modern economic growth started in the former. Particularly in Japan's case, the long seclusion policy of the Tokugawa Era contributed much to keep the traditional elements distinct.

On the other hand, modern economic growth first took place and spread in the West. Japan's case is its Asian offspring. The dualistic growth in Japan is thus coloured by a sharp contrast

---

[3] I follow the concept "Economic backwardness" coined by Gerschenkron. Alexander Gerschenkron, *Economic Backwardness in Historical Perspective*, Harvard University Press, 1962. However, this does not necessarily imply that the *specific type* of borrowed technology which seems to me to be crucial in the Gerschenkron model is applicable to Japan's case. See K. Ohkawa, Capital Formation in Japan—A review article of Henry Rosovsky, *Capital Formation in Japan*, 1868–1940, *Economic Development and Cultural Change*, Vol. XII, No. 1, October 1963.

between indigenous Japanese and Western elements. In this sense her dualistic growth appears in sharp relief presenting a variety of interesting problems to be analysed economically and socially.[4]

From the economic point of view, the most important Asiatic feature is high population density given as the initial condition of modern economic growth. This appears as a very unfavorable man-land ratio in the traditional agriculture of most, if not all, countries of Asia. This is a historical heritage from the pre-modern epoch and makes the initial conditions quite different from the Western experience. In this respect, Japan is not exceptional but rather a typical case of dualistic growth with a high population density.[5]

Analytical Problems

The dualistic growth defined and described in the preceding section is a historical concept. An attempt to articulate historical concepts and analytical tools of a theoretical nature appears to be one of the recent trends in the field of economics. This is a desirable but hard task. In most essays contained in this volume efforts are made in this direction. Here I would like to present an overall view of the crucial problems which may arise in the analysis of dualistic growth.

First, on the type of analytical approach I would say that a macro-model has very limited usefulness. A two-sector model

---

[4] Some of them have been investigated by us. See, H. Rosovsky and K. Ohkawa, The Indigenous Components in the Modern Japanese Economy, *Economic Development and Cultural Change*, Vol. IX, No. 3, April 1961.

[5] I am not referring to the rate of population growth during modern economic growth. Japan's experience is reminicent of the Western pattern and no peculiarity is found, broadly speaking, with respect to its pattern of population growth since the Meiji Restoration. The population explosion which took place in other Asian countries after World War II is aggravating the population pressure in these countries. This is a big problem but differs in nature from the present context.

at least is needed to grasp the mechanism of dualistic growth effectively. A simplification can be made by a dichotomy: the modern sector vs. the traditional sector. Actually, the modern and traditional elements which constitute different technologies, human behavior and institutional organization are intermingled in a complex manner, forming a wide range of intermediate combinations. Analytically, however, it seems unavoidable to make a simplification at the sacrifice of these realities in order to make an useful and convenient bridge between historical and analytical approaches.

For the process of capital accumulation in the modern sector the standard analytical tools can be applied in principle whereas for the traditional sector a special device will be needed to make an effective approach which allows traditional elements which may differ from one country to another. The place and function of landlordism and the pattern of agrarian structure are particularly important since agriculture is the major traditional sector. It seems difficult, however, to make a generalization in Asian perspective except for two basic features: a high population density and a production characterized by self-employment.

Modern economic growth as seen from the viewpoint of a two-sector model is a long process of expanding the modern sector and of contracting the traditional sector. It goes without saying that the growth pattern of the modern sector is a central problem of our analysis but this is not the sole problem for us. We have to deal also with the pattern of transformation of the traditional sector and the interrelated growth mechanism between the two sectors. The interrelated growth mechanism is a complex matter but it can be said to be composed of two elements: one is the influence which the growth pattern of the modern sector will exert on the pattern of transformation of the traditional sector; and the other the influence which the latter will exert on the former.

The relation between technological progress and wage performance is a central problem for economic growth in general and provides a simple illustration of the interrelated growth mechanism mentioned above. On the one hand, for a country of economic backwardness technology borrowed from advanced countries requires a high level of capital intensity. In such a country, on the other hand, the modern entrepreneurs can employ labor at a low wage rate which originates from the traditional sector where surplus labor exists. This leads to selecting of a technology of a low level of capital intensity. These two contradictory forces will operate in the course of dualistic growth: a contradiction between technological requirements and factor price inducements. Given a rate of capital accumulation, a higher capital intensity in the modern sector will absorb a smaller amount of labor from the traditional sector thus tending to accumulate more surplus labor, which in turn will retard the transformation of the traditional sector. Between the two sectors, the technological gap and hence the productivity gap will be widened as economic growth goes on. To the contrary, lower capital intensity in the modern sector has the favorable effect of absorbing more labor from the traditional to the modern sector and of inducing the transformation of the traditional sector. In this case, technological and productivity gap between the two sectors may be less wide. However, on the other hand, the modern sector will not cope with international competition because of its low technological level. Between these two patterns of growth, it seems to me, there may be no clear-cut *a priori* solution based on some kind of optimum conditions.[6]

I said before that dualistic growth must be a long process. Its historical length depends upon the initial conditions and the

---

[6] The so-called classical model of economic development assumes that a constant subsistence wage is given to the modern sector from the traditional sector. From our point of view, this is an extremely simplified version of dualistic growth. Its solution is simply a process of capital widening expansion in the modern sector.

subsequent pattern of growth and hence may differ from one country to another. Japan's experience tells us that it lasted almost a century. This experience deserves attention. For the purpose of the present discussion, the whole process can be demarcated by three growth phases, each of which has distinct characteristics. During the initial phase which lasted until the beginning of this century, the transformation of the traditional sector in terms of productivity growth, if not in production organization, proceeded considerably side by side with the inauguration of the modern sector. Technology borrowed from advanced countries was essential in developing the modern sector but the rates of technological progress and of productivity growth as between the two sectors were not greatly different. During the subsequent prewar period, however, continued growth of the modern sector and a retardation of the traditional sector took place. This is the second phase, the characteristics of which we called "differential structure". "The structural change which starts to affect the Japanese economy slightly in 1905 and powerfully since 1919 is a specific form of the general phenomenon of economic dualism which we call differential structure. To us, differential structure, besides the usual different levels of productivity and capital intensity in modern and traditional sectors, the rapid growth of modern sectors and the lagging growth of traditional sectors — in other words a *growing gap* in the structure of the economy."[7] To the socio-political as well as economic consequences of the differential structure particular attention has been drawn.

The third phase covers the postwar period after the economy had recovered from the war effects. The impact of the war was

[7] A citation from K. Ohkawa and H. Rosovsky, "A Century of Japanese Economic Growth" op. cit. (pp. 14–15) In this paper, the term "differential structure" was used in terms of a two-sector model: the modern and the traditional sector. In other papers contained in this book, this term is used in a somewhat different context but essentially, I believe, there seems to be no inconsistency.

so great that Japan's experience may not be taken as typical. But it stands out clearly that the traditional sector began to be dissolved during this phase. This does not necessarily imply, however, emergence of a new tendency of narrowing the gap of productivity growth between the two sectors, although the wage differentials, which characterized the second phase, tended to be narrowed between the two sectors. What form the remaining part of this phase will take in the future is yet to be seen.

The papers contained in this volume will deal with various aspects of these phases but I have still no comprehensive answer to the challenging problems of dualistic growth as a whole.

PART I

ECONOMIC GROWTH AND DIFFERENTIAL STRUCTURE

THE PATTERN
OF JAPANESE LONG-TERM
ECONOMIC GROWTH

Introduction[1]

The modern economic growth of Japan following the Meiji Restoration in 1868 began in a densely populated state with a peasant handicraft economy, at a time, when most of the present advanced countries already had modernized their economy to a considerable extent. These historical features of the initial condition, among other things, must undoubtedly lead to a particular pattern of economic growth differing from the Western type. For one thing, we can say that today Japan is the only highly industrialized economy which still embodies numerous economic activities in the sectors of the traditional type. The study of

---

[1] This paper was written while I was staying at the University of California, Berkeley. I would like to thank the Center for Japanese Studies for its generous hospitality. I have benefited a great deal in the various discussions I have had with Professor H. Rosovsky and would like to acknowledge my debt to him for many helpful suggestions.

Reprinted by permission of the International Association for Research in Income and Wealth, from V.K.R.V. Rao and K. Ohkawa eds., Asian Studies in Income and Wealth, *Asia Publishing House, Bombay, 1965 pp. 48–70. The paper was originally presented to the first Asian Conference on Income and Wealth, Hongkong, 1960. Since then the statistical data have been revised. They are, however, retained as they were. Where necessary, the implication of the revision will be noted as* **P.S.** *in the footnote.*

the Japanese growth pattern, therefore, will shed light on the problems of economic development of the present underdeveloped countries in the densely settled areas, particularly in Southeast Asia.

The pattern of economic growth can be approached in several ways, depending upon the specific aim one may have in mind. But in any case, it is desirable to define "pattern", as this term has often been loosely used. The purpose of this paper is to analyze the Japanese long-term growth process from the supply side, particularly from the viewpoint of the changes in labor-capital-output relationships in the light of technological development. It seems to me that the most crucial phase of a growth pattern can be defined as the structural changes in the factor combination in relation to output increases.

Recently considerable progress has been made in the historical macro-quantitative study of Japanese economic growth, although many unresolved points still remain. Also some relevant cross-section data have recently become available. These data are considered sufficiently reliable for the broad descriptive analysis that follows.[2]

By using a two-sector (agriculture and non-agriculture) approach, we will first try to clarify the long-term changes in the growth rate of output, breaking it down into the growth rates of two components— the output per labor force and the labor force. In this respect, particular attention will be directed to the

---

[2] Since the publication of *The Growth Rate of the Japanese Economy since 1878* by K. Ohkawa and others (Tokyo: Kinokuniya, 1957), we have been engaged in a research project to further explore basic data at the Institute of Economic Research, Hitotsubashi University. This research was supported by the Rockefeller Foundation. This project is still unfinished and much remains to be done before a comprehensive revision can be made of the old data through the entire long-term period after the Meiji Restoration up to the present. Therefore, in this paper the older series contained in the volume cited above were mainly used. Tentative result from this research, however, were taken into consideration as a means of checking the old data, and care was taken not to go beyond a broad interpretation.

non-agricultural sector, but we will principally use these two components as basic tools in order to clarify our problems.

Next, we will try to find certain relationships between the rate of increase in output per labor force and that of capital intensity for the non-agricultural sector. For a broad picture of the incremental changes in capital intensity, we will make use of the movements of the capital-output ratio. This will be done by observing identical relationships in the rates of increase of several terms, instead of by a functional approach. As is well known, within the framework of the macro-empirical approach it is very difficult, if not impossible, to use a certain type of production function with full confidence, particularly in the case of weak investment or capital data. As a rough substitute, I hope that these speculative observations will serve to clarify the broad outlines of the growth pattern.

Thirdly, in order to interpret the results of the above observations, certain specific relationships among output, labor, and capital will be introduced in the light of data obtained by cross-section surveys. To attain a consistent understanding of the growth patterns suggested by both the time series and cross-section data is our ultimate task, and this will be worked out for the long-term swings, including the Post-World War II period.

Over-all Pattern of Growth

It has often been suggested that the most outstanding feature of Japanese economic growth is its rapidity or what is even more important, the rapidity in the increase of per-capita national income.[3] It must be admitted that the reliability of international comparison of growth rates depends very much on the degree of

[3] In Japan this point was for the first time presented in "Nihon Keizai no Bunseki" (*The Analysis of the Japanese Economy*), Vol. I, edited by S. Tsuru and K. Ohkawa (Tokyo: Keiso Shobo, 1954).

data reliability in individual countries as well as on conceptual comparability, so that we should keep in mind the ranges of statistical errors and biases of various kinds. As far as the comparison of average growth rates in the long run is concerned, however, the risk may be minimal. Professor S. Kuznets' comprehensive research on the long-term rates of growth of many countries,[4] seems to confirm that the United States, Canada, Sweden and Japan were the most rapidly growing nations in terms of national product, and that, in terms of growth rates of per-capita national income, Sweden and Japan showed the most rapid growth in this group.

This raises a question. By what process has Japan sustained such a high rate of growth? The discussion that follows attempts to answer the question from the particular viewpoint mentioned above.

To begin with, let us observe the long-term movement of the growth rates of national product. As is shown in Table 1[5] ($\bar{G}$ in Column 1) and illustrated in Chart 1 (the aggregate), two and a

[4] Simon Kuznets, "Quantitative Aspects of the Economic Growth of Nations. 1. Levels and Variability of Rates of Growth." *Economic Development and Cultural Change*, Vol. V, No. 1, October 1956. He deals with the data from the later decades of the 19th century to the Post-World War II period.

[5] These data for both national income and labor force used in the Table are all taken from our volume cited above. The figures of both output and labor force for the non-agricultural sector were estimated tentatively as the weighted average of the figures for secondary and tertiary industries. (In this discussion agriculture includes foresty and fishery, and all the other activities are included in non-agriculture). The weights are, respectively, the income-percentage and the percentage of gainfully occupied population in each sector at the mid-period. The rate of increase in output per labor force (g) is estimated simply as G (the growth rate of output)—n (the growth of labor force).

The rate of investment was calculated from Professor H. Rosovsky's worksheets, the original data for which were mainly prepared in collaboration with Mr. K. Emi at the Institute of Economic Research, Hitotsubashi University. This does not include inventory changes. As for concept, scope and method of estimation, see Henry Rosovsky, "Japanese Capital Formation: The Role of the Public Sector," *The Journal of Economic History*, Vol. XXI, No. 3, September 1959. Because of lack of data, the rate of investment is calculated as gross investment/domestic net product and the marginal capital-output ratio is obtained by a simple procedure—investment rate/growth rate of output.

half long swings are discernible: the first from 1885 to 1905, the second from 1905 and the third seems to start from 1945. The trough in 1945 is of course caused by war damage, but the exact reason is not yet clear for the trough around 1905.[6] The procedure of computation was as follows: the averages of net national product in constant prices for 10 years, moving in overlapping five-years (1878–87, 1883–92,...) were first taken as the unit and then the annual compound rates of growth between these two successive units were calculated. The years in the chart represent the mid-point of each unit-period. To discuss the real long swings in the rate of growth in detail, more refined statistical techniques are necessary but even these rough figures may suffice for the present discussion, as our prime aim is not to deal with long swings as such.[7]* In the same Table (G_a, G_n in Columns 3

[6] To clarify this point a further analysis of the breakdown into major sectors is desirable. For example, from 1898–1902 to 1903–12 the retardation of domestic manufacture in terms of net output is particularly noticeable. It must be admitted that our estimate of the output for this sector is especially weak because we had to use indirect methods, but still the slow-down of the growth rate of domestic manufacture during this period seems to be a fact. In the factory production also, items such as "food, beverage" and "textiles" showed retardation from 1898–1902 to 1903–07, while "machinery and chemicals" had sustained a speedy growth. (See Part II, Secondary industry in our volume cited above).

[7] To discuss the problem of long swings more properly, the revision of the deflators, among other things, is particularly urgent. Our national income series were deflated by a wholesale price index because of lack of better deflators at that time. Generally speaking, real national income of this type tends to be undervalued in the boom period and over-valued in the depression period because the prices of consumer goods do not fluctuate as much as the wholesale prices. I made a tentative check on this point by using a new cost-of-living index recently constructed by Mr. S. Yamada and Miss Y. Ando. The result is more or less all right as far as our present discussion is concerned. It may be a problem to be examined further, however, whether there was another trough around 1930 before Japan entered into the war-time economy. In this paper, however, I would like to treat the inter-war period as one set without making a breakdown.

After completing my manuscript I learned that in Japan Prof. M. Shinohara has made a more elaborate study of the long swings in the Japanese economy. He used parts of the results of our project supported by the Rockefeller Foundation, as well as relevant time series other than national income, and found three long swings including the third trough around 1930 throughout the long growth process before World War II. I was pleased to know that his result seems to suggest no substantial differences with mine. As for the causes of the long swings, however, he believed and 4) and Chart 1, the shares in aggregate growth rates by both agriculture and non-agriculture are shown. The behavior of the share of the non-agricultural sector reveals swings similar to the aggregate, while that of agriculture suggests that its effect is minor on the aggregate output growth pattern except during the first swing when this sector played an influential part in the aggregate swing. Thus, the analysis that follows can concentrate mainly on the non-agricultural sector as changes in its growth rate can almost be taken to represent the aggregate pattern of growth.[8] Sectoral observation is too hazardous for the period after 1940 in the Chart, because of the discontinuity of the data.

The actual growth rate of output being composed of two parts—the growth rate of the employed labor force and that of output per employed labor force—the word "employed" will be omitted

that the effects of war and monetary contraction are most important and thus indicates a different line of approach from ours. (M. Shinohara, "Nihon Keizai no seicho to choki hado" (The Growth and Long Swings of the Japanese Economy—a mimeographed paper issued by the Institute of Statistical Research, Tokyo, 1960).

* P.S. The long-swings have later been confirmed in a revised shape by use of the improved data. See K. Ohkawa and H. Rosovsky, "Postwar Japanese Growth in Historical Perspective", in L. Klein and K. Ohkawa eds., *Economic Growth: the Japanese Experience since the Meiji Era*, Economic Growth Center, Yale University, 1968.

[8] As for the importance of agriculture during the first swing, see K. Ohkawa, "The Role of Agriculture in Early Economic Development", presented to the Round Table on Economic Development with Special Reference to East Asia by the International Economic Association, Gamagori, Japan, April 1960. [Later published in Kenneth Berrilled., *Economic Development with Special Reference to East Asia*, Macmillan, London, 1964.] In brief, agriculture raised its output per worker almost parallel with that of non-agriculture by introducing various types of technological improvements within the traditional framework.

In the discussion of output per worker or productivity, we should be cautious about the so-called "shift-effect" caused by the labor-flow from the sector of lower productivity to that of higher productivity. If we do include agriculture, the major sector of low productivity, in the present discussion, this kind of effect will certainly be substantial. For example, from 1878–82 to 1908–12 the aggregate rate of growth of output per worker is estimated as 3.2 per cent per annum, but those of the major sectors–agriculture, manufacture, services, are 2.6, 2.3 and 2.3 per cent, respectively. The gap between the aggregate and the sectoral figures will give us a rough idea of the magnitude of the shift-effects. This is another reason why our discussion is concentrated on the non-agricultural sector.

18

for brevity on the following pages—, the long swings observed above can be broken down into these two parts. These figures for the non-agricultural sector are shown in Table 1 (n, g in Columns 6 and 7) and illustrated by Chart 2. (The discussion of the Post-World War II period will be deferred to the later pages.) It is interesting that the growth rate of output per labor force is mainly responsible for the ups and downs of output growth rates in the long process, while the growth rate of the labor force always pushes the trend almost straight down, suggesting that its major effect lies in changes in the level of output growth rates. If we describe these facts on the average for the two phases of long swings suggested above, it is quite clear that in the first phase, the growth rate of the labor force is definitely higher than that of output per labor force, while in the second phase one can observe a reverse relationship. This suggests that the changes in rates of both labor supply and labor productivity had played important roles alternately in changing the pattern of growth throughout these years. In the discussion that follows, first the supply of labor and next productivity will be analyzed, both as incremental changes.

In general, the long-term behavior of labor supply is influenced mainly by three factors: the natural rate of increase in working age population, their participation rate in the labor force and international migration effects. In Japan the effect of the last factor was trifling, since she could not send a substantial number of emigrants abroad, and this is one of the peculiar features of labor supply in Japanese economic development as compared with most Western experience.[9] As for the long-term change in

[9] For the years following World War I, the story is not so simple. For example, according to Irene B. Tauber, during the years 1920–1940, 18.2 per cent of the increase of Japanese males of working ages (15–59) were removed by civilian emigration from Japan; of these 46.3 per cent were replaced by immigration of colonials mainly Koreans, (Mimeographed Rapporteur of Conference on Urban-Rural Relations in the Modernization of Japan, Carmel, California, U.S.A., August 1959). Such qualifications, however, do not affect much our discussion in the main text.

Table 1.*   Growth Rates of Output, Labor Force and Output
Per Labor; Rates of Investment and Capital-output
(All units in percentage except C)

Period		1 $\bar{G}$	2 $\bar{n}$	3 G_a	4 G_n	5 G	6 g	7 n	8 n_1	9 n_2	10 I	11 C
0.	1883–87	4.3	1.4	1.3	3.0	6.5	2.3	4.2	0.6	3.6	—	—
1.	1888–92	4.9	1.2	2.3	2.6	5.5	1.7	3.8	0.8	3.0	22	3.9
2.	1893–97	5.5	0.9	2.2	3.3	6.7	3.2	3.5	0.9	2.6	18	2.6
3.	1898–1902	3.0	0.7	0.9	2.1	4.0	1.1	2.9	0.7	2.2	18	4.4
4.	1903–07	2.9	0.5	0.7	2.2	4.0	1.2	2.8	0.9	1.9	18	4.5
5.	1908–12	3.6	0.4	0.5	3.1	5.5	3.2	2.3	0.7	1.6	23	4.2
6.	1913–17	4.0	0.4	0.6	3.4	5.2	2.8	2.4	1.0	1.4	20	3.8
7.	1918–22	5.2	0.7	0.8	4.4	6.6	4.1	2.5	1.4	1.1	27	4.1
8.	1923–27	5.6	0.8	0.2	5.4	7.6	6.0	1.6	0.6	1.0	24	3.1
9.	1928–32	4.8	0.8	0.3	4.5	5.7	4.0	1.7	0.8	0.9	21	3.7
10.	1933–37	4.3	1.0	0.4	3.9	4.8	2.7	2.1	1.2	0.9	25	5.2

REMARKS: (i)   Notations: $\bar{G}$, aggregate growth rate of output. G_a and G_n, growth share by agriculture and non-agriculture, so that $G_n + G_a = \bar{G}$. G, growth rate of output in non-agriculture; $\bar{n}$ and n, growth rates of labor force in aggregate and non-agriculture; n_1 and n_2, shares originating in non-agriculture and shares originating in agriculture in the growth rate of labor force in non-agriculture. g, I and C, rate of increase in output per labor, rate of investment and capital-output ratio all in non-agriculture, respectively.

(ii)   There is some inconvenience in a continuous computation between pre- and post-war years. A tentative calculation of G by the same method for the later years shows–1.8 for 1938–42,—3.5 for 1943–47 and 5.9 for 1948–52. The data for these years are taken from the appendix table in "*Kokumin Shotoku Hakusho*" (National Income White Paper) 1959, Economic Planning Agency.

(iii)—, data are not available.

(iv)   For other explanations of data and computing method, see footnote 5.

*   *P.S.*   The primary data of output, labor and investment used in Table 1 and Chart 1 have been revised. See each volume concerned of the Chōki keizai tōkei (*Long-term Economic Statistics of Japan since* 1868), edited by K. Ohkawa, M. Shino-hara and M. Umemura Tōyo Keizai Shimpōsha, Tokyo, 1965–1972. The overall pattern described here, however, can still be justified broadly, although the figures of $\bar{G}, G_n$, n, n_2 and g turned out to be over-estimated for early years particularly for the period from 1883–87 to 1903–07.

the participation rate, we have not enough reliable data to present a more or less definite measurement, but it is almost safe to say that this rate showed a slowly decreasing trend over time —a phenomenon experienced in the process of economic develop-

Chart 1.　Change in the Growth Rates of Output

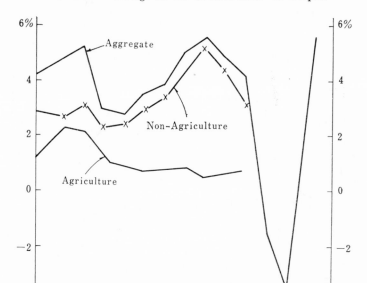

Remarkes:　See P.S. in pages 18 and 20.

ment in most advanced countries.　This definitely had a partial effect on the sharp downward trend of the growth rate of labor force described above.

The major determinant of the direction of this trend, however, seems to be the first factor—natural rate of increase in working-age population, and for the discussion of the non-agricultural sector, the crucial point is the process of out-migration of rural population to urban districts.　We will, therefore, focus our attention on this factor.　Statistically, there are considerable difficulties in quantifying the changes in and shifts of the "labor force," in terms of modern definitions, both for conceptual and factual reasons.　It will be, however, not difficult to understand, depending on

21

Chart 2.   Rates of increase in Output-Labor Ratio (g) and in Labor
Force (n) in Non-Agricultural Sector

several estimates, that almost all the increase (net of replacement)
in the labor force produced in the agricultural sector had mig-
rated to the non-agricultural sector, leaving the total labor force
engaged in agriculture almost unchanged (or very slightly decreasing) throughout the whole period under discussion except
the years during and immediately after World War II.[10]

[10]   M. Umemura made an attempt to estimate the flow of labor force between
agriculture and non-agriculture.   According to him, for example, out of 159,000
(the increase of labor force in non-agriculture), 134,000 was the outflow from agriculture in 1880, and in 1920, this was 168,000 out of 289,000 and in 1953, 162,000 out
of 757,000.   The percentage declined as 85, 58 and 22.   See M. Umemura, "Sangyo-
kan rodoido to sono koka," (Flow of labor between industries and its effect), Chap.
III, Section 2 in S. Tohata, and K. Ohkawa, *Nihon no keizai to nogyo* (Japanese
Economy and Agriculture) (Tokyo: Iwanami Shoten, 1956).

According to Namiki, from 1872 to 1920, the increase of he working population in
non-agriculture comprised almost all migrants from agriculture, and it was estimated
around 8 million, and since the number of factory workers employing more than five
workers was approximately 2 million in 1920, the bulk of the outflow of labor from
agriculture went into spheres other than factory.   (M. Namiki, "The Farm Population

Thus the incremental increase of the labor supply to the non-agricultural sector has been composed of two parts; one, migrants from agriculture to this sector (A) and the other, the net increase produced within this sector (N). Under the general assumption of an unchanged labor force in agriculture and of constant rates of increase in labor force in both sectors, it is quite natural that the share of A will decrease and that of N will increase and it is also obvious that the growth rate of the labor force in non-agriculture will decrease as time goes on, if we add another assumption to the above model that the rate of increase in producing the labor force is greater in agriculture than in non-agriculture. This is a universal phenomenon experienced with various modifications in the course of the economic development of presently advanced countries. Japan's case, however, presents us with a most impressive example,—a rapid effect of forces of this kind in a comparatively short period. As can be naturally expected, in Japan after the emancipation from feudal restraints, the spurt of population increase occurred mainly in the rural districts because at that time the urban population was still proportionately very small and its age-and-sex structure was not favorable to the acceleration of population increase. Besides, in Japan almost all the labor force shifted from rural to urban districts by single units,

in the National Economy before and after World War II," a paper for the same conference mentioned in footnote 9.)

These studies give the background of my estimation in growth terms. The estimation was simple: first, for the period 1883–87 we assumed that 85 per cent of the increase in labor force in the non-agricultural sector was supplied by the labor force shifted from agriculture. This is 0.95 per cent increase per annum in terms of the assumed constant agricultural labor force, and 2.6 per cent in terms of non-agricultural labor force; second, it was assumed that this 0.95 per cent continued for the whole period, and this was converted to the rate of increase in the non-agricultural sector by using the ratios of agricultural labor force to non-agricultural labor force in each period. Therefore, we disregarded the fact that the rate of natural increase was actually accelerated slightly in the later years and that the size of the labor force actually engaged in agriculture had slightly decreased and that there was a slight reverse flow from urban to rural districts. These may be misgivings for a more refined discussion on the demographic studies, but for our present aim of more or less broad interpretations, they may not be serious.

instead of family units, so that it accelerated a young age-structure in the urban area, which naturally had a very small effect on the production of working age population in this area. This feature contributed much to the wide difference in magnitudes between A and N in the ensuing years.

The figures presented in Table 1 were estimated under certain assumptions in order to quantify the facts described above in a convenient form for discussion in the growth-term formula.[11] The rates of increase of parts A and N are denoted by n_2 and n_1 (in Columns 9 and 8), both in terms of rates of increase in the total labor force in the non-agricultural sector. It is most notable that A continued to provide the dominant share almost throughout the entire period before World War II, but that towards the latter part of the period starting around 1908-12, the major reason for the slowing down of the rate of increase in the labor force in this sector was the relative decrease of labor supply from agriculture with a significant rise in the self-increase of labor in this sector towards the end of this period, 1933-37. Thus, it is quite clear that the changes in relative magnitude of this shift has been mostly responsible for the dramatic changes in the pattern of labor supply over a relatively short interval preceding World War II.

The significance of this phenomenon will be discussed in relation to the changes in the rates of increase in output per labor in the following pages. I would like to make here one point, in particular, about its effect on the growth pattern in early economic

---

[11] The importance of the rate of increase in non-agriculture in relation to that of total population is demonstrated in F. Dovring, "The Share of Agriculture in a Growing Population," *Monthly Bulletin of Agricultural Economics and Statistics*, August/September 1959, Vol. VIII, No. 8/9. Though his discussion is developed from the viewpoint of agricultural problem, his idea is relevant to our problem, and his data are useful in making international comparisons. According to his estimates of the long-term growth process, the compound rates of annual increase in population or employment in the non-agricultural sector in most advanced countries of the Western type ranged from 1.3 to 2.7 per cent except for the United States, whose rates were exceptionally high (4.2 for 1850–80, 3.6 for 1880–1910). By the way, his figures for Japan (2.6 for 1890–1915 and 1.8 for 1915–40) are doubtful.

development. On the average, during the first phase, the output growth rate of the non-agricultural sector was 5.4 per cent while the rate of increase in labor force was 3.5 per cent. This means that this initial high rate of growth was achieved largely (two-thirds) through the increase of the labor force. In other words, during this phase, productivity increases were still minor (one-third) in its incremental contribution to the economic growth. This fact naturally suggests a particular growth pattern for this phase, which will be elaborated in the later pages.

Productivity Growth and the Role of Capital

"Output per labor force" as used here is not a productivity concept by itself, but is relevant to it. This term implies that all the contributions to the increased output stemming from factors other than the input of labor should necessarily appear in the changes of this ratio. In this sense, here we would like to use this ratio as an index of productivity in terms of labor. The changes in this output-labor ratio are often discussed in relation to two main factors, capital intensity and technological change. Without knowing the type of specific production function, we cannot weigh quantitatively the effects of these factors. In the discussion that follows, an attempt will be made to describe the relationships between the output-labor ratio and capital intensity both in growth terms in the course of the long swings described above. In order to do so, first we must answer the question: how can we know the changes in the rate of increase in capital intensity?

The capital problem is very difficult, and usually we have very little data which can be used directly to measure the rate of capital accumulation in a manner similar to the measurement of labor force. The relevant data we do have for the Japanese economy are investment rates and capital-output ratios in incremental form.[12] Hence, the problem is to find a method for the indirect measurement of capital increase, in particular, in relation to the labor increase, by using these terms.

As in the case of labor, we have an identical relationship $G = k+h$, where k is the growth rate of capital stock and h the growth rate of "capital productivity" (the reciprocal of the capital-output ratio), though statistically the case of capital is quite different from the case of labor because we have no direct data for either k or h. As for the *ex-post* data for an arbitrary period, however, there must be an identity $k+h=g+n=G$, so that we can specify the following three cases:

if $h<0$, then $k-n>g$ $(G<k)$
if $h=0$, then $k-n=g$ $(G=k)$
if $h>0$, then $k-n<g$ $(G>k)$.

The concept of capital intensity usually concerns labor input rather than labor stock. If we disregard the difference between the rate of increase in labor stock and that of labor input (which might not be substantial in the present discussion), $(k-n)$ is nothing but the growth rate of capital intensity, and since the capital-output ratio will be increasing, unchanged or decreasing, corresponding to whether h is $<0, =0,$ or >0 (and the growth rate of output will be smaller, equal or larger as compared to the rate of capital accumulation), we can observe the relationship between the growth rate of capital intensity and that of the output-labor ratio by the actual data for the movements of the capital-output ratio. In reality, however, our data for the capital-output ratio are given only as average figures for each period in incremental form. Therefore, in order to apply the above formula to our case, we must assume that the changes in the incremental capital-output ratio can represent the movements of the average

---

[12] If we have good data of capital stock in constant prices, it might be better to use direct measurements of capital intensity, but this is still not the case for Japan as yet [see P.S., p. 27].

capital-output ratio, although, in principle the former can differ from the latter.

Let us look at the relevant figures shown in Table 1. The incremental capital-output ratio, inventory investment excluded (C in Column 11), seems to change from period to period, ranging from 2.6 in 1888–92 to 5.2 in 1933–37. But, broadly speaking, the fluctuations seem to show neither a definite upward nor a downward trend throughout the whole period. For instance, the average of the four early figures is 3.9 and that of the six later figures is 4.1. We cannot see substanital changes between the first and the second periods, though there might be a sign of slight increase.[13] If our view is adopted, it is possible to use the assumption of unchanged capital-output ratios as a long-term trend in our case and to say that rate of increase in the output per labor can broadly represent the rate of increase in capital intensity.*

[13] Because of lack of adequate data of capital depreciation for the years before 1930, our figures of the capital-output ratio give the ratio of gross domestic fixed capital formation to the net domestic product. In the discussion of long-term behavior of the capital-output ratio, it is controversial whether we should use a net or gross concept. I think the latter is preferable as a first approach in this case. If we keep in mind the degree of reliability of our statistical data, however, this issue seems to raise no serious problem in our discussion. According to the official estimates (Economic Planning Agency, *Kokumin shotoku hakusho* (National Income White Paper, 1959), the percentages of capital depreciation to the net national product at market prices are 7.1 for 1930–33, 7.5 for 1934–36, 8.3 for 1937–4.0 in the pre-war period, and 7.0 for 1951–54, 9.5 for 1955–58 in the post-war period. Although these figures are for the aggregates instead of for the non-agricultural sector and there is a minor difference between net national product and net domestic product, they can give us an idea of the difference between the net and gross calculations. If we assume that the percentage of capital depreciation was smaller in the earlier years (supposing the figure for 1952–54 was exceptionally low) and take up three hypothetical cases— 4.0, 7.0 and 10.0, then the capital-output ratio 4.0, for instance, will be modified to 3.8, 3.7 and 3.6, respectively. This is a simple calculation and different from the method used in the main text, but still I would say that such a slight decreasing trend has no substantial effect on our broad interpretation in the main text.

* *P.S.* The Capital Stock data are now available. No basic alteration is needed for the findings above. See "Shihon Stokku" (*Capital Stock*), Vo. 3 of the *Long-term Economic Statistics of Japan*, op. cit.

We can see that the rate of increase in the output per labor has changed very much between the first and second phase as already touched upon in the last section; its range is 1.1—3.2 per cent in the first phase, while in the second phase it is from 2.7 to 6.0 per cent. This suggests that both the capital intensity and labor productivity had increased rather slowly during the early years and that they increased much faster (about two times on average) in the later years. This distinction characterizes the patterns of growth in each phase. Taking the facts noted in the last section into consideration, we would like to say that in the early years until around 1903–07 the high rate of increase in the labor force, accompanied by a moderate increase in capital intensity, was the crucial factor for the then rapid growth rate of output, while during the period from around 1908–12 the accelerated increase of capital intensity, accompanied by a moderate rate of increase in the labor force, became the dominant factor for the accelerated growth rate of output. Further from the standpoint of technical development, it can be suggested that in the first phase improvement of simple, labor-intensive techniques of the traditional type was dominant, while in the second phase introduction of capital-intensive techniques of the modern type became more important, each corresponding to the different behavior of the rates of increase in capital intensity in each phase.

Thus, speaking in average terms about the second phase, out of a 5.9 per cent growth rate of output, 3.8 per cent or about two-thirds was achieved through the growth of productivity, while only the remaining one third was due to the increase of labor force. Taking these facts together, I would like to characterize the two periods as follows: a *labor-growth* pattern dominated the first phase and that towards the second phase it developed into a *productivity-growth* pattern.

Such a broad characterization, however, would be misleading if we do not pay closer attention to the changes in the figures from period to period, because, as previously mentioned, the capital-output ratio sometimes changes considerably from period to period. The next step, accordingly, is to clarify the relationships between the changes in the capital-output ratio and the upward or downward movements of the growth rate of output per labor in the process of the long swings.

A reverse relationship between the changes in the capital-output ratio and those in the rates of increase in output per labor can be discerned for the early years, while in the later years we can not necessarily see such a clear reverse relation. For example, from 1888–92 to 1893–1902 (these years belong to the upward period of the first long swing) the rate of increase in output per labor rose considerably (from 1.7 to 3.2 per cent) but the capital-output ratio decreased at the same time, so that the rate of capital accumulation must have been lower than the growth rate of output, and accordingly the rate of increase in capital intensity cannot necessarily be assumed to increase by the above-suggested rate. On the other hand, from 1893–97 to 1898–1902 (the period covering the downward trend in the first long swing) the capital-output ratio increased, while the rate of increase in output per labor decreased. In this case, the rate of capital accumulation was faster than the growth rate of output, so that the rate of increase in capital intensity must be higher than the rate suggested by that of output per labor. Therefore, for the early years we cannot discuss the rates of increase in the capital intensity by too heavily depending on the figures of rates of increase in output per labor.

Next, for the relatively long period from 1898–1902 to 1918–22, we may say with confidence that the rate of increase in capital intensity had been accelerated to a considerable extent. This period, as pointed out in the previous pages, constitutes both the downward part of the first swing and the upward part of the second swing. It is interesting that the capital-output ratio varied only slightly throughout this period. From 1908–12 on-wards both the rates of investment and rates of output-growth were accelerated with the capital-output ratio almost unchanged, so that we can say that the rate of increase in output per labor (an increase from around 1 to 4 per cent) expresses more or less the real upward trend in the rate of increase in capital intensity.

After that, however, the picture has changed again. Toward 1923–27, the output growth rate was still rising, but the rate of investment decreased resulting in a smaller capital-output ratio, and this was followed by the downward part of the second swing. During this period the capital-output ratio showed an upward trend, while the rate of increase in output per labor began to decline. We may say that the rate of increase in capital intensity did not decrease so much as indicated by this rate.

In sum, what can be said about the relationship between the output-labor ratio and capital intensity? For the long swings it may best be summarized as follows: First in the upward part of the long swing, the acceleration in the rate of increase in the output-labor ratio occurred almost at the same rate as that of capital intensity, due to the acceleration of capital accumulation under conditions of almost unchanged rates of increase in the labor force. Second, in the downward part of the long swing, the rate of increase in the output-labor ratio was overtaken by that of capital intensity. Third, near the peak of the long swing, the rate of increase in the output-labor ratio was faster than that of capital intensity. These propositions may not appear too sub-stantial, but it is beyond our present scope to get into an analysis of the particular causes of these changes. They seem, however, to suggest that our assumption of an unchanged capital-output ratio is plausible for the long-term growth process and that the deviations of this ratio from the "normal" trend should be taken to correspond negatively to the fluctuations in the growth rate of output per labor.[14]

Dualistic Growth

In the foregoing discussion we have ignored the changes in the economic structure which necessarily occurred in the growth process. The term "differential structure" has often been used recently to express the present feature of the Japanese economy in the sense that it includes a large sector of pre-capitalistic production of the traditional type side by side with the large-scale, capitalistic production of the modern type, thus embodying a wide range of differentials in productivity, wage rates etc. This is an undeniable fact. As far as our present problem is concerned, our main interest is to clarify the real process by which such a structure has developed as the result of the specific pattern of economic growth described previously.

From observations of various data, we can almost confirm the following facts relevant to our present aim. In the comparison of large-scale and small-scale manufacturing establishments, the

[14] The following chart was constructed to give a quantitative illustrtaion of the thesis proposed in the main text. If the assumption of unchanged capital-output ratio is valid, the relation between the rate of increase in labor productivity and that in capital intensity must be expressed by the 45° line (α) passing through the origin. The dotted points (the number shows each period in their historical order designated in Table I) are given to illustrate their movements around the above line. The figures of rate of increase in the capital intensity were tentatively calculated on the assumption that the average growth rate of

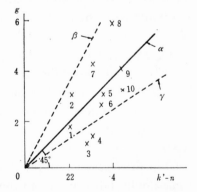

output throughout the whole period (G') is equal to the "normal" rate of capital accumulation (k') and that the rate of increase in capital productivity (h') can be obtained by a relation $h'=G'-k'$. Therefore, this is nothing but a simple presentation withot theoretical reasoning, but will be helpful in understanding the idea developed in the text. The line α seems to be more likely than β (downward capital-output ratio) or γ (upward capital-output ratio).

31

Table 2. Differential Structure of Manufacture in 1932

Capital class	Average No. of workers	Output per worker	Average wages	Labor's relative share	Average capital-output ratio	Capital intensity
1,000 yen	*					1,000 yen
		yen	yen	%		per worker
2— 5	3.5	492	304	62	2.3	11
5— 10	6.7	639	373	57	2.0	13
10— 50	14.5	852	453	53	2.1	18
50—100	29.3	949	524	55	2.6	25
100—500	67.9	1,101	566	51	3.1	31
Over 500	409.8	1,574	671	43	6.1	96

REMARKS: Reproduced, excluding capital classes under 2,000 yen, from Table 6 on page 258 of M. Umemura, "Chingin kakusa to rodo shijo" (Wage Differentials and Labor Market), Section VIII in S. Tsuru, K. Ohkawa, eds. *Nihon Keizai no Bunseki* (Analysis of Japanese Economy), Vol. II (Keiso Shobo, Tokyo, 1955). This was estimated by Umemura from *Kogyo Chosa* (Survey of Manufacturing) compiled by the Ministry of Commerce and Industry in 1932. The coverage is restricted to six prefectures where six large cities are located. All figures are per annum. Salaried workers are included in *. Capital intensity is calculated by multiplying the figures of output per worker by capital-output ratios.

capital-output ratio, the output-labor ratio and capital intensity, all these three magnitudes are greater in the large-scale establishments than in small-scale ones. Actually, in most data, scale of establishment is measured in units of number of workers, but better data in which the scale is taken in terms of capital amounts are also available, although they are scarce. The above propositions are, in principle, in terms of capital-scale.

It is quite understandable that output per worker in large-scale establishments should be larger due to greater capital intensity, for this involves a reasonable technical relationship which is often used in the discussion of the production function. There may be some doubt, however, about the bigger capital-output ratio in the larger firm, as this implies a lower profit rate in the large-scale establishment. In reality, if the wage differential between large-scale and small-scale establishments is sufficiently small compared to the differentials in output per worker (i.e., labor's relative share is smaller in the former than in the latter), the profit rate can be higher in the former.

To illustrate the above propositions, Table 2 is presented here and although the reliability is not too high, this is the only data of this kind available for the inter-war period. No detailed explanation is necessary for the fact that as we go from the small-scale to the large-scale class, output per worker, capital intensity and capital-output ratio all show increasing trends almost without exception and that the wage differentials among them in relation to productivity differentials indicate that large-scale enterprises show possibilities of larger profits as is revealed by the figures of labor's relative share.

As for the post-war data of this kind, the Economic Research Institute, Economic Planning Agency, recently made a comprehensive study.[15] Similar results were obtained only more precisely by this research. Three kinds of data—the survey of national wealth and its annex data, the basic survey of small and medium-scale enterprises and the statistics of incorporated enterprises—were tabulated and analyzed, and in all cases they found out that the formula $Y/L = a \log K/L - b$ is the best-fitting curve (where Y, net or gross value added, L, number of workers, and K, amount of capital, a and b, parameter and constant). It is obvious

[15] Prof. K. Miyazawa and others, "*Kibobetsu shihonkozo to seisansei kakusa*" (Capital Structure by Scale-class and Productivity Differenitails), a mimeographed paper, February 1960. [Later published as No. 6 of the Study Series, June, 1960]

[16] It is not easy to give theoretical explanations with confidence for the coexistence of large-scale and small-scale enterprises in terms of our definition. A very simple idea, however, might be suggested here. Under assumptions of differential supply price of labor, uneven distribution of ability among enterprisers to command the necessary fund for investments and a given set of knowledge on the possibilities of adopting certain types of technique, we can say that enterprisers will choose different types of techniques, in order to maximize their profit rates as is shown by the simple

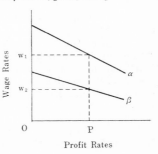

from this equation that the capital intensity, output-labor ratio, capital-output ratio, all will increase as the scale grows larger.[16]

If we can extend these relationships found in manufacturing to the non-agricultural sector as a whole, it will provide a better understanding of the growth pattern and its changes. We have seen that in the early years until around 1903–07, the rate of increase in capital intensity was small in relation to that in labor force. This does not imply an even distribution of capital-labor combinations, but does suggest the dominance of small-scale establishments and their high rate of growth. In discussing the growth pattern during this early phase on a previous occasion, I called it the period of "dual development" in order to specify the feature of such a formative stage.[17] In using this term we tried to characterize a growth process in which a substantial part of the aggregate growth rate in terms of output is achieved by the traditional sectors while the modern sector shows initially an impressively rapid growth although its place in the economy in terms of output is still not dominant. If we define the traditional sectors as composed of a great number of small-scale establishments whose output growth will be attained by a moderate increase in capital intensity, and the modern sectors as composed of a relatively small number of large-scale establishments, whose output growth will be attained by a comparatively big increase in capital intensity, then in the course of dual development as a whole, the capital intensity must increase slowly as compared with

Chart. The two lines α and β express the different technological character of production process.

So far as the amount of capital shown in these data are used, the average profit rates tend to be smaller in the larger-scale enterprises although the wage differentials in relation to productivity differentials favor the large scale enterprises. This is also true of the data for 1932 mentioned above. Is this really a fact? We can elucidate only one point: in the smaller-scale enterprises the "wage earnings" for self-employment of enterprisers are included in the profit shares, which nominally raises profit rates.

[17] It was treated preliminarily in K. Ohkawa, "The Role of Agriculture in Early Economic Development" cited above (footnote 8).

the rapid increase of labor force. This was exactly the case in Japan. In other words, the rapid growth in terms of output was mainly achieved by an intensive utilization of young, single laborers, mainly migrants from rural districts, combined with moderate improvements of labor-intensive techniques, and with small amounts of capital. In fact, the bulk of the ou.flow of labor from agriculture went into spheres other than factory (see footnote 10). This is the only explanation which can be consistent with the fact that the rate of investment was kept almost unchanged during this period (see Column 10 in Table 1). Therefore, the upward part of the first swing should be distinguished from the later ones in the pattern of growth.

As long as such a pattern of economic growth continues, the aggregate capital-output ratio can be kept at low magnitudes, as is demonstrated, during the earliest years. However, from around the turn of the century it began to increase. This might be the outcome of some slowing down in the improvement of production techniques of the traditional type, together with the effects of increased social over-head investments, on which I cannot dwell here.

Turning to the second period after around 1908–12, the modern sector became more and more important in terms of output growth. In reality, this was achieved by a greater acceleration in the rate of increase in productivity than in the number of laborers. The introduction of modern production techniques, which require greater capital investment, must be the main cause of the accelerated growth rates during this period. The rate of investment was increased from 18 to 27 per cent around the peak of the second swing as clearly seen in column 10 in Table 1. On the other hand, the role of the traditional sector declined, and it is to be noted that this corresponds to the decline in the rate of increase in the labor force, due to the decreased rate of labor-flow from agriculture. In fact, this labor-flow from agriculture was the

35

main condition of developing the traditional sectors in non-agricultural sector. Thus, around the beginning of the 1930's, the "differential structure" of the Japanese economy was firmly established in the sense that large-scale capital was accumulated in the modern capitalistic sector while in terms of employment the traditional sector was still dominant, particularly if agriculture is included. Therefore, the accelerated rates of increase, both in capital intensity and output per labor during this phase which we discussed in the previous pages, should be understood to be a combination of a higher rate achieved in the modern sector and a lower rate prevailing in the traditional sector.

I am afraid that such a brief explanation may lead to some misunderstanding since such a multi-layer structure embodies a complex of various inter-relationships in its growth process, which should be analyzed in further detail. Here I would like to demonstrate only that an aggregate approach without attention to the structural problems cannot be successful in analyzing the growth pattern of a country like Japan. However, I would like to point out two things in this respect. One is the fact that the capitalistic sectors themselves have changed their methods of production from the labor-intensive to the capital intensive type both in intra- and inter-industry shifts. Transformations within the textile industries and shifts from light to heavy industries are notable examples. Our dichotomy does not intend to deny this fact, but rather takes it for granted because this aspect of the problem has already been discussed by other authors.

The other is the factor-proportion thesis. In the case of a late-comer to modern economic growth like Japan, in spite of the abundance of relatively cheap labor, the modern sectors are forced to adopt techniques which permit almost no elasticity in proportions of the factor combinations, in order to meet the intense international competition. This fact is highly responsible for the dualistic nature of our structure as is often pointed out. The

simple illustration in footnote 16 has no intention merely to demonstrate the importance of wage differentials. In the historical
development described above, we understand that the illustrated
mechanism was more or less in action and has gradually increased
its significance.[18]

Now, if we take all these facts into consideration, it may appear
that we will have some difficulty in reconciling the thesis of an
unchanged capital-output ratio proposed in the last section to
the structural changes described in this section. This comes
from the fact that, in the course of economic development, as
the proportion of large-scale enterprise becomes larger in the
aggregate or the shift from labor intensive to the capital-intensive
techniques of production progresses, the aggregate capital-output
ratio must necessarily rise, or in other words the rate of increase
in labor productivity must necessarily fall behind the rate of
increase in capital intensity. Therefore, to be consistent, we have
to assume a factor or factors which will act as a counter-balance
to the increasing capital-output ratio stemming from the structural
changes. At this juncture I do not have sufficient factual evidence
to identify such counter-balancing factors, but I would suggest
that either in the social-overhead sector or through private industries, there may be technological and institutional developments of a capital-saving nature which could, in effect, reduce
the aggregate capital-output ratio. If we can assume such effects,
the capital-output ratio could be unchanged in the long run

---

[18] In these two respects, it may be interesting to refer to Gustav Ranis, "Factor
Proportions in Japanese Economic Development," *American Economic Review*, September, 1957, Vo. XLVIII, No. 5. His crucial point is the change in relative factor
prices. Statistically, his data are not without doubt since a formation of a long-
term price series of investment goods in Japan is still a problem to be solved. But
his analytical viewpoint is very close to ours. The difference lies rather in emphasis;
he gives us an impression that change in factor prices and the adaptation to them were
worked out uniformly in each historical stage (I believe this is not his intention). Our
crucial point lies in the differential structure, which embodies differentials of relative
factor prices concurrently.

despite changes in the structure.* I would be inclined to assume the existence of such capital-saving effects.

Postwar Growth Pattern

A full discussion of the war and post-war period would require a separate and extensive analysis since the effects of the War on the Japanese economy were too enormous and radical to be treated in a simple manner. It would be not so hazardous, however, to touch the post-war period within certain defined limits set by our present discussion. Statistically, there are certain difficulties in linking the post-war data to the pre-war figure. This is another reason why we treat this period separately.[19]

It is convenient to separate the period during which the rehabilitation effects were still dominant from the period in which the growth process has been more or less normalized. For this purpose, 1952 might be an appropriate year by which these two periods should be demarcated. In the former period, 1946–52, the growth rates of output, labor force, and output per labor force were 16.1, 7.1 and 9.0 per cent, respectively, for the non-agricultural sector; all appear to be abnormally high rates. They cannot be explained fully, however, by abnormal factors only since they imply post-war structural changes in the pattern of economic growth set into motion immediately after the war.

---

* *P.S.* The revised data reveal a slight increase in the prewar ratio until the end of the thirties, followed by a decrease in the postwar ratio. This is partly due to the revision made for the national income statistics.

[19] The data of Post-World War period were all taken from M. Kawakami, "Kokumin soseisan to keizai seicho" (Gross National Product and Economic Growth), Chap. II in *Kokumin shotoku* (National Income) edited by K. Ohkawa (Tokyo; Shunju-sha, 1960), especially from Table 8, p. 90.

In the text, we did not work out the breakdown into sub-sectors within non-agricultural sector. One thing deserves special attention here is the elastic nature of service industry in employments. The Post-World War II jump in the rate of increase in labor force was most evident (5.6 per cent per annum in 1952-57) in this sector.

For the period 1952–57, the corresponding figures of growth rates are estimated as 9.7, 5.1 and 4.6 per cent, respectively, which suggest something common to the former period if we compare these figures with those of the pre-war long-term process. The greatly accelerated growth rate of output is composed of two equally important components, the accelerated rate of increase in the labor force and also the accelerated rate of increase in the output-labor ratio. The former is the combined result of rehabilitation and the change in age-structure due to the changes in the post-war demographic pattern. Immediately after the war the labor force in agriculture increased abnormally, but recently it has begun to show a decreasing trend, and its percentage to the non-agricultural labor force has decreased accordingly. Thus, its share of contribution to an increasing labor force has greatly diminished while the non-agricultural sector became much more self-sufficient in this respect (see Umemura's estimate, footnote 10)—a shift in the principal source of labor supply from rural to urban districts. (This shift in origin poses the important problem of the changes in the structure of labor market, on which we cannot elaborate here.)

In spite of this, the significant fact is that the rate of increase in the labor force to be employed in this sector has greatly increased (5.1 per cent as mentioned above), which even in the first phase Japan had never experienced, and this is believed to be a more or lesss sustained phenomenon since the present high rate of increase in working-age population is estimated to continue at least for the coming several years. Thus, as for the rate of increase in labor supply, we can say that following the first long period of rural origin sustained mostly for the pre-war period, it has now shifted to the second period of urban origin. This means a step toward the third stage where labor supply will become smaller in relation to capital supply, but still during this second period the pressure of labor supply will continue to be a basic feature of the Japanese economy.

It is remarkable that in spite of the great pressure of the labor supply, the rate of increase in the output per labor force in 1952–57 reached the highest figure (4.6 per cent) in the whole process of economic growth under consideration, except for the pre-war peak in the second swing. We have seen that during the pre-war period, the larger rates of increase in productivity were achieved by smaller rates of increase in the labor force, and in the post-war period we are facing a new situation. In analysing this new situation, it should particularly be noted that there seems to be no substantial difference in the capital-output ratio between the pre-war and post-war period.

Because of a certain lack of comparability in concepts and methods of estimation, there are difficulties in comparing post-war data of national income and capital formation with those of pre-war days, which we used in the previous discussions. It may not be so hazardous, however, to attempt a tentative comparison of the capital-output ratios by using the preliminary estimates of the Economic Planning Agency for the pre-war years since 1930 in comparison with the official estimates for the post-war years by the same Agency.[20] The aggregate capital output ratio for 1952–57 is estimated to be 3.3, while the corresponding pre-war figures come out to be 3.0 for 1928–32 and 3.7 for 1933–37. These are all measured as the ratio of the rate of gross investment, inventory excluded, to the growth rate of net national product. I would say that these figures may be good enough to give evidence to the almost unchanged capital-output ratio between pre- and post-war periods. (The differences between these figures and those in Table 1 may be mainly due to two causes: one is the different manner of treating government expenditures, in partic-

---

[20] Both of these data are reproduced in the volume "*National Income*" edited by K. Ohkawa cited above.

ular, military expenditures, and the other is the effect of agriculture, as in this estimate agriculture is not excluded because of the lack of continuous data for the pre-war years).

This estimate, if admitted, not only endorses the proposition made in the previous section but also enables us to understand the post-war growth pattern by the same thesis continuously throughout the whole growth process despite the war break. Thus we can say that the post-war rate of increase in capital intensity became higher on average, as suggested by the higher rate of increase in labor productivity as compared with pre-war periods, and that the rates of increase both in labor force and in capital intensity have been raised at the same time. This naturally suggests an accelerated rate of investment and in reality we see it is estimated as high as 32 per cent for the non-agricultural sector according to the category rearranged to be more or less comparable with the pre-war period. We have seen that the rate of investment was accelerated from the first to the second phase. Now it made a second acceleration from the second to the third phase. This re-acceleration of the investment rate is basically supported, among other things, by the reaccelerated supply of labour force.[21]

In structure, the rate of capital accumulation and the rate of introduction of capital-using techniques are accelerated in the domain of large-scale enterprises while in the fields of medium and small-scale enterprises, much of the increased labor force is employed thus, making possible the high rate of increase in the total employment of the economy. As a result, the differentials in productivity are apt to be enlarged although the progress of labor-intensive techniques is again accelerated to some extent.

---

[21] To be comprehensive in the discussion of these points, we have to elaborate on the features of and the changes in the wage-profit formulation and of savings rate. But these topics would have required an extensive treatment and deserve separate analysis.

Thus the once-established differential structure is now developing in an enlarged scale.

In conclusion, we can say that in the post-World War II phase, the pattern of economic growth of Japan combines two elements, the labor-growth dominant pattern, experienced in the first period, and the productivity-growth dominant pattern, begun in the second phase.

THE DIFFERENTIAL
EMPLOYMENT STRUCTURE

Introduction[1]

When economists discuss the characteristics or features of the Japanese economy, it is usual to speak of the rapid growth rate, the high rate of savings, labor's low relative share and the like. Here, however, I would like to deal with the structural aspects. It is often said that the Japanese economy is a combination of both Western-type industry and Asian-type agriculture. In reality, in less than a century since the Meiji Restoration in 1868, industrialization has developed very rapidly along the line of building up a Western-type factory system; and nowadays, large-scale factories are producing many modern commodities to compete with advanced countries. But, at the same time, there still remain many small-scale firms employing large numbers of workers, and also a large number of very small-scale farms throughout the country. Thus the Japanese economy is unique in its industrial structure, which is quite different both from advanced economies of the Western type and from backward economies of the Asian type.

[1] Hearty acknowledgement is due to Dr. Alan Gleason for editing my English and giving helpful comments, and Messrs. T. Noda and T. Sasaki and Miss Y. Ando for helping me in editing and arranging tables and charts.

Reprinted from The Annals of The Hitotsubashi Academy, *Vol. IX No. 2, April 1959, pp. 205–217.*

Table 1. Distribution of Wage-earning Workers according
to Size of Establishment in Manufacture (%)

Countries	Japan	U.S.A.	U.K.	West Germany
	(1954)	(1954)	(1949)	(1955)
Number of workers				
1— 9	23.1	3.8	4.8[1]	2.7
10— 49	29.2	12.5	11.3[2]	11.4
50— 99	9.0	9.4	10.1	10.0
100—499	17.1	29.1	32.6	30.8
500—999	6.5	12.5	13.1	13.1
100 and over	15.1	32.6	28.1	32.0
Total	100.0	100.0	100.0	100.0

Source:
Japan ....Survey of Establishments
U.S.A. ....Census of Manufacture
U.K. ....Production Census
West Germany...Statistical Yearbook
Remarks: 1. 1–10. 2. 11–49.

As is shown in Table 1, in Japan the number of workers employed by small-scale firms of less than 50 employees comprises a
little more than half of the total number of workers in manufacturing; while in the more advanced countries it is only 15–16 per
cent. It is noted that the percentage of workers employed by the
largest-scale firms in Japan is low as compared with that of
medium-scale firms.

Data of a similar kind are not available for other industries,
but it is clear that there is also a large number of very small
establishments in other sectors, especially in service industries,
in which family enterprises prevail widely as in the case of agriculture. The composition of labor force according to employment status given in Table 2 will be a great help in illustrating
Japan's characteristics in this respect.

The number of hired wage-workers in Japan comprises only
40 per-cent (50 per cent in the case of males and 30 per cent in
the case of females), while the numbers of the other two categories,

Table 2. Composition of Labor Force according to Employment Status

(%)

	Japan	U.S.A.	U.K.	France	West Germany
	1956	1950	1951	1954	1950
(Male)					
Self-employed	33.3	19.8	8.4	25.9	18.8
Wage-worker	49.6	78.7	91.5	67.7	76.7
Family-worker	17.1	1.5	0.1	6.4	4.5
Total	100.0	100.0	100.0	100.0	100.0
(Female)					
Self-employed	14.8	5.9	4.3	14.4	7.1
Wage-worker	29.6	91.1	95.2	59.1	60.4
Family-worker	55.6	2.9	0.5	26.5	32.0
Total	100.0	100.0	100.0	100.0	100.0
(Total)					
Self-employed	25.7	15.9	7.2	21.9	14.8
Wage-worker	41.4	82.1	92.6	64.7	70.8
Family-worker	32.9	1.9	0.2	13.4	14.4
Total	100.0	100.0	100.0	100.0	100.0

Source: Japan from "*Labor Force Survey*"; other countries from "*Yearbook of Labor Statistics*", (I.L.O.)

self-employed and family-workers, total almost 60 per cent, a very high figure as compared with that of more advanced countries. Thus, the predominance of small-scale firms is closely related to the widespread existence of family firms, where unpaid family workers play a great role in carrying out production of goods and services.

Such an employment structure is a historical product of the capitalistic development of the Japanese economy up to the present, in the sense that this structure has established its root in an economy where the traditional pattern of production still remains nation-widely. A structure such as this has often been characterized as a "dual economy" which means that both the modern capitalistic element and the old traditional element co-exist side by side. I am not opposed to this characterization.

However, as far as employment is concerned, I think it is more appropriate to describe such a situation as a *differential employment structure* for reasons which will be explained later. It is primarily this structural problem that I would like to discuss in this paper. It is my view that in the case of Japan's type of structure, the concepts of employment or unemployment which have so far been developed will not necessarily be valid in their applications.

Empirical Observations

First, let us begin by illustrating the actual employment and wage situation in Japan through an analysis of a curious statistical result. In the area of international comparisons of labor's relative share, a very simple measure, namely, the ratio of income per wage worker to the national income per capita of all people gainfully occupied is often used. The numerical values of this ratio are roughly 120 per cent for Japan (in 1953), 60 per cent for U.K. (in 1950), 80 per cent for U.S.A. (in 1951) and 90 per cent for West Germany (in 1950). The highest value for Japan seems strange at first glance, but actually it merely reflects the very low level of income of the non-wage working classes, in particular that of unpaid family workers. This is because of a hidden bias in the method of computing the ratio, a bias resulting from the implicit assumption that all non-wage workers will get the same average wage as earned by wage-workers. Because of the high degree of unreality of this assumption in Japan, the ratio gives a result according to which the total income earned by labor exceeds the total national income! This can be demonstrated by the following simple equation where the notation is as follows:

N, total labor; N_w, hired wage-worker; N_e, non-wage workers $(N=N_w+N_e)$; Y, national income at factor cost; E, non-wage income as computed by the above-mentioned assumption; W, wage income; R, relative per capita share of national income per worker received by wage-workers.

$$R = \frac{W}{N_w} \bigg/ \frac{Y}{N} = \frac{W}{Y} \cdot \frac{N}{N_w}$$

$$= \frac{W}{Y}\left(1 + \frac{N_e}{N_w}\right) = \left[\frac{W}{N_w} \cdot N_e + W\right] \bigg/ Y$$

Since, $E = \frac{W}{N_w} \cdot N_e$, we have $E + W > Y$ in the case of Japan where $R > 1$.

Where there is little difference in the average incomes of wage-workers and non-wage workers, the formula gives useful results. But, in cases such as Japan, where unusually wide differentials exist, the formula gives a quite unreasonable result.

Secondly, it is noticeable that within the wage-workers' group, wage differentials show a large dispersion because of the larger proportion of low-wage workers as compared to the more or less normal patterns of the advanced countries. For example, the frequency distribution of wage rates in Japan is quite different from that of the U.S.A., as may be clearly observed in Chart 1. In Japan's case there is a strong bias toward the low level group,

Chart 1.   Frequency Distribution of Wage Rates

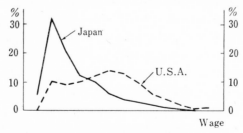

Remarks: Quoted from Ministry of Labor's Survey.
Source: Japan from the "Special Survey of Individual Wages," U.S.A. from "Monthly Labor Review."   Both relate to manufacture.
Unit: Japan, monthly wage earnings; U.S.A. wage rates per hour (both in April 1954).

47

Table 3.　Wage and Productivity Differentials in Manufacturing Industry

Scale (number of workers)		Value added per worker (A)	Wage earnings per worker (B)	(B)/(A) %
1	4—9	197 (28)	87 (32)	44
2	10—19	236 (33)	107 (40)	45
3	20—29	265 (37)	117 (43)	44
4	30—49	303 (42)	126 (47)	42
5	50—99	364 (51)	141 (52)	39
6	100—199	450 (63)	158 (59)	35
7	200—299	532 (75)	176 (65)	33
8	300—499	594 (83)	199 (74)	34
9	500—999	683 (96)	217 (80)	32
10	1000 and over	714 (100)	270 (100)	37
	Average	364	144	40

Remarks:　Unit:　thousand yen.　Figures are per year in 1955.　Figures in brackets show indices.
Source:　Kōgyō tokeihyo (*Manufacturing Census*, Ministry of International Trade & Industry.

while the U.S.A.'s distribution is rather smooth. Incidentally, the coefficient of dispersion is very high, being 102 in Japan's case as against 43 in the case of the U.S.A. These statistics show respectively the existence of a large number of low-wage workers and of sizable wage differentials.

Now, we would like to take up comprehensive data relevant for our purpose, which are summarized in Table 3 and illustrated by Chart 2. These data show that both productivity and wage differentials form almost straight lines sloping downwards from bigger enterprises to smaller ones and that the slope of the productivity line is steeper than that of the wage line. The latter fact is natural even in the case where the relative share of labor is the same for each scale of establishment, but here it is observable that the difference of slope is larger than in such a case. The productivity level of the workers in the smallest firms (4 to 9 workers) is less than 30 per cent of the level of the largest firms (more than a thousand workers) while the wage level of the smallest firms' workers is little more than 30 per cent of the largest

Chart 2.   Wage and Productivity Differentials in Manufacturing Industry

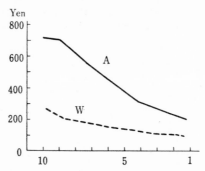

Remarks: (A) Added value per worker (net value productivity).   (W) Wage.
The numbers on the horizontal axis denote classes in terms of number of the
workers as designated in Table 1.

firms' level.   This is really a remarkable differential and it prevails
throughout manufacturing industry.

Next, we calculate corresponding data for agriculture shown
in Table 4.   Here also we find a wide range of income and productivity differentials for various farm household income groups.
The lowest group produces an income only 17 per cent of that
of the highest group, a difference which is even larger than that
of manufacturing industry.   In Japanese farming, incomes earned
by jobs off the farm constitute a considerable part of total farm
income.   The figures in the last column which include these incomes, however, do not change the wide differential tendency
as shown by the percentage figures in the table.

These two sets of data are difficult to compare because in one
case, scale is measured in terms of income and, in the other case,
in terms of number of hired workers.   It seems useful, however,
to show them together rather than separately in order to illustrate
the employment structure of the whole economy.   It is assumed
that the tertiary sector follows the same pattern.   In this way
the following points may be noted:

49

Table 4. Productivity and Income Differentials in Agriculture

Income class (ten thousand yen)	Agricultural net income produced per-agricultural worker	Farm net income (including non-agricultural) per worker
1 under 10	32 (17)	51 (14)
2 10—15	48 (26)	151 (40)
3 15—20	60 (32)	137 (36)
4 20—25	68 (36)	165 (44)
5 25—30	77 (41)	188 (50)
6 30—40	90 (48)	205 (55)
7 40—50	106 (57)	224 (50)
8 50—70	129 (70)	263 (70)
9 70 and over	186 (100)	375 (100)
Average	96 (52)	96 (52)

Remarks: Unit: thousand yen. Average annual figures for 1955 period. Fiures in parentheses show indices.

Source: Nōka kezai chōsā (*Farm Economy Survey*). Ministry of Agriculture & Forestry.

(1) The net value productivity of the lowest income class in manufacture is very close to that of the highest income class in agriculture. In reality there are many manufacturing firms the scale of which is even smaller than the class just mentioned, namely the class of less than three workers about which we have no adequate data available as to value productivity. In view of this situation, it will be assumed that the productivity curve as illustrated in Chart 2 is more or less a continuation of the productivity curve which could be inferred from the figures in Table 4. However, the distribution of the income from the product at this border line class differs greatly between manufacture and agriculture. In manufacture, wage earnings per year are 87 thousand yen and labor's relative share is around 44 per cent; while in agriculture, average product per worker, which is almost the same as wage earnings in manufacture, is a mixed income for the farm household consisting of rent, profit, and interest as well as wages, if we neglect the very small amount of wage payment

for hired workers. On the side of small-scale manufacture, there are also a considerable number of self-employed and family workers, but in this case the proportion of hired labor is much larger. Where the total family income in manufacture is estimated to be around 700 thousand yen, which is very close to the family income of the top classes in agriculture, there may be a kind of border line between capitalistic enterprise (we mean, in this case, an enterprise in which most of the workers are hired) and family enterprise in which almost all the workers are self-employed.

(2) The average wage earnings in manufacturing firms falling in the two smallest-size groups are around 90–100 thousand yen, which is almost equal to the level of farm income for the average size enterprise in agriculture.

(3) Turning to the highest class in manufacture, the wage earnings per worker are 220–270 thousand yen, which exceeds slightly the total income per worker for the highest class in agriculture. If we consider the qualitative difference between workers in manufacture and agriculture, these two figures are not significantly different. On the other hand, the income of a proprietor who belongs to the lowest class (say hiring less than 3 workers) might be assumed to be near the level of wage earnings of the highest class workers, though adequate data are not available as yet.

These observations may be enough to suggest that small proprietors' income, mixed income of the upper level family farms, and wage earnings of upper class workers, are not determined independently but are closely related to each other in the general framework of the demand for and supply of employment.[2]

[2] Of course, a mechanical comparison of urban workers and farmers in terms of money income alone is lacking in accuracy. The so-called "psychic income" gained by farmers, as well as the consumers' price difference between urban and rural districts and so forth should be taken into account in a comparison of real income. Consideration of these factors would reduce the differentials but probably not weaken seriously the broad conclusions drawn from the data presented.

Some Analytical Observations

Chart 3 is used to illustrate continuous wage and productivity differentials as observed in the previous section in order to provide a basis for a theoretical model. Both wage and productivity figures are shown on the vertical axis and the scale of enterprise in terms of capital stock per worker (capital intensity) is shown on the horizontal axis. We have no good data available as to the capital intensity classification. However, I think a capital intensity scale is theoretically better than the number of workers classification already adopted in the previous table. Taking into consideration some data on the capital intensity classification of incorporated companies, we assume here that the above-mentioned differentials will also be valid for a capital intensity classification and that there is a close correlation between capital intensity rank and number of workers rank. In other words, the smaller the enterprise in terms of the number of workers the lower the capital intensity will be.

Line A denotes continuous differentials of average net value productivity and line W continuous wage rate differentials. On the horizontal axis, attention is drawn to two points; first, M_1,

Chart 3. Productivity and Wage Differentials

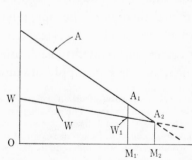

representing the border line between capitalistic enterprise and family enterprise, and second, M_2, denoting the marginal point of family enterprise, in the sense that the net productivity is just sufficient to cover wages. The two points A_1 and A_2 on line A show the average net value productivity at M_1 and M_2 respectively. The important features of this chart are: first, the degree of wage differentials is much smaller than that of productivity differentials, secondly, capitalistic enterprise and self-employment enterprise do not constitute two independent sectors but comprise a continuous, interrelated economic structure.

I would like to discuss first the capitalistic enterprise sector, where large scale enterprises and medium-and-small-scale enterprises co-exist. According to the statistical data available, the following relationships are decidedly clear. Using the notation α and β, representing large-scale enterprise and small-scale enterprise respectively, (1) the average net value productivity of α is greater than that of β, (2) the wage rate of α is higher than that of β, (3) the capital intensity of α is larger than that of β. (These relationships have already been mentioned above).

By denoting capital stock as K, number of labor force employed as N, output as Y and wage rate as ω, the above relationships can be arranged as follows:

$$1)\ \frac{Y_\alpha}{N_\alpha} > \frac{Y_\beta}{N_\beta}, \qquad 2)\ \omega_\alpha > \omega_\beta, \qquad 3)\ \frac{K_\alpha}{N_\alpha} > \frac{K_\beta}{N_\beta}.$$

Now the average profit rate of enterprise can be expressed by the terms mentioned above as follows; $\dfrac{Y-N\omega}{K}$, which can easily be changed to the expression $\left(1-\dfrac{N\omega}{Y}\right)\Big/\dfrac{K}{Y}$, where $\dfrac{N\omega}{Y}$ is labor's relative share and $\dfrac{K}{Y}$ is the capital coefficient. If we represent these latter two terms by R and C, an equal rate of average profit for enterprises α and β can be expressed as follows;

$$\frac{1-R_\alpha}{C_\alpha} = \frac{1-R_\beta}{C_\beta}, \text{ or } \frac{1-R_\alpha}{1-R_\beta} = \frac{C_\alpha}{C_\beta}.$$

This equation simply enables us to show the relationship between both types of enterprises in terms of the capital coefficient and labor's relative share. If the equality is to be maintained, it is clear that if $C_\alpha \lessgtr C_\beta$, then $R_\alpha \gtrless R_\beta$.

Next, let us assume that both α and β enterprises as going concerns adopt certain techniques which can be described by a production function $[Y=(K, N)]$ at a given wage level and capital price. This means, in other words, that the average productivity of labor Y/N, capital intensity K/N, and capital coefficient K/Y or C are all determined by production functions. From actual observation of the statistical data available we can introduce the following quantitative relationship between enterprises α and β with respect to the capital coefficient, namely, $C_\alpha > C_\beta$. As for relative share, $R_\alpha < R_\beta$ is observable from actual data. Hence, in theory, it is possible to assume an equilibrium state between α and β based on the conditions $C_\alpha > C_\beta$ and $R_\alpha < R_\beta$. This means that in the case of α, the disadvantage of having a greater capital coefficient due to technological requirements is apt to be compensated for by the advantage of the smallness of labor's relative share, which shows that in larger-scale enterprises, the ratio of the wage rate to productivity is smaller than in the case of smaller-scale enterprises. In actuality, the profit rate of α may be greater than that of β in the long run when the degree of $R_\alpha < R_\beta$ is apt to be greater than that of $C_\alpha > C_\beta$ and this depends mostly on the wage differentials in relation to the productivity differentials.

Although this is a very rough sketch of the economic structure in which we are interested, employment under conditions of wage differentials should, I believe, be analysed in terms of the framework of such a structure. Since it is reasonable to suppose that the marginal productivity of labor of α enterprise is higher than that of β, it is quite obvious that the demand price of labor should show a differential at a competitive state. In reality the larger-scale enterprises can hire labor at a level lower than the assumed

Table 5. Wage Distribution by Establishment Scale and Workers'
Age in Manufacturing Industry

Unit: yen a month

Age \ Scale	Average	1,000 and over	500 ~ 1,000	100 ~ 500	30 ~ 100	10 ~ 30
Average	13,659	17,435	14,816	12,478	10,807	9,379
under 18	5,175	5,993	5,450	4,960	4,799	3,726
18—20	7,072	8,027	7,229	6,784	6,579	6,084
20—25	9,728	11,119	10,334	9,322	8,622	7,799
25—30	14,276	16,784	15,462	13,616	11,825	10,294
20—35	17,478	21,337	19,640	16,270	14,046	11,662
35—40	19,727	24,715	22,208	17,811	14,727	12,042
40—50	20,884	27,363	23,992	19,017	15,405	12,135
50—60	19,140	28,032	22,933	18,712	14,683	12,077
60 and over	13,263	17,892	20,709	15,850	12,923	10,614

Source: The Ministry of Labor, *Survey of Wages for* 1954.

demand price because the supply price of labor is apt to be suppressed to a lower level by the existing competition among the workers who accept work at lower rates in this situation.

In theory, it is not easy to give a full explanation of the competitive relationship between workers of larger-scale enterprises and smaller-scale ones. However, as is illustrated by Table 5 and Chart 4, the wage differentials between larger-scale and smaller-scale establishments according to the age difference of workers is well worth noting. For low-age workers the differential is very slight, while for middle-age workers, the differential is very wide, and this is mainly responsible for the average differential between larger-scale and smaller-scale establishments. In connection with this fact, I am inclined to point out that there is a sort of imperfect competition as far as the movement of labor between α and β is concerned, and that this becomes greater as the workers get older. However, as a whole, the very existence of low wages in smaller firms can act so as to make lower the wage level of larger firms.

55

Chart 4.   Wage Distribution by Establishment Scale and Workers'
Age in Manufacturing Industry

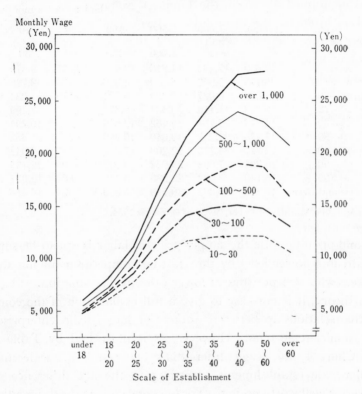

Monthly Wage
(Yen)

over 1,000

500~1,000

100~500

30~100

10~30

Scale of Establishment

Thus, within the capitalistic enterprise sector as a whole, we
have three kinds of differentials—productivity, wage rate and
profit rate. Referring again to Chart 3 above, let us turn our
attention to point M_1 on the horizontal axis. At this border
point, the profit per worker (which is denoted by $A_1 W_1$ in the
chart) is just enough to maintain the concern, as the amount
of profit will be almost equal to the ordinary level of wage earnings
of workers. In other words, this marginal enterpriser is in a
competitive situation with workers in the sense that if the wage

level rises relative to his profit, he will be ready to become a hired worker himself and such a marginal enterprise will disappear.

As mentioned above, in the Japanese economy the number of workers hired by the capitalistic enterprise sector is only about 40 per cent of the total labor force, so that the importance of the sector of family enterprise is very great. Now, we move to the consideration of this sector, which is mainly composed of agricultural and, to some extent, service industries. In this sector, each independent small proprietor is working as a manager as well as a worker and depends on his own family labor force. Generally speaking, the marginal productivity of labor in this sector must be lower than that of the capitalistic sector because if it were not lower such persons would not remain in a state of self-employment. However, they will get all the net product other than rent and interest paid to outsiders, so that if we assume for the sake of simplicity that they own all capital as well as land required to carry on their enterprise, it turns out that average productivity of labor instead of marginal productivity is the income indicator.

Though we have little data on the tertiary sector, much empirical study has been done on the agricultural sector with regard to the matters relevant to this problem. A wide range of differentials for average productivity is observable in agriculture in terms of cultivated area of land, almost corresponding to the differentials already discussed in terms of the income classification in Table 4. Again for the sake of simplicity, if we neglect the small amount of capital, which also differs according to the land scale, it may be assumed that the labor productivity differential is mainly determined by land scale in the case of cultivated land of homogeneous quality. In reality, this means that the ability differential to enlarge the land is primarily responsible for this productivity differential.

Let us look at the border point M_2 on the scale line in Chart 3, assuming that this scale line is also applicable to the land-scale differentials. If we assume the so-called marginal labor productivity concept to be considered in terms of a man-year unit, at point M_2, we would presumably find a worker with almost no capital, and with average productivity theoretically equal to marginal productivity at a level which is a minimum in a sense that if, at this point, another laborer engages in production, his product will be lower than the income required to keep the level determined by the continuous differential line of wage or minimum income.

The concept of the so-called under-employment or disguised unemployment in agriculture is a controversial issue. Some insist that in such a case the marginal productivity of labor must be zero, while others assert that it should be positive. However, the problem of a zero or positive marginal productivity is not the crux of the issue. In a theoretical setting it might be possible to define the conditions under which marginal productivity of labor is zero. This might be done if we assume a certain institutional framework of self-employed farmers who are maximizing their total net product under certain assumed conditions. However, if we take, for example, a man-year unit instead of a man-hour or man-day unit, the whole picture changes, because the marginal worker must produce at least enough to maintain his minimum standard of living. Hence his productivity over a year period, must be positive.

The so-called disguised unemployment is usually defined as the employment characterized by an unusually low level of marginal productivity and this definition has generally been applied to the conditions of the farming population in most Asian countries. This is not an useful concept. The main reason is that it stems from a too-much generalization from Western experience. In a country like Japan, where capitalistic enterprises have emerged

and developed, accompanied with the traditional ways of production and living, it is a basic structure that there always exists
a gap between the marginal productivity of labor in modern
industry and that of the traditional pattern of self-employment
enterprises. Again let us observe Chart 3. The zone between
M_1 and M_2 represents the sector of self-employment enterprises,
so that point M_1 is also the border line between the sectors of
capitalistic and self-employment enterprise. The controversial
issue concerning the conditions determining labor mobility between these sectors will not be discussed here in detail. It will
suffice to say simply that, in a static situation, the wage differentials in the capitalistic sector will correspond to the differentials
of family *mixed* income in the self-employment sector as a whole,
to the extent that the new labor force coming from the lower
income families (the source of the labor supply to smaller-scale
enterprises) has a lower labor supply price.

Conclusion

The situation which has been described and analysed in the
preceding sections is called a *differential employment structure*. The
main causes for this particular structure are two: 1) the inequality
of capital distribution among individual enterprises, and 2) the
peculiar pattern of supply curves of labor, which are not uniform
among various groups of workers. I quite agree with the assertion that the level of the wage rate in relation to productivity will
be determined by the relationship between the rate of capital accumulation and the rate of increase of labor supply. It is to be
noted, however, that in an economy where the supply of labor as a
whole is apt to exceed the demand which comes from the development of the capitalistic sector and where the man-land ratio is
unfavorable to man, the differential employment will be an inevitable result because of the two reasons mentioned above.

Much has been said on the problems of structural unemploy-ment as against Keynesian unemployment due to a shortage of effective demand, disguised unemployment and the like. Re-cently, in relation to the development of theoretical and empiri-cal approaches to the economic conditions in underdeveloped countries, studies on these problems have developed rapidly. However, once we recognize that the differential employment structure to be the basic feature of the Japanese economy, as distinguished from the fairly homogeneous structure of employ-ment in Western economies, almost all the discussions based on the notion of *un*-employment appear to be of limited usefullness. The productivity of labor engaged in various industries, including family enterprises, shows a wide range of continuous differentials (even within the same industry) and the wage rates or incomes of working people also have wide continuous differentials. These differentials must be said to be a structural characteristic since the situation has not changed over a long period and can be un-derstood to be at a sort of equilibrium. It is difficult to analyze such phenomena in terms of the concepts which have drawn out from the experience of the economies of homogenenous structure. The general pattern of labor supply and demand permits employ-ment at remarkably different wage levels, and thus makes the proportion of unemployed exceedingly small.[3]

---

[3] Actually, in Japan according to the official statistics of the labor force, the percentage of unemployment is only around 1.5 per cent even in recession periods, and I think this is mostly unemployment of a frictional nature. But most scholars con-sider that this is due to the existence of considerable disguised unemployment. In fact, according to several surveys, the number of the so-called disguised unemployed was estimated to be 2 to 8 million, depending upon different criteria of measurement. It is not necessary to enter into the technical problem of measurement here. The only point to which I would like to call attention is the inevitable arbitrariness or multiplicity of the measurements of disguised unemployment due to the very nature of the economy. For example, if we take up a representative definition of disguised unemployment according to which the marginal productivity of labor is lower than that of "normal" employment, we are puzzled to find that there is no normal level of labor productivity with which the so-called lower productivity of labor can be compared.

ANALYSIS

OF THE DIFFERENTIAL

STRUCTURE

Differential Structure

In recent articles I have used the term "differential structure" (Keisha kōzō) to characterise the structure of Japanese economy. I use this term here because of lacking a more appropriate expression. "Multi-layer structure" might be an alternative. Finally there is a similar term, like "dual structure": (*Nijyu kōzō*). The co-existence of huge and tiny enterprises can be called a dual structure. Between these extremes, however, a number of medium-small scale enterprises actually exist and the structure is multi-layer rather than dual, having continuous differentials between the two extremes in terms of scale of production units, productivity, wages etc.

The phenomenon of such continuous differentials, in my view, is much more important than it appears at first glance. The problems of capital-labor allocation, availability of different technologies, the income formation pattern and distribution etc.—these are all characterized by the differential structure. The purpose of this paper is to clarify the characteristics of this structure.

A revised English version of "Keisha Kōzō no Bunseki", Keizai Kenkyū, *Vol. 10, No. 3, July 1959, pp. 193–199.*

First, the empirical findings will be observed for the capitalist sector in terms of the combination of production factors, relative income shares and type of technologies in order to determine the relationships with the scale differentials. Second, the relationships will be analyzed in searching for the possibility of interpreting these as forming a state of equilibrium. In so doing, particular attention will be drawn to the factors which are responsible for forming the differential structure. Third, by use of a simple production function the significance of the technological differentials will be discussed. Particular attention will be paid to interpreting the "macro-productivity function" in the light of our findings about the differential structure. Lastly, the self-employed sector will be treated with special reference to labor employment. Between this sector and the capitalist sector, a specific form of equilibrium state will be discussed with respect to the labor employment situation.

Relationships Derived from Empirical Facts

Several important relationships are derived from the empirical data as follows.

i) The capital-labor ratio (i.e. capital intensity) is higher in larger-scale than in smaller-scale enterprises.

$$K_a/L_a > K_b/L_b, \text{ (at the same time } K_a > K_b),$$

where K and L stand for capital stock and labor and the suffixes a and b for larger-scale and smaller scale enterprises. The scale of the enterprise is classified in terms of capital amount.

ii) The average labor productivity is higher in larger-scale than in smaller-scale enterprises.

$$Y_a/L_a > Y_b/L_b,$$

where Y stands for output (added value). Wage rates (w) have a similar relationship.

$$w_a > w_b.$$

But the ratio of the wage rate to average labor productivity is smaller in larger-scale enterprises than in smaller-scale enterprises.

$$\omega_a \bigg/ \frac{Y_a}{L_a} < \omega_b \bigg/ \frac{Y_b}{L_b}.$$

iii) The capital-output ratio is bigger in larger-scale enterprises than in smaller-scale enterprises.

$$K_a/Y_a > K_b/K_b.$$

All these relationships are derived from observing various data such as *Kogyo tokeihyo* (Manufacturing census), *Hojin kigyo tokei* (Statistics of corporate enterprises) and the supplementary survey of *Kokufu chosa* (National Wealth Survey, 1955).[1]

The rate of return on capital (r) is expressed as follows using the notions mentioned previously:

$$r = \frac{Y - wL}{K} = \frac{1 - \dfrac{wL}{Y}}{\dfrac{K}{Y}} = \frac{p}{c},$$

where p and c stand for the relative income share of capital and the capital-ontput ratio. Therefore we have a simple relation

$$p_a/c_a \lessgtr p_b/c_b$$

for the rates of return on capital between larger-scale and smaller-scale enterprises. We already know that $c_a > c_b$ and $p_a > p_b$. The latter follows directly from the fact that the labor's relative income share is smaller in larger-scale than in smaller-scale enterprises. This suggests that the rate of capital return is not necessarily higher for larger-scale enterprises and that there is a possibility of a competitive equilibrium with respect to the rates of capital return between enterprises of different scale. The

---

[1] It is not intended here to discuss in detail statistical aspects of the data. However, I have to mention the following two points. First, the unit is sometimes the "establishment" rather than the enterprise. The difference between the two is ignored for the sake of simplicity. Second, there are cases where the data is classified in terms of the number of employed workers, instead of the amount of capital. Again for simplicity, the difference which may arise due to this classification difference is ignored.

following implication can then be drawn from this relationship: Larger-scale enterprises use technologies which require a higher level of capital intensity and this produces a higer level of average labor productivity. The wage rates paid for employing workers to carry out such a type of production is higher on the average than in the case of smaller-scale enterprises. Labor's relative income share is, however, lower in larger-scale enterprises so that capital's relative income share can be higher compared to smaller -scale enterprises. On the other hand, the amount of capital technologically required for producing a unit amount of output is bigger in larger-scale enterprises, and this tends to make for a smaller rate of capital return as compared to the case of smaller-scale enterprises.

It is my view that these are more important than they appear at first glance. Suppose that the wage differentials are given due to one cause or another, this situation must be one of the most crucial parameters in entrepreneurial decision-making. A wide range of wage rate differentials for available workers will be seriously considered in order to select the most appropriate technologies for maximizing profit. The different types of technologies are here considered simply in terms of the capital-labor ratio. It is a well known proposition that a higher wage rate should be associated with a higher level of the capital-labor ratio and *vice versa*, either in historical or international comparisons. The present case is a co-existence of such an association within an economy.

Chart 1 is intended to illustrate such a situation of coexistence[2]. Two different technologies, α and β, are compared in terms of a combination of wage rates (on the vertical axis) and capital

[2] This chart is drawn following the suggestion made by Komao Tanaka in his comment on my article "Kajōshūgyō to keisha kōzō (Excess Employment and the Differential structure (in K. Ohkawa ed., *Kajōshugyō no bunseki* (The Analysis of the Excess Employment), 1959.

Chart 1.   Co-existence of Different Technologies

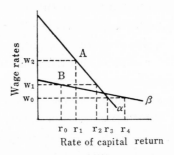

return (on the horizontal axis).   Technology α is assumed to represent the larger-scale enterprises and technology β the smaller-scale enterprises.   The points the vertical axis intersects lines α and β indicate the level of output per labor unit (Y/L in our notation) to be obtained by each technology.   The selection of technologies is illustrated as follows.   Suppose a low wage rate w_0 is given, the rate of return on capital is r_4 for technology β and r_3 for technology α.   Since r_4 is higher than r_3, the former technology will be adopted.   At a higher rate of wages, w_1, however, the rate of capital return is r_0 for technology β and r_2 for technology α; since the latter turns out to be higher than the former, technology α will be adopted.   If only a single wage rate prevails in the labor market (and no differentials in interest rates), the most profitable technology will be determined uniquely.   The present case is illustrated by a co-existence of say, w_0, w_1, w_2 in the chart which shows that it is possible to think of the same rate of capital return for technologies α and β associated with a different level of wage rates.

The so-called differential structure can now be understood as a state of competitive equilibrium.[3]   The factors which are respon-

---

[3]   In the main text, a proof has been given for a static competitive equilibrium. This is not intended to ignore the fact that historically larger-scale enterprises grew

sible for forming such a structure are as follows: First, the differentials in the power to commanding capital; second, the differentials in wage rates and third, differentials in technological knowledge and capability. The scale of enterprises have been defined in terms of the amount of capital used for production operations. Either owned or leased, this implies, *de facto*, the resulting differentials in the power to command capital. The factors underlying wage differentials are complex. The quality difference of labor due to such factors as sex, age, education etc. is no doubt responsible for the higher wage rate in larger-scale enterprises because the composition of workers employed by these enterprises manifests itself, on the average, in a higher level of quality than in the case of smaller-scale enterprises. Even after eliminating such a quality difference, however, there still remains a considerable degree of wage differential which is of particular concern for our analysis. This is a special form of surplus labor, which manifests itself not in unemployment but in low-wage employment. A wide range of availability of technological knowledge and capability has been made possible historically through the particular combination of the modern technologies borrowed from advanced countries and indigeneous technologies domestically developed.

---

faster than smaller-scale enterprises. It is quite possible that the rate of capital return tends to be higher for larger-scale enterprises than for smaller-scale enterprises, even apart from the effects of monopolistic elements. In our terminology the condition for forming such a situation is given as follows

$$\frac{Y_a - w_a L_a}{Y_b - w_b L_b} > \frac{K_a}{K_b}.$$

This relation can easily be derived from $p_a/c_a > p_b/c_b$. The total capital-returns ratio on the left must be larger than the capital ratio on the right. So long as this inequality condition is fulfilled, a higher rate of capital return will be sustained for larger-scale enterprises. This is quite probable with respect to the dynamic process of economic development, resulting in the cumulative process of enlarging the power of these enterprises to command capital.

Functional Observations

It appears that we can assume a productivity function

$$\frac{Y}{L} = F\left(\frac{K}{L}\right)$$

from the empirical findings mentioned above. Let us first examine this possibility by assuming that the confirmed relationships between a and b enterprises exist continuously for the entire range of different scales of enterprises. Expressing Y/L by y and K/L by k, we assume conditions $F' > 0$ and $F'' < 0$ for $y = F(k)$ as is illustrated by Chart 2. This function satisfies the relations we confirmed previously such as $k_a > k_b$, $y_a > y_b$ and $c_a > c_b$, as has been analyzed in detail by Ara.[4] Therefore, if all the enterprises of various scales are assumed to be at equilibrium at the points where the condition of profit maximization is fulfilled, the curve in the chart would represent the macro-productivity function in the sense that these equilibrium points, continuously connected,

Chart 2.   Macro Productivity Function

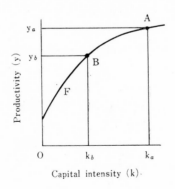

Capital intensity (k)·

[4] K. Ara, "Capital Theory and Economic Growth", *The Economic Journal*, Vol. LXVIII, No. 271, September 1958.

Chart 3. Different Productivity Functions By Scale

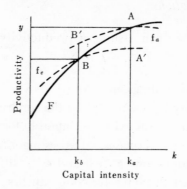

Capital intensity

form a schedule of production behavior for the enterpreneurs taken as a whole.

Measurements of the production function using cross-section data assume in theory an existence of such a single macro-production function. It is clear, however, that this is not valid for our case. A single production funcion cannot represent the technologies which differ by scale of enterprises. According to the simple treatment developed in the preceding section, we have to assume at least different parameters of a specified function for different scales of enterprises. This is illustrated by Chart 3.

Through two points A and B, two productivity functions f_a and f_b are drawn (dotted lines) in order to illustrate the situation we face. At each point a state of equilibrium maximizing rates of capital return is assumed.[5] Now it is supposed that all

[5] The rate of return on capital can be given in the following form.

$$\frac{Y - wL}{K} = \frac{\dfrac{Y}{L} - w}{\dfrac{K}{L}} = \frac{y - w}{k}.$$

If we differentiate this equation with respect to k and equated to zero, we have $y = F'k + w$, This is transformed to $F' = \dfrac{dy}{dk} = \dfrac{y - w}{k}$. This equation tells us that the maximum rate of capital return is equal to F'.

the equilibrium points, such as A and B, compose the curve F, which has previously been observed. The difference of schedules is illustrated as follows. For the level of capital intensity k_a, point A', instead of point A, is now supposed for enterprise b. Likewise, for the level of capital intensity k_b, point B' instead of point B, is now supposed for enterprise a. The equilibrium wage rate, w_a, is given on the vertical axis at the point of intersection with the extrapolated line tangent to f_a at point A. Likewise w_b will be given corresponding to point B. These should be equal to the marginal productivity of labor of scale a and b enterprises respectively. These cannot be equal, and it is this inequality which represents the differentials in the marginal productivity of labor and equilibrium wage rates.

The schedules illustrated above by curves f_a and f_b are hypothetical as we have no knowledge based on empirical findings. Therefore, we should be cautious in applying such an idea to empirical analysis. The above-illustration assumes a wide range of schedule, but actually this must be fairly limited. The limitation may come from either the availability of capital or the entrepreneurs' ability to use technological and organizational knowledge. To the extent that the limitation is actually greater, the schedule curves in the chart should be drawn within a shorter range. In the extreme case we would come back again to a single productivity function drawn between points A and B, This, however, cannot be justified. Even if the actual range is very narrow, it is our view that the functions such as f_a and f_b should separately be assumed.[6]

---

[6] In the original version this aspect of limitation was not adequately described. On revising this point I have benefited greatly from recent discussions I had with Yukihiko Kiyokawa.

The Self-employment Sector

All the previous discussion has dealt with the capitalist sector. Now we turn to the self-employment sector. The differentials of marginal productivity in labor and wage rates are particularly relevant to the relationship which we shall examine between these two sectors.

This sector is distinguished from the capitalist sector in that profit maximization behavior does not prevail and the so-called "mixed income" is dominant. The latter poses a particular problem for us because the allocation of production factors cannot directly be discussed by means of marginal principle. Actually, even in this sector a wide range of differentials of productivity is witnessed in terms of the scale of production unit. It is not intended here to discuss in detail the actual situation of this sector referring to the empirical data concerned. Instead, our purpose is to clarify conceptually what is the place and role played by this sector in the general framework of the differential structure.

For simplicity, this sector is represented by agriculture and we assume that the productivity funcion

$$\frac{Y}{L} = f\left(\frac{B}{L}\right)$$

can describe its production behavior. B stands for land, capital being supposed complementary enough to be included in B. From the empirical observation of Japanese agriculture we think it is possible to assume $f'>0$ and $f''<0$. Corresponding to the treatment in the preceding sections, it is possible to suppose a curve which connects all the equilibrium points of farm enterprises subject to only one different condition: equilibrium means in this case an equality between the marginal productivity of labor and the marginal self-evaluation of labor. It is to be noted

Chart 4.   Demand and Supply Prices of Labor

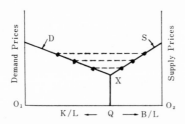

that in this sector the major factors responsible for forming the differential structure are i) the differences in the power to command land area and ii) the level differences in the marginal self-evaluation of labor.   Actually, the data classified by farm-operation scale can provide us with the empirical basis of presenting these propositions.

Let us begin with a simple idea.   It would be possible to assume that the differential structure thus defined with respect to this sector will shape a labor supply curve with respect to the supplies of labor from this sector to the capitalist sector.   Chart 4 is intended to describe the situation of this sector in this respect.   Starting from point Q on the horizontal axis, the land-labor ratio, B/L, is supposed to increase.   Correspondingly, the supply price of labor will increase as is illustrated by curve S.   On the horizontal axis, K/L in the capitalist sector is supposed to be larger in the opposite direction.   Corresponding to this, curve D illustrates a tendency of increasing wage rates.   Dotted lines connecting the corresponding points on curves S and D are intended to show a formation of equilibrium wage rates at each different level.

This presentation appears to explain the process of forming the differentials in equilibrium wage rates by pointing out the possible correspondence between the differentials in the demand price and the supply price of labor.   This is far from the case, however, because in reality the level of marginal productivity of labor is, on the average, lower in the self-employed sector than in the capitalist sector, and it is misleading to that the marginal productivity of labor is equal between the two sectors at point Q.

The inequality of the marginal productivity of labor between the two sectors has been one of my basic notions in develpoing a two-sector model. In treating a state of equilibrium with respect to the demand-supply of labor between the two sectors, the *average* productivity, instead of the marginal productivity of labor in agriculture, has been proposed as the appropriate notion. The idea is as follows. Surplus labor, that is the labor force which is not employed by the capitalist sector, is all obliged to engage itself in the self-employed sector where the marginal productivity of the surplus labor should naturally be lower than that of the capitalist sector. This phenomenon has been called an "excess employment" (Kajyo syūgyō) situation because the excess employment is the cause of a lower level of marginal productivity of labor with a tendency of decreasing returns. Despite the over-occupation of the labor force in agriculture, urban-farm incomes can be at equilibrium if we take the household unit as the basis for comparison because the latter obtain non-wage incomes. In this sense, the average productivity of the latter should be compared with the marginal productivity of labor in the capitalist sector.[7]

Taking this notion into consideration, Chart 5 is drawn.[8] On the vertical axis, productivity and wages are taken for Sector 1

[7] This was originally developed in K. Ohkawa "Nōgyō no keizai bunseki" (*Economic Analysis of Agriculture*), Taimeido, Tokyo, 1955.

[8] The chart in the original version was rightly critisized as misleading by Yasukichi Yasuba in his Discussion Paper "Modern Economists' Views on Japanese Economy," D.P. 014, *KIEP*, Kyoto Institute of Economic Research, Kyoto University. I have presented here a revised version. The chart Yasuba himself presented in his paper, however, seems to be misleading in that the intersection of M_2 and a downward extrapolation of M_1 (in Chart 5) marks the level of "Excess employment" labor in sector 2. (See his chart in footnote 41, pp. 20).

Chart 5. An Excess Employment Situation in the Self-employment Sector

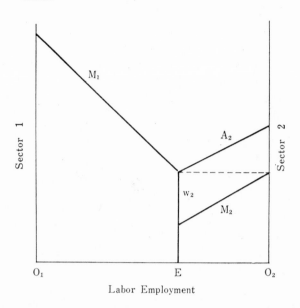

Labor Employment

(the capitalist sector) on the left and for Sector 2 (the self-employed sector) on the right. M_1 and M_2 stand for the marginal productivities of labor for sector 1 and sector 2; A_2 and w_2 stand for average productivity of labor and the prevailing wages in sector 2. On the horizontal axis, O_1E and O_2E show respectively the size of labor employment in sectors 1 and 2.

In this chart, at point E, an equality is realized between M_1 and A_2, the level of M_2 being much lower than that of M_1. According to the conventional notion of the optimum allocation of labor, this would be a state of disequilibrium. According to our scheme, however, this is a sort of equilibrium, the disequilibrium being implicitly involved. In this sense this has been called the *disguised equilibrium* in my above-cited book. It was a simple approach based on the average observation with a two-sector model. Here it is intended to introduce this notion into the scheme of the differential structure. For sector 1, M_1 represents the wage differentials at a state of equilibrium whereas for sector 2 the prevailing wage rate, w_2, is drawn parallel to the horizontal axis, producing an increasing gap between its level and that of M_2 as the labor occupied in this sector increases. Only at point O_2 do we have $w_2 = M_2$. Therefore, all the labor occupied in Sector 2 is defined as "excess employment." This is only for the sake of simplicity. Actually, it would be possible to include the piont beyond O_2 but this is ignored as it does not influence the present discussion. What we want to note here is the following. In the self-employment sector the minimum level of the wage rate will prevail so long as the marginal productivity of labor is lower than the minimum level of the marginal productivity of labor in the capitalist secter. In other words, the miminum level of the average productivity of labor in the self-employment sector conforms to the lowest level of wages in the capitalist sector.[9]

Having thus established a link between the two sectors, let us now discuss the mechanism of forming the differentials in equilibrium wage rates in the capitalist sector. In doing so, one preliminary point must be made to avoid a possible misunderstanding. My notion of "disguised equilibrium" has originally been intended to establish an analytical frame within which postwar Japanese agriculture could usefully be investigated in relation to the growth of the rest of the economy. The abolishment of the persistent institution of landlordism was of course one of the important conditions for applying this notion. But, in my present view, it is much more important to note that this notion

[9] This is of course a great simplification of the complexities with which we face in the real world. In an empirical approach it is of course indispensable to distinguish different prices of labor supply due to various status of the labor force in the self-employment sector, as agricultural economists specializing in this fields have done.

should only be applied to the historical phase where the wage rates are determined endogenously. In other words, this should not be applied to the phase where the subsistence wage is assumed to be given exogenously to the capitalist sector.[10]

Now, with regard to the main subject, there are two point I would like to make. First, speaking generally, the demand side, rather than the supply side, must be influential in changing wage differentials. As has previously been suggested, a higher level of capital intensity requires a higher quality level of workers. This is undoubtedly responsible for forming the wage differential. The wage differential proper which still exists after making allowances for the quality difference is, in my view, to be explained in association with the demand-supply relation of the labor force.[11] When the "surplus" becomes greater, the minimum level of wage rates will be lower and *vise versa*. An increase in the excess-supply of labor, according to our scheme, will make the minimum level of the average productivity of labor lower in the self-employment sector whereas a mitigation of the excess supply will bring forth a reverse effect. In either case we can suppose another state of equilibrium.

Second, with respect to the supply side, it may not be appropriate to ignore entirely the effect of the differentials of average productivity on the supply price of labor to the capitalist sector. The members of the farm-household whose level of productivity is relatively higher will require higher wage rates if they want to

[10] In the original version this point was not clearly stated, and I may be responsible for misleading readers as to my thinking. For example, in reviewing my paper "Agriculture and Turning Points" (contained in this volume), Y. Yasuba, in the paper cited above, critisized me saying "what has happned to his model of disguised equibrium, which is the prototype of Jorgenson's model" (pp. 26). The text is revised to be clearer.

[11] How can such wage differentials exist for workers of the "same quality"? The answer will be given in pointing out that for larger-scale enterprises workers are not of the same but higher quality judged from the long-term point of view. It will require an extra training cost to replace them by workers newly employed.

migrate to the non-agricultural sector. However, this may not be so influential in forming the wage differentials in the capitalist sector because the incentives for them to migrate may be much less as compared with the case of farm-households which belong to the lower strata.

WAGES,

PRODUCTIVITY AND PRICES

Introduction

The purpose of this note is to analyse the relationship between wages, productivity and commodity prices with a very simple two-sector model: Sector I of high productivity and Sector II of low productivity.

It is a widely recognized fact that the present Japanese inflation is characterized by differential rates of increase in commodity prices: a high rate of increase in Sector II and a low rate of increase, or even decrease, in Sector I. Statistically, this manifests itself in producing a sharp contrast between the consumer price and wholesale price indices: a distinct rise in the former vs. relative stability in the latter, because broadly speaking, the former represents the commodity prices of Sector II, whereas the latter those of Sector I.

This pattern of inflation, in my view, suggests the significance of *structural* causes, and the conventional macro-thesis of either "demand pull" or "cost push" cannot appropriately be applied. Our structural approach will be tried in testing the hypothesis: that the rise of commodity prices is caused by a combined effect of i) chronic productivity differentials in favor of Sector I and ii)

A revised English version of "Chingin, Seisansei, Bukka" Keizai Kenkyū, Vol. *20*, No. *4. November 1969*, pp. 356–359.

a new tendency of wage differentials to narrow between the two sectors in favor of Sector II. The implication of this hypothesis is as follows. Historically, the productivity differentials and the wage differentials have been built up closely interrelated, forming the differential structure of the Japanese economy. The historical pattern of commodity prices until around 1960 can be interpreted without making any specific hypothesis: a faster rate of productivity growth of Sector I tended to decrease its output prices, relatively, whereas a slower rate of productivity growth of Sector II did not manifest itself in raising its output prices remarkably because the cheaper wage-cost, due to the sustained wage differentials, kept output prices at a relatively low level. It can be said that a sort of balance had been kept with respect to price performance so long as no basic changes took place in the economic structure. Since around 1961, however, a sustained high rate of growth of the economy brought forth a basic change in wage differentials despite the continued differentials of productivity growth and I believe this is the core of the problem.

This note is not intended to develop a comprehensive analysis of the problem but merely to clarify some of the basic factors which, I believe, are responsible for forming the mechanism. First, a most simplified model will be developed as a framework for analysis. Second, each equation will be tested by empirical observations.

A Simplified Model

Our model is presented below in a most simplified form.

(1) $$\dot{w}_1 = a + b\dot{y}_1$$
(2) $$\dot{w}_2 - \dot{w}_1 = F(U)$$
(3) $$\dot{p}_2 = c + d(\dot{w}_2 - g_2),$$

where the suffixes 1 and 2 stand for Sector I and Sector II and the dot (like $\dot{w}$) denotes the rate of increase.

Equation (1) is intended to explain linearly the rate of money wage increase in Sector I ($\dot{w}_1$) by the rate of increase in the value productivity of labor in this sector ($\dot{y}_1$). Equation (2) takes up the wage differential in the form of rate of the change ($\dot{w}_2 - \dot{w}_1$) to be explained by the degree of surplus labor (U), the definition and measurement of which will be explained later. In equation (3), rate of change of the output prices in Sector II (p_2) is intended to be explained by the difference between the rate of increase in wages ($\dot{w}_2$) and that of productivity growth in real terms (g_2) in this sector.

A model of three equations with six variables implies that the three variables, y_1, g_2 and U are to be given exogenously. The performance of productivities (g_1 and g_2) and the situation of the demand-supply of labor (U) can legitimately be assumed to be given in such a simple, partial model. It is a more serious matter, however, that the performance of output prices in Sector I (note that $p_1 + g_1 = y_1$) is assumed to be given. Not for logical but for practical reasons, this can be allowed because the rate of change in p_1 has been minor during the period under review. Viewed from this point, the model is to aim at analyzing the price performance of Sector II. Particular attention is drawn to equation (2) in which the rate of unemployment is not used. This may appear to go against the recent fashion but closer inspection shows that this is not the case. The degree of surplus labor, which particularly pertains to Sector II, is used merely as an indicator of the changes in the demand-supply situation of labor in a similar sense as the rate of unemployment, taking into consideration of the structure of the Japanese economy. The variable to be explained in this equation is the wage differential rather than the wage itself. This is different from the conventional approach: the wage rate in Sector I is simply related to the value productivity of labor and, in relation to $\dot{w}_1$, thus determined, $\dot{w}_2$ is considered to be determined, being associated with U.

Given $\dot{g}_2$ and $\dot{w}_2$ in equation (3), $\dot{p}_2$ will be determined, implying that a rise of wages is the cause of an increase in the output prices in Sector II. This is the opposite relationship as compared to Sector I and appears to assume a causality similar to the thesis of "cost-push". However, we do not think that this is really a cost-push phenomenon. The true causality is as follows: an increase in productivity in Sector I→ an increase in wages in Sector I→ an increase in wages in Sector II (through a decrease in U as a result of the expansion of Sector I)→ an increase in the imbalance between wages and productivity in Sector II→ an increase in the output prices in Sector II. Nowhere in this process is an independent rise of wages assumed[1].

What is implied in our simple model can be further explained as follows. First, let us clarify its implications in comparison with a single-sector model. If we eliminate Sector II, a combination of equations (1) and (2) will lead to the function

$$\dot{w} = F(\dot{y}, U), \text{ or } \dot{w} = F(\dot{p}, \dot{g}, U),$$

which will be similar to the conventional approach except that the rate of unemployment is replaced by U. In this dimension the controversial issue has been in what sense the productivity term can be used to explain the rate of wage changes. Some says it is a demand term because it can represent enterprisers' ability to pay wages while others assume that it is a supply term because workers will demand wages taking productivity perfor-

---

[1] In Sector II the so-called "mixed income" is dominant. Because of this fact, the use of w_2 may be criticized as being unrealistic. We admit this in principle, but in practice the performance of the wage rate can effectively be used as a proxy. Another criticism may be that the support prices of farm products such as rice, wheat etc. must be the cause of a rise of rural wage rates. This suggests a reversed causality— from p_2 to w_2. An extended version of this view is found in the assertion that a rise of wages in Sector II is the cause of a rise of wages in Sector I. I cannot share such a view because it assumes the driving force behind rising prices to come independently from Sector II—a hypothesis which is opposite of our own.

mance as a standard. I am not ready to present any rigorously defined proposition in this respect. Here, equation (1) is presented on the empirical basis that the increase in productivity and the increase in the wage level has long been associated historically. This implies a basic recognition that in the modern sector a rise of wages depends upon an increase in the productivity of labor as seen in a broad historical trend.

Second, with respect to Sector II, the historical meaning of equation (2) is different: a tendency of wage differentials to narrow can take place over a historical span of limited range in which the situation of the demand-supply of labor is subject to a distinct change—that is a period of the particular form of the differential structure.

Empirical Tests

There are three points I would like to make as preliminaries. i) From the nature of our model, empirical evidences should be posed in terms of longer swings to be found after eliminating short-term fluctuations. ii) Econometric measurement is not our aim so that the degree of statistical fitness will not be the sole judgement. Rather we will attempt to describe broadly the relationships of the selected variables. iii) Some of the data which will be used are of a tentative nature, being subject to future revision so that the interpretation should be done broadly. (The sources and remarks on the charts will be described in the *Statistical Notes* which appear at the end of this paper).

Equation (1)

To begin with the postwar period, Sector I is represented by manufacturing. Investment performance being taken as the criterion, two swings are identified: an upward swing for 1955–61 and a downward swing for 1961–65. Chart 1 shows the relation between the rate of increase in the value productivity of labor

Chart 1. Relation between $(\dot{w}_1)$ and Value Productivity $(\dot{y}_1)$ in Terms of Rate of Increase: Manufacturing (A), 1955–1965.

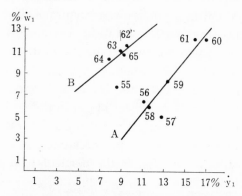

Table 1. Relation between the Rate of Productivity Growth $(\dot{y}_1)$ and the Ratio of Wage to Productivity (w_1/y_1): Manufacturing, 1886–1964

Period	$\dot{y}_1$	Year	w_1/y_1
1886–1908(U)	5.97%	1886(T)	34.9%
		1898(P)	22.2
1898–1905(D)	2.40	1905(T)	32.0
1905–1919(U)	9.72	1919(P)	25.0
1919–1931(D)	3.62	1931(T)	27.8
1931–1938(U)	6.84	1938(P)	22.2
1945–1961(U)	10.03	1954(T)	33.1
1961–1964(D)	8.89	1961(P)	27.9
		1964(T)	27.4*

Remarks: i) U and D stand for the upswing and downswing phases; T and P stand for the trough and peak years of swings. ii) The figure of w_1/y_1 is intended to show only the relative changes as this is not the labors' relative share which counts working days. iii) The postwar data are presented for comparisons. The figure marked by * is not directly comparable because of different coverage.

Source: reproduced from Tables 1–5 and 1–6 in K. Ohkawa and H. Rosovsky, "Postwar Japanese Growth in Historical Perspective: A Second Look" in L. Klein and K. Ohkawa eds., *Economic Growth: The Japanese Experience Since The Meiji Era*, Richard D. Irwin, 1968.

$(\dot{y}_1$ on the horizontal axis) and the rate of increase in money wages $(\dot{w}_1$ on the vertical axis). Broadly speaking, the former is relatively bigger for 1955–61 than for 1961–65 whereas the latter is bigger for the downswing than for the upswing. In other words, since the year of peak, 1961, $\dot{y}_1$ tended to decline while $\dot{w}_1$ did not. The two lines A and B are drawn roughly in the chart in order to suggest the changes in the value of a and b, particularly the former. Without recognizing such a shift, it seems impossible to witness any regularity between the two variables. We understand that the postwar empirical facts endorse equation (1) with shifts through swings.

How about the prewar period? What has been found in the above also appears to be recognized broadly for the prewar years, although data availability is limited. Table 1 presents the relevant figures which give evidence not directly, but indirectly for equation (1): the tendency $\dot{y}_1 > \dot{w}_1$ is seen during upswings and the reverse tendency $\dot{w}_1 > \dot{y}_1$ is seen during downswings. Through this swing regularity, we can conceive a similar shift performance of equation (1) as we found previously for the postwar years.

To give a satisfactory interpretation of this phenomenon is beyond the scope of this note. What it implies, however, can be understood as follows. We see the so-called time-lag of wage increases behind productivity increases during upswings whereas the well-known downward rigidity of wages during downswings seems to exist. The time-lag phenomenon appears to be easily explained in relation to the flexible supplies of labor: as value productivity increases, enterprisers do not necessarily need to raise wages because workers are available with lower wages. The downward rigidity of wages, however, appears to be contradictory to the flexible supplies of labor. A more consistent interpretation of both upswing and downswing is thus required. The enterprisers' behavior of employing workers in a longer run dimension seems to be relevant. Wages are kept relatively stable despite productivity fluctuations. This is particularly so in view of the peculiar employment-wage system of modern Japanese enter-

83

prises. At any rate what is important to the present discussion is that equation (1) is valid in the long run dimension and that its shift through swings is understandable in view of the relative stability of wage performance.

Before closing the discussion on equation (1), particular attention is drawn to the performance of wages in recent years. With respect to the downward period, 1961–65, most economists have asserted that the tendency of wages to increase at a faster rate than that of productivity must have been caused by the new situation of "labor shortage". According to our analysis, however, this assertion cannot readily be accepted. The tendency $\dot{w}_1 > \dot{y}_1$ has been a repeated phenomenon through all downswings as we found in the preceding discussion. As will be seen in the following section, the performance of wage differentials appeared

Chart 2. Relation between Wage ($\dot{w}_1$) and Value Productivity ($\dot{y}_1$) in Terms of Rate of Increase: Manufacturing (B). 1955–1968.

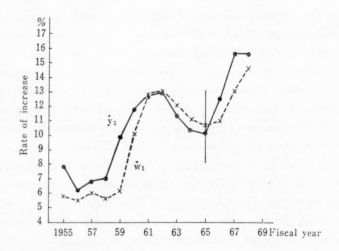

Remarks: The vertical line drawn for 1965 indicates differences in data before and after that year (See *Statistical Notes*).

to differ from its historical regurality during this particular period and accordingly we see the effects of "labor shortage". But to be decisive in this respect, we have to look at the post-1965 period of upswing.

The value productivity of labor has again turned out to increase at a faster pace than wages since 1965. Chart 2 is shown to illustrate this in comparison with the previous postwar years.

I am much inclined to conclude that the historical regularlity has still been sustained almost up to the present despite a distinct change in the demand-supply relationship in the labor market. This poses the important question as to why this is so. I will return to this point after having discussed the performance of Sector II.

Equation (2)

Let us begin by measuring U, the indicator of labor surplus. The conventional rate of unemployment is extremely small in Japan, being less than one per cent in recent years. This has often been understood as indicating "full employment". It is true that an "excess demand" situation has been witnessed for new entrants into the labor market according to the available statistics. However, this does not necessarily imply a full employment situation in the structural sense because there is still a rich source of labor shift from the sector of low productivity to the sector of high productivity. For example, in 1968–69 there was an increase of 950 thousand workers in the non-agricultural sector whereas the labor force decreased by 510 thousand in agriculture: roughly, the labor shift contributed 54% of the total additional workers in the non-agricultural sector.

In view of such a situation the sum of unemployed and underemployed people is taken and its ratio to the total hired employment (self-employed and family workers excluded) is defined as U. It is difficult to have a reliable measure of the underemployed, but a proxy can be found. Short-time workers in the self-employ-

Chart 3.   Relation of Two Indicators of Labor Availability

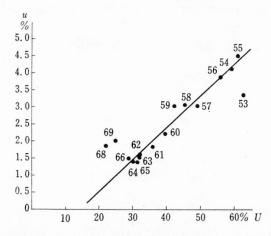

Remarks: Years are indicated in abbreviated form, e.g. 53=1953.

ment sector are tentatively estimated from the *Labor Force Survey*. In Chart 3 this indicator is shown as U in comparison with u, the unemployment rate, each as a percentage of the total hired employment.

The two indicators show a broad association, and to that extent u can be used as a proxy of U.   This may explain why the use of u has often been successful in certain econometric studies.   A closer look, however, reveals some disassociation of the two, particularly for the later years.   It is important to note that U itself shows a tendency to decline sharply, roughly from 60 to a less than 30 per cent level over a very short interval.   Undoubtedly a drastic change has been taking place on the right hand side of equation (2).

Next, regarding the wage differentials, proxies of w_1 and w_2 are taken from manufacturing and agriculture.   Wages in agriculture may fluctuate due to the factors peculiar to this sector.   The statistics of wages in the tertiary sectors, however, are less reliable

Chart 4. Changes in the Wage Differentials and the Degree of Labor Availability.

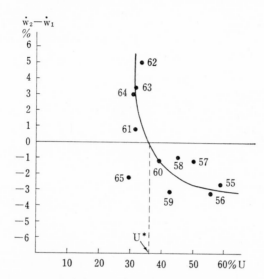

and we use agricultural wages as a second best choice. Chart 4 shows the relationship between $\dot{w}_2 - \dot{w}_1$ and U. During the upswing of 1955–61, $\dot{w}_1 > \dot{w}_2$ was the case whereas the reverse has been the case during the post 1961 downswing. The point where $\dot{w}_1 = \dot{w}_2$ is marked by U^*. After passing this point, the curve shows a sharp increase in $\dot{w}_2 - \dot{w}_1$ responding to a relatively small decrease in U.[2]

No data are available to measure U for the prewar years and for the time being it is impossible to observe equation (2) in a long-run dimension, as in the case of equation (1). The following is an indirect, partial approach which may be useful to judge prewar performance. The ratio w_2/w_1 measured by the same proxies as before is readily available and is shown for the years

[2] The fact that $\dot{w}_1$ exceeded $\dot{w}_2$ in 1965 does raise certain doubts. Whether this is exceptional or suggests a slow down in the tendency of wage differentials to narrow is yet to be seen.

Table 2. Wage Ratio (Agriculture/Manufacture): Selected years

	Trough Years		Peak years
1886	69.9%	1898	76.5%
1905	69.6	1919	73.3
1954	37.3	1961	42.0
1964	48.6		

Source: Ibid Table 1.

of peak and trough in Table 2. The postwar figures are added for comparison.

The tendency $\dot{w}_2 > \dot{w}_1$, during upward phases, and its reverse $\dot{w}_1 > \dot{w}_2$, during downward phases, are regularly seen until 1954. It can reasonably be supposed that U became smaller during upward and larger during downward phases, so that a shift pattern of equation (2), like in the previous case of equation (1), is quite likely to take place. What draws our particular attention is its performance since 1961. The tendency $\dot{w}_2 > \dot{w}_1$ manifested itself despite the phase of downswing of the economy. This provides evidence for the historically unprecedented structural change which took place in the labor market. The new tendency of wage differentials to narrow—an important element of our hypothesis, is thus given an empirical basis.

Equation (3)

The last is to test equation (3) empirically. Here again agriculture will be used as a proxy of Sector II entirely with respect to wages, labor productivity in real terms and output prices. Chart 5 is intended to show a closely associated performance between $\dot{p}_2$ and $\dot{w}_2 - g_2$. Such an association was not recognized in the prewar years. Agricultural prices show a certain peculiarity and other sectors of low productivity (such as commerce and service industries) should be tested further. Consumer prices elevant to these industries have increased rapidly. The whole-sale prices of manufactured goods produced by medium-small

Chart 5.   Output Prices and the Wage-Productivity Gap in
Terms of Rate of Increase: Agriculture

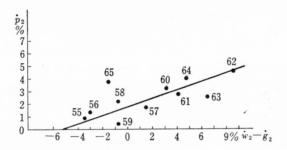

scale enterprises have tended to rise.   Even without giving
detailed statistical evidence for these facts, it is intuitively clear
that Chart 5 can well represent the general phenomenon that the
rate of increase in the output prices of Sector II is explained by the
degree of gap between the rate of increase in money wages and
that of productivity in this sector.

Two points deserve further comment.   First, it goes without
saying that a rise in prices must be supported by a stronger
demand.   Actually the shift in the demand curves for the goods
and services produced in Sector II has been occurring at a fast
pace because of the high rate of growth of per-capita income derived by a faster rate of expansion of Sector I.   Second, the self-
employed sector is the major component of Sector II.   A rise of
output prices in the self-employed sector is a form of maintaining
a balance between the mixed income in this sector and the workers'
wage income in Sector I.   Not through labor migration but formation of output prices, a tendency towards a sort of equilibrium
has taken place.   This is one aspect of the "disguised equilibrium", the concept of which I have developed elsewhere.[3]

[3]   See "Analysis of the Differential structure" contained in this volume.

Concluding Remarks

By way of conclusion I would like to mention two major points. First, the whole process we investigated can be summarized as follows. 1) A faster rate of growth in the sector of higher productivity implies an increase in the rate of productivity growth in this sector. 2) Through the mechanism simply described by equation (1) the rate of increase in money wages in this sector will be accelerated with swing variations. 3) Concurrently, the rate of labor shift from the sector of low productivity to the sector of higher productivity will be accelerated, resulting in a smaller size of labor force available for the expansion of the latter sector. 4) A combined effect of 2) and 3) above will bring forth an accelearation in the rate of increase in the money wages and incomes in the sector of low productivity, resulting in narrowed differentials as compared to those in the sector of high productivity. 5) The gap thus derived and widened between wages and productivity will be responsible for the tendency for output prices to rise in the sector of low productivity, being supported by a rise in demand. 6) These succesive processes are backed up by the basic fact that an acceleration in the rate of productivity growth in the sector of higher productivity does not necessarily accompany a parallel acceleration of productivity growth in the sector of low productivity, but rather tended to produce a wider differential of productivities between the two sectors. The last point has not been examined in this note but is the basic feature of the differential structure.

Let us treat this issue with an opposite supposition—that is a deceleration of the growth rate in 1) will bring forth eventually a slower rate of increase in the output prices in the sector of low productivity. In this sense, a sort of trade-off relation can be recognized between the degree of inflation and the rate of growth of the economy. However, this is different in nature from the trade-off relation defined in a macro-setting.

Second, the one-way track nature of our model should further be examined. As has been summarized above, no feedback is assumed from 6) to 2), that is a rise of consumer prices has no effect on the performance of money wages in the sector of high productivity. In my view, this is a legitimate assumption in light of the factual evidence we have for manufacturing. To mention the simple statistics, the index of real wages deflated by the index of consumer prices in 1970 is 152.4 as against 197.1 for the index of real labor productivity, 1965 being taken as 100. This suggests that a big gap has been produced between the rate of productivity growth and that of real wage increases. It would be intuitively supposed that no sizable gap would take place if money wage would increase in a full response to a rise in consumer prices.[4]

Towards the end of our discussion on equation (1), a question was posed—why the swing regularity in the related performance of the wage-productivity relationship has not been altered, even recently? The importance of this question must have been further emphasized after having confirmed the recent tendency of wage differentials to narrow quickly; this new phenomenon appears to have no effects on the regular performance of the wage-productivity relationship in the sector of high productivity. My speculative answer to this question is that the lack of feedback from a rise of consumer prices is certainly the essential cause of the sustained regularity in the wage-productivity relationship.

---

[4] Both indices are from the series published quaterly by Nihon Seisansei Hombu (the Japan Productivity Center). Incidentally, as in other advanced economies, consumer prices have often been found as one of the explanatory variables of money wages in postwar Japan. Such econometric measurements, however, cannot directly explain why the wide gap mentioned above could take place between productivity and real wages.

And this may explain the reason why a vicious circle of wage-price increases has not occurred up to the present.

Statistical Notes

Manufacturing wages (w_1)—Average monthly cash earnings of regular workers. Agricultural wages (w_2)—Average daily wages of casual and day workers. Source: Economic Research Institute, Economic Planning Agency, *Keizai Bunseki*, No. 27 March 1969.

Value productivity of manufacturing (y_1) and agriculture (y_2) are calculated from product value and the labor force employed respectively in each industry. The former is industrial components of NDP, taken from the *Annual Report on National Income Statistics*, 1969, Economic Planning Agency and the latter from the *Labor Force Survey*, Bureau of Statistics, Prime Minister's Office.

Agricultural price (p_2) is from the *Survey of Prices in Agricultural Community*, Ministry of Agriculture and Forestry. Agricultural productivity (g_2) is calculated by y_2/p_2.

The number of short-time workers, the major component of U, is estimated from the *Labor Force Survey*, taking the workers of less than 24 hours a week both in agricuture and non-agriculture. A breakdown into two classes, 1–14 and 15–34 working hours, is available only since 1962 so that a weighted sum has not been tried.

The above-mentioned data have been used for all the charts except Chart 2 for which the series of w_1 any y_1 are from different sources. Until 1966 they are from the worksheets of A. Ono & R. Minami (later published in Nijyū kōzōka no bukka hendō (Price Changes in the Dual Structure,) *Kikan Riron Keizaigaku* (The Economic Studies Quarterly) Vol. 22, No. 2, August 1971, originally based on *Kōgyō Tōkeihyō*, Ministry of International

Trade and Industry). The series since 1967 are my tentative estimation based on the data provided by the Japan Productivity Center.

All the data have been used in a three-year moving average in order to eliminate short-term fluctuations.

PART II

SUPPLIES OF LABOR AND GROWTH PHASES

THE PHASE OF UNLIMITED

SUPPLIES

OF LABOR*

In his path-breaking articles [5] [6] Arthur Lewis presented a modern version of the classical system, from Smith to Marx, in terms of his concept of "unlimited supplies of labor" at subsistence wages. His idea was to establish the kind of economics which would throw light upon the economic development problems of under-developed countries with surplus populations, because the neo-classical assumption of a limited supply of labor, in his understanding, would not be applicable to the problems of these countries. Since then, not a small number of authors have followed this line of thought in the field of economic development. Some of them succeeded in their efforts to develop and refine Lewis' original presentation. This paper attempts to make a further contribution along this line.

We shall be primarily concerned here with a generalized model of the phase of unlimited supplies of labor. This theoretical

* We have received valuable criticism of preliminary drafts from many persons. We wish to acknowledge particularly suggestions from Mataji Umemura, Yuichi Shionoya, Shigeru Ishiwata and James A. Kokoris.

A revised version of a joint paper with Ryoshin Minami in *Hitotsubashi Journal of Economics*, Vol. 5, No. 1, June 1964, pp. 1–15. I would like to express my deep gratitute to Ryoshin Minami who has generously allowed me to include this paper in this volume. Revisions pertain only to the form of presentation and I am solely responsible for them.

approach is taken due to our belief that the basic assumptions hitherto made in building two-sector models of the Lewis type seem to be not necessarily flexible and general enough to be consistent with historical realities. First, attempts will be made to examine the basic assumptions in general. In defining the characteristics of the subsistence sector in particular, special efforts will be made in order to specify the operational assumptions to be used for the discussion that follows. Secondly, we shall describe the main results of our investigation through the different characteristics of several cases, which are based on different assumptions respectively. In doing so, even cases of increasing wage rates will be discussed. Lastly, mathematical treatments of these models will be given to provide a more or less rigorous presentation. Because of technical limitations, our models will be built on rather simple assumptions, and yet we hope that these will contribute to clarifying the general nature of the phase of unlimited supplies of labor, and in particular, to illuminating the problem of possible solutions of various equilibrium growth paths.[1]

The Basic Assumptions

The economy is assumed to be composed of two sectors: capitalists sector (sector I) and subsistence sector (sector II), following Lewis' original model. In examining the features of these sectors and the assumptions which are relevant to the discussion that follows, no particular difficulties are involved with regard to sector I.

The features of sector I can be assumed in a most simplified form. With a certain stock of technological knowledge available, the capitalists, (in whom are combined the functions of both enter-

---

[1] For simplifying the discussion, the problem of output-equilibrium between the two sectors is not examined here. This does not imply that the possible changes in the terms of trade are unimportant. An illuminating analysis is given, among others, with respect to agriculture by Ranis and Fei [12].

prise and finance) carry out the production process by using available capital and labor. They follow the principle of profit-maximization and at the equilibrium state of perfect competition the wage rates equal the marginal product of labor, leaving no surplus for income distribution. The economy grows by their investments for production, being financed by their own savings out of profits, so long as the labor force is readily available. All the workers' earnings are assumed to be spent for their consumption. An equilibrium growth path can be discussed in a very simple form under these conditions, if we further assume a sustained equilibrium of savings=investments.

In the growth process of sector *I* described above, the rate of capital accumulation (ratio of investment to capital stock) will be determined by the two variables: profit rates and savings ratio. Given the savings ratio at a certain level and allowing no change, only the level of profit rates concerns us here. How can the profit rate be determined? It can only be endogenously determined within sector *I*, when either the amount of labor available or the wage rate to be paid is given from outside this sector. This answer constitutes the core of our problem.

Suppose a certain production function can represent the production process with a given technology. It would be easy to ascertain that our simple system is composed of four equations: production function, equality between wage rate and marginal product of labor, equality between profit rate and marginal product of capital and equilibrium of savings=investment. The number of variables contained in this system, however, are five: output, capital, labor, wage rate and profit rate; the output elasticities of capital and labor being both assumed given. Hence, one more variable is required from outside in order to complete the system. Which variable have we to select? The answer should depend upon the nature of the problem one may wish to analyze.

Lewis stressed the importance of giving the wage rate from outside, instead of the labor force, which is assumed as given in the neo-classical system. Following him, we define the basic feature of sector I to be its complete dependence on the wage rate which is determined outside the sector. To substantiate the given wage rate, Lewis introduced the classical notion of subsistence wages, which in our view seems to imply some vagueness, conceptually. This will be discussed in detail later, and it is sufficient at the moment to note that the unchanged wage rate based on the subsistence level is given central importance in his model.

Once sector I is given a certain level of the wage rate, the rate of profit and accordingly the rate of capital accumulation is determined in the system. At the same time the demand for labor at that wage rate will be determined. So long as the supply of labor to this sector exceeds the demand, we can say that an unlimited supply of labor exists at that wage rate. The sources of labor supply will be discussed in later pages. If all the required conditions mentioned above are adequately fulfilled in order to provide the capitalists with sufficient profit rates to initiate their enterprises, then the economy of sector I, it is argued, will expand in a sustained manner as capital accumulation continues until the sources of unlimited supplies of labor are exhausted. If we assume an economy which is completely free either from the diminishing returns due to natural resource limitations or from the effects which exogenous factors would bring into the economy, it is quite possible to identify a sustained equilibrium growth path with unchanged wage rates. Throughout the entire path of such an expansion a capital-widening process takes place, the capital-labor ratio being held constant.

These are the main features of the phase of unlimited supplies of labor, centering on sector I. In our view, there is no conceptual difficulty with this approach.

Next, let us turn to a discussion of the features of sector *II*. Unlike the case of sector *I*, we have to face some difficulties in simplifying the appropriate assumptions which are required for characterizing this sector. This should be done in a way so as not to depart too far from historical realities. For one thing, the conventional use of the somewhat vague concept "subsistence level" is subject to different interpretations. For another, the historical and institutional circumstance, inherited from the pre-modern epoch, vary from one country to another. Nevertheless, with some hesitation, we have to make several bold assumptions for the sake of simplifying the basis for subsequent analysis.

It is most convenient, we believe, to begin with the problem Lewis himself left un-solved. After referring to the classical notion of subsistence level, he suggests a more objective index, namely, the average product of the peasant. But he doubts the applicability of this objective standard by recognizing the case of tenant-peasants for, as he observed, the rent will probably be adjusted so as to leave them just enough for a conventional level of subsistence. May we cite his own conclusion. "It is not, however, of great importance to the argument whether earnings in the subsistence sector are determined objectively by the level of peasant productivity, or subjectively in terms of a conventional standard of living. Whatever the mechanism, the result is an unlimited supply of labor for which this is the minimum level of earnings [5, p. 409]." It is our contention that the mechanism of the "objective standard" can imply different results from those of the mechanism of the "subjective standard." In this section, however, we take up only the subjective standard, leaving the discussion of the objective standard to the subsequent section. Here we would like to begin with a simple assumption that a certain level of minimum subsistence is inherited historically at the beginning of modernization from

101

the pre-modern epoch and that this level continues to prevail due to inertia during the phase under consideration.

First all, sustained sources of unlimited supplies of labor must be provided from sector *II*. To meet this requirement throughout the entire phase under consideration, there must always exist a certain number in the labor force of this sector who are willing to be employed by the capitalists in sector *I* at unchanged subsistence wage rates. Two elements are contained in this situation: one is an ever-lasting source of the labor force and the other a maintenance of incentives for their outmigration. Here we are concerned with the latter, leaving the discussion of the former to later pages. The incentive is assumed to be given by the differentials between subsistence wages and earnings of labor employed in sector *II*. The differentials should be considered with appropriate allowances such as the extra living costs required for urban life and the psychological resistance or social inertia to out-migration, etc. These considerations, however, would not alter the nature of the problem nor the assumption that the differentials must be large enough to sustain incentives for migration.[2] Implicit is a potential of earnings in sector *II*, which must be necessarily lower as compared with the subsistence wages of sector *I*.

Second, such workers whose earnings are lower than the subsistence level should be kept in sector *II*. To explain why

[2] In this respect, it is important to make a distinction between the head of households and dependent family workers. In the case of household head, the possibility of having job opportunities for his dependent family workers in sector *I* is an important additional factor to be considered in the discussion. Mazumdar presents an interesting argument in this respect in the light of Indian experience [7]. As will be stated later in the text, however, we maintain that during the phase under consideration the source of unlimited supplies of labor concerns solely the dependent family workers. If outmigration of household heads accompanying their family workers is required even in the initial phase of economic development for one reason or another, as Mazumdar argues, the situation of demand and supply of labor would present a completely different picture. In the light of Japanese experience throughout the prewar economic development, however, the main body of outmigrated labor has consisted of dependent family workers [11].

this is possible it is most convenient to assume that typically this sector is composed of traditional households or extended families,[3] that is, unseparated units of production and consumption. The heads of households are responsible for both carrying out production and maintaining all family members. Let us take a typical case of peasant farming. With given technological knowledge and a small amount of capital goods (which can be assumed, in theory, part of land because of their complementarity with land), the household head carries out farming on his own land by using his own family workers. Some sort of maximization principle (which must be different from the principle assumed for sector *I*) can be defined in one way or another, but we hesitate to do so here.[4] The minimum specifications required are that the household head maintains his dependent family workers whose production contributions are lower than the subsistence level and that he offers no resistance to their outmigration to sector *I* if they can find jobs there.

Having thus specified the features of sectors *I* and *II*, let us discuss the relation between the two. Chart 1 shows a schematic presentation of what has been said thus far. At point *E* on the horizontal axis the average product per worker *(AP)* equals the subsistence level*(SL)*. In reality a certain margin *(AP>SL)* may be required at least to maintain the household at a traditional level of production and consumption corresponding to the sub-

---

[3] An interesting description of people's behavior is presented by Bauer and Yamey with respect to the extended family system [2]. The main concern here, however, is not the extended size of the family but the paternal behavior of the household head. With respect to the latter feature, the prewar Japanese pattern was typical especially as it was characterized by the existence of the right of primogeniture. For the sake of simplicity we have assumed that no landlords exist in sector *II*. If they were to be incorporated in the discussion, various functions could be attributed to them in accordance with the institutional conditions of the economy under consideration. This would not, however, alter substantially the core of our statement that follows.

[4] Some principle of maximizing total output can be assumed, for example. This would be an attempt along the line of thought which is well-presented by Georgescu-Roegen [4].

Chart 1

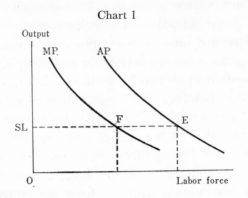

sistence level of individuals. For simplicity, however, the margin can be assumed as zero. Given a decreasing return of the production curve, it is assumed that the household cannot maintain more dependent workers beyond this limiting point. At this point the marginal product of labor (*MP*) is lower than *SL*. If this point is sustained continuously as capital accumulation goes on in sector *I*, we can define the simplest phase of unlimited supplies of labor. This is only possible by assuming that all the increase in the labor force due to population growth is absorbed by the expansion of sector *I*. Such a case is special and cannot be assumed in general, but can be used as a standard for our discussion.

The simplest case mentioned above implies two major elements which are relevant to the significance of point *E*: i) the initial condition historically given and ii) the difference between the rate of increase in the demand for labor in sector *I* and the rate of increase in the supply of labor due to population growth. With respect to i), any points located to the left of point *E* can represent the initial condition so far as *SL>MP*. Its location between two points *E* and *F* may differ from one country to another. With respect to ii), any *a priori* assumption cannot be made. If the difference is plus, the number of the labor force in sector *II* tends to decrease as capital accumulation goes on in sector *I*. If the difference is minus, reverse is the case. The simplest case mentioned above is featured by that i) the initial condition is given at point *E* and ii) the difference is zero. What concerns us here is that despite these possible variations it is possible to define in general the phase of unlimited supplies of labor by the boundary demarcated by points *E* and *F* in Chart 1 in that the supply price of labor will be kept unchanged at the same subsistence level.

We want to make further comments. First, with regard to point *E*, the system assumes population growth as an exogenous variable. Unlike the Ricardian system, as we interpret it, the system contains no relationship between the subsistence level and population changes since the latter is assumed not affected by the changes in the former. Given the rate of population growth and the demand for labor which is determined by the growth mechanism of sector *I*, the surplus labor, if any, is merely assumed to remain in sector *II* at the unchanged subsistence level, irrespective of the resultant changes in productivity there. The subsistence sector is treated as if it were a sponge which can absorb the labor force unlimitedly (a residual thesis). In this respect the limiting point *E* in Chart 1 is intended to indicate a boundary condition for the labor-absorbing function of sector *II*.

Second, let us assume that the number of labor force in sector *II* tends to decrease as capital accumulation goes on in sector *I*. *F* in Chart 1 marks the turning point towards the next phase. If capital accumulation goes on beyond this point, the supply price of labor henceforth will be determined not by the subsistence level but by the marginal product of labor. It is argued by Lewis and some other authors that the mechanism of the economy is now characterized by neo-classical thought: the wage rates and the allocation of the labor force between the two sectors are determined in accordance with the principle that

105

the marginal productivity of labor should be equal in both sectors.

Alternative Assumptions

Throughout the previous discussion, it was assumed that a constancy of the subsistence level is possible despite changes in productivity. This assumption is given by dint of the historical inertia applied to the subjective standard. We believe that this is not the only possible assumption which can be made. Alternative approaches can be pursued by adopting different assumptions, and it is desirable to do so to arrive at a generalized model. Among these, the objective standard previously mentioned will be discussed first together with its relationship to the subjective standard. Secondly, and this is more important, a general case which includes increasing subsistence wages will be taken up.

To begin with the objective standard, the picture appears quite different from that described in the previous section. In order to meet the requirement of an unchanged level of subsistence wages, a constant average productivity of labor (and accordingly its marginal productivity) should be maintained in household production. This would be impossible, in general, if we assume the schedule illustrated by Chart 1 in the previous section. Even under a permissible assumption of an unchanged technology, labor producitivity and accordingly the supply price of labor would increase as the number of family workers decreases following a greater demand for labor as a result of capital accumulation. However the objective standard can be applicable in the special case where productivity changes can practically be assumed nearly zero. In reality, in the initial phase of economic development, the demand for labor by sector I is relatively very small as compared with the total labor force employed in sector *II*. Therefore, labor supply from this sector is possible to a certain extent without causing any substantial effects to its productivity level. So long as this is practically possible within this narrow range, the supply price of labor can be assumed constant. Moreover, if the pattern of economic growth is such that any point between *E* and *F* in Chart 1, given at the initial condition, is more or less sustained continuously for the subsequent phase, then the average productivity in sector *II* will not virtually increase at least due to the decrease in the labor force in this sector. The notion of unlimited supplies of labor can practically be applicable based on the objective productivity standard, assuming unchanged supply price of labor.[5]

It is admitted that the standard of living is a vague concept, but we cannot avoid this concept in order to develop the thesis of unlimited upplies of labor. The previous assumption of an unchanged subsistence level, however, can be modified in order to be closer to the historical reality. The labor supply schedule, illustrated by Chart 1, implies two dimensions: one is that potentially it is applicable at every point in time of the historical process of economic development and the other that historically it expresses a locus of successive equilibrium points under an unchanged situation during economic development. With respect to the former the assumption of an unchanged subsistence level can be valid. Concerning the latter, however, it cannot necessarily be supported. During the long process of economic development, the various factors responsible for maintaining

---

[5] The objective standard may also be understood in terms of per-head consumption. Enke suggests an interesting idea in this connection [3]. Subsistence wages, he argues, concern not the level of productivity of household production but the consumption level of individuals. Because of the peculiar behavior of traditional households, the latter level in practice, changes a little despite substantial changes in productivity. It does suggest a practical range within which a constant level of consumption can theoretically be assumed. It seems doubtful, however, that such a fact can be assumed as a general basis for establishing the notion of unlimited supplies of labor in the long run observation.

historical inertia may substantially change. It would be more realistic to assume that the subsistence level will increase. If the surplus labor, whose marginal productivity is lower than the subsistence level, still exists, the mechanism of the economy may remain the same with this modification. The subsistence level may be raised due to technological progress in sector II to the extent that the historical inertia cannot retain it. The trend of an increasing subsistence level, however, can occur independently, at least in theory, from technological progress. Again referring to Chart 1, suppose an upward shift of the subsistence level. Other things being equal, points E and F will move to the left, the new SL line being crossed by both the AP and MP curves at the higher levels. At this new level, however, the range of unlimited supplies of labor can be defined with respect to the new level of subsistence in a similar way as was done previously. If such a shift occurs continuously as a historical process, it will result in an increase in subsistence wages due to a shift of the subsistence level. It brings forth the process of capital deepening in sector I, more capital being used in relation to labor. The capital widening process thus disappears in the system. If we follow Lewis' original concept of unchanged subsistence wages, such a situation cannot be called the phase of unlimited supplies of labor. However, so long as it maintains the basic feature of the system, that is, the complete dependence on the wage rate which is determined outside sector I, this must be called, in our view, the phase of unlimited supplies of labor.

Now, these considerations lead us further to the next problem of a generalized model. In practice, the given variables in the system, such as population, technology as well as the subsistence wage are all subject to changes during economic growth. The theory of unlimited supply of labor, therefore, should be tested by taking these changes into consideration in order to identify the scope of its validity.

What about the effects of technological progress in general? In the previous section we assumed that the system is given a certain level of technological knowledge and that there is no technological progress in either sector. If technological progress takes place in sector *I*, what effect will this have on the system? If technological progress takes a simple type of neutral shift in the given production function,[6] it is obvious that all the benefits brought about will accrue to the capitalists. Given a constant savings ratio, technological progress of this type will simply accelerate the growth rate of such an economy. This has already been pointed out by Lewis on the assumption of no technological progress in sector *II*. One may consider a case in which no technological progress is assumed in sector *II* because it is composed of subsistence households. In reality, however, traditional agriculture can make technological progress and this may contribute to a considerable extent to developing the economy as a whole.[7] Therefore, it is worthwhile examining the effects of technological progress in sector *II*. In general, in order to approach reality more closely, we have to consider the case where technological progress takes place in both sectors at unequal rates of shift.

Now, with population growth and technological progress, how can the boundary condition be satisfied in the case of an in-

---

[6] An assumption of a neutral shift of the production function in sector *I* is too simple to represent historical reality. The problem of technological unemployment of the Marxian type may be raised here. If this is dominant, the sources of unlimited supplies of labor would be continuously reproduced to the extent that the economy could never arrive at the turning point. In our view, however, such an assumption does not fit well with historical reality.

[7] In particular, in the light of Japanese experience with the initial phase of economic development, traditional agriculture based on household production grew at a considerable rate in terms of both output and productivity; technological progress had taken place and the level of living and wage rates increased to a certain extent. These responses occurred together with the increase in population [10]. In view of this, it seems that the features of models of the Lewis type are too rigorous to be applied to such historical realities.

creasing subsistence level? An attempt to arrive at the answer will be given in the next section.

Lastly, we want to say a few words on the turning point towards the next phase. The economy will arrive at this point in the long run, if economic development continues to raise the marginal productivity of labor in sector *II* to the extent that it equals the subsistence level, irrespective of whether the subsistence level remains constant or increases. In principle, the nature of the turning point in our generalized model remains the same as in Lewis' case. In our view, however, after the turning point, although the supply price of labor is now increasing, the economy will not necessarily eliminate the subsistence sector; there may still remain a considerable labor force to be absorbed by sector *I*. In this respect, such a historical phase draws particular attention, being distinguished from a genuine phase of limited supplies of labor. However, this would have required an extensive discussion and deserves separate analysis.[8]

Mathematical Presentation of a Generalized Model

Under the condition of unlimited supplies of labor, the real supply price of dependent laborers in sector *II* (w_2, the suffix 2 is for sector *II*) is equal to the subsistence level (SL);

$$w_2 = SL(t),$$

and at the same time the marginal productivity of labor is lower and the average productivity is higher than SL. If the production function in sector *II* is given as

$$Y_2 = A_2(t) F_2(N_2, R_2),$$

the following relation must be satisfied;

---

[8] In the light of the current situation of the Japanese economy, we are particularly interested in a phase of this type. Elsewhere, Ohkawa has called it the phase of semi-limited supplies of laobr. Enke presents a similar view and his analysis gives valuable suggestions [3]. Smithies' illuminating anaylsis of an economy with a flexible supply of labor is also suggestive in this respect [14].

$$\delta \frac{Y_2}{N_2} < SL < \frac{Y_2}{N_2} \quad \text{or} \quad \delta \frac{Y_2}{SL} < N_2 < \frac{Y_2}{SL},$$

where Y_2, X_2 and R_2 denote real output, employment and natural resources respectively. R_2 is assumed constant. δ and ε are output elasticities of labor and natural resources (assumed constant); i.e.,

$$\delta \equiv \frac{\partial Y_2}{\partial N_2} \Big/ \frac{Y_2}{N_2}, \quad \varepsilon \equiv \frac{\partial Y_2}{\partial R_2} \Big/ \frac{Y_2}{R_2},$$

where we assume linear-homogeneity of the production function

$$\delta + \varepsilon = 1$$

and

$$\delta, \varepsilon > 0$$

or decreasing returns to each factor. $A_2(t)$ denotes the shift in the production function. For simplicity's sake, we define it netural "technological progress"; the rate of shift is assumed constant. It must be noted that SL is not necessarily constant, but may rise overtime. For simplicity, however, we assume the rate of increase in SL as constant.

On the other hand, the production function in sector I for which the suffix is 1 can be stated as follows:

$$Y_1 = A_1(t) F_1(N_1, K, R_1),$$

where Y_1, N_1, K and R_1 denote respectively real output, employment, capital stock and natural resources in sector I. We assume linear-homogeneity and decreasing returns to each factor, or

$$\alpha + \beta + \gamma = 1,$$

where α, β and γ are output elasticities of labor, capital and natural resources (assumed constant); i.e.,

$$\alpha \equiv \frac{\partial Y_1}{\partial N_1} \Big/ \frac{Y_1}{N_1}, \quad \beta \equiv \frac{\partial Y_1}{\partial K} \Big/ \frac{Y_1}{K}, \quad \gamma \equiv \frac{\partial Y_1}{\partial R_1} \Big/ \frac{Y_1}{R_1}.$$

Technological progress, expressed in $A_1(t)$, is assumed to go on at a constant rate. The equilibrium state of the economy is represented in the relations below;

$$w_1 = \alpha \frac{Y_1}{N_1}, \quad q = \beta \frac{Y_1}{K},$$

111

where w_1 and q denote the real wage rate and profit rate in this sector. In other words $w_1 N_1$ is labor income, qK profit income, and the residue $Y_1 - (w_1 N_1 + qK)$ is paid as rent to the owner of natural resources. Assuming savings and investment take place only in profit income, we have

$$\dot{K} = sqK,$$

where s is average propensity to save out of profit.

The conditions of equilibrium between the two sectors are

$$w_1 = w_2$$
$$L(t) = N_1 + N_2,$$

where L is labor supply in the economy given from outside the system.

Hence we have a model of economic growth as the following:

(1) $Y_1 = A_1(t) F_1(N_1, K, R_1)$

(2) $w_1 = \alpha \dfrac{Y_1}{N_1}$

(3) $q = \beta \dfrac{Y_1}{K}$

(4) $\dot{K} = sqK$

(5) $Y_2 = A_2(t) F_2(N_2, R_2)$

(6) $w_2 = SL(t)$

(7) $w_1 = w_2$

(8) $L(t) = N_1 + N_2.$

The model has a unique solution, because the number of variables, $Y_1, Y_2, K, N_1, N_2, w_1, w_2$ and q are equal to the number of equations, if the initial values of N_1, N_2 and K are given.

From the equations (2) (6) and (7) the real wage rate in sector I is determined at the level $SL(t)$. Capital stock is given from (4). Capitalists employ a certain number of laborers to the extent that the profit rate reaches a maximum, under the conditions of given real wage rate, capital stock, natural resources and the production function (1). As the labor supply is given, employment in sector II is determined as a residue in equation

112

(8), and the output in this sector can be known from the production function (5).

Rewriting these equations in growth rate terms, we get

(1)′ $G(Y_1)=\bar{G}(A_1)+\alpha G(N_1)+\beta G(K)$

(2)′ $G(w_1)=G(Y_1)-G(N_1)$

(3)′ $G(q)=G(Y_1)-G(K)$

(4)′ $G(K)=sq$

(5)′ $G(Y_2)=\bar{G}(A_2)+\delta G(N_2)$

(6)′ $G(w_2)=\bar{G}(SL)$

(7)′ $G(w_1)=G(w_2)$

(8)′ $\bar{G}(L)=WG(N_1)+(1-W)(GN_2)$,

where W is defined as the ratio of employment in sector I to total employment; i.e.,

$$W \equiv \frac{N_1}{N_1 + N_2}.$$

From the equations (1)′ (2)′ (3)′ (4)′ (6)′ and (7)′, we get

(9) $G(q)= \dfrac{s\bar{r}}{1-\alpha}\Big\{\dfrac{1}{s\bar{r}}\,[\bar{G}(A_1)-\alpha\bar{G}(SL)]-q\Big\}.$

Defining the relation as follows

(10) $\bar{q} = \dfrac{1}{s\bar{r}}\,[\bar{G}(A_1)-\alpha\bar{G}(SL)],$

equation (9) becomes

$$G(q) - \frac{s\bar{r}}{1-\alpha}\,(\bar{q}- q).$$

The general solution of (10) is

$$q(t)=\frac{\bar{q}}{1-\dfrac{q(0)-\bar{q}}{q(0)}e^{-s\frac{\bar{r}}{1-a}\bar{q}t}},$$

where

$$\lim_{t\to\infty} q(t)=\bar{q},$$

because $\dfrac{s\bar{r}}{1-\alpha}>0$. It means that the equilibrium $\bar{q}$ is stable.

In this equilibrium state, the growth rates of output and input in sector I take the levels shown below;

$$\bar{G}(Y_1)=\bar{G}(K)=\frac{1}{\gamma}\left[\bar{G}(A_1)-\alpha\bar{G}(SL)\right]$$

$$\bar{G}(N_1)=\frac{1}{\gamma}\left[\bar{G}(A_1)-(1-\beta)\bar{G}(SL)\right].$$

It may be useful to define three cases as follows:

Case A; $\bar{G}(A_1)>\alpha\bar{G}(SL)$

Case B; $\bar{G}(A_1)=\alpha\bar{G}(SL)$

Case C; $\bar{G}(A_1)<\alpha\bar{G}(SL)$

Case A: The equilibrium levels in profit rate and the growth rates of output and capital are positive. The growth rate of employment in sector I is smaller than that of capital. In other words the economy attains steady growth with capital deepening.[9]

In the case assumed by Minami elsewhere [8] [9], in which a constant real wage dominates, the states of equilibria are expressed as follows;

$$\bar{q}=\frac{1}{s\gamma}\bar{G}(A_1)$$

$$\bar{G}(Y_1)=\bar{G}(K)=\bar{G}(N_1)=\frac{1}{\gamma}\bar{G}(A_1),$$

or the economy develops along the course of capital widening. Case B: In this case we have the relations,

$$\bar{q}=\bar{G}(Y_1)=\bar{G}(K)=0, \quad \bar{G}(N_1)<0.$$

This might be called a sort of 'quasi-stationary state' in the sense that profit rate, output and capital remain constant, but with capital deepening. Assuming no technological progress and constant wages, however, we get

$$\bar{q}=\bar{G}(Y_1)=\bar{G}(K)=\bar{G}(N_1)=0,$$

or a situation in which output, capital and employment are all stagnant; in other words, the stationary state dominates. Case C: In this case, as the equilibrium level in profit rate becomes negative, the model does not work.

---

[9] Employment in sector I increases, remains constant or decreases, if
$$\bar{G}(A_1)\gtreqless(1-\beta)\bar{G}(SL).$$
Hence, it decreases in Cases B and C; i.e.,
$$\bar{G}(A_1)\lesseqgtr\alpha\bar{G}(SL)$$

We have assumed thus far that production in sector I depends on three factors; labor force, capital stock and natural resources subject to the following codition:

$$\alpha + \beta + \gamma = 1.$$

It may be useful, however, to investigate the state of equilibria in the case where production depends only on labor and capital, not on natural resources. This implies an assumption of zero elasticity of output with respect of natural resources; i.e.,

$$\alpha + \beta = 1.$$

Under these assumptions, equation (9) becomes

$$(9)' \quad G(q) = \frac{1}{\beta} [\bar{G}(A_1) - \alpha \bar{G}(SL)].$$

We have now the following three cases:

Case A: The growth rate of profit is positive, or the model has no unique solution. Assuming constant wages, (9)' becomes

$$G(q) = \frac{1}{\beta} G(A_1).$$

This may be similar to the case of given wages, as we interpret it, in the Fei-Ranis model [13].

Case B: The profit rate keeps its initial value $q(0)$, because its growth rate is zero. Hence the growth rates of other variables reach the following levels:

$$\bar{G}(K) = \bar{G}(Y_1) = \bar{G}(N_1) = sq(0).$$

This case, also assumed in K. Ara's model [1],[10] is consistent with steady growth accompanied by capital widening.

Case C: This model has no unique solution, the growth rate of profit being negative.

In summary, we can say the following:

1) The model has a stable solution under the conditions of neutral technological progress and increasing wage rates.

If the growth rate of technological progress is higher than the product of output elasticity of labor and the growth rate of real

[10]   The model depends on the more restrictive assumptions: no technological progress and constant wage rates.

wages, the model has a solution characterized by steady growth and capital deepening. In the special case of technological progress with constant wages, it results in a steady growth with capital widening.

If the growth rate of technological progress is equivalent to the product of output elasticity of labor and the growth rate of real wages, then the 'quasi-stationary' state with capital deepening manifests itself. Assuming constant wages in this case, the stationary state with capital widening appears.

If the growth rate of technological progress is lower than the above product, there is no enonomically meaningful solution. 2) The conclusions above may be changed, if we assume that output elasticity of natural resources is negligible.

In the case where the growth rate of technological progress is not equivalent to the product of the output elasticity of labor and the growth rate of real wages, there is no solution. If the equality is satisfied, the economy develops steadily along the course of capital widening.

We have investigated economic growth in the capitalists sector. Now we will be concerned with economic growth in the subsistence sector. From (8)′ we get a relation in which the growth rate of the labor force in sector II is determined, if the growth rate of labor supply is given outside the system and that of employment in sector I is determined in the following state of equilibrium;

(11) $\bar{G}(N_2) = \dfrac{1}{1-W} \bar{G}(L) - W\bar{G}(N_1).$

Assuming the relation

$$\bar{G}(A_1) > \alpha\bar{G}(SL),$$

the equilibrium growth rate of employment in sector I becomes

(12) $\bar{G}(N_1) = \dfrac{1}{\gamma} [\bar{G}(A_1) - (1-\beta)\bar{G}(SL)].$

Substituting this equation into (11), we get

(13) $\bar{G}(N_2) = \dfrac{1}{1-W}\bar{G}(L) - \dfrac{W}{\gamma} [\bar{G}(A_1) - (1-\beta)\bar{G}(SL)].$

116

This means that the growth rate of employment in sector I is larger and that in sector II is smaller, if the growth rate of technological progress and output elasticity of capital are higher and that of the wage rate in sector II lower. The growth rate of employment in sector I is independent from that of labor supply, while its growth rate in sector II depends on it. Relations (5)' and (13) determine the growth rate of output in sector II; i.e.,

$$(14) \quad \bar{G}(Y_2) = \bar{G}(A_2) + \frac{\delta}{1-W} \Big\{ \bar{G}(L) - \frac{W}{r} \times$$
$$[\bar{G}(A_1) - (1-\beta)\bar{G}(SL)] \Big\}.$$

The model developed in this section describes the phase of economic growth in which the real wage rate is historically given. The boundary condition of this phase, as mentioned above, is

$$\delta \frac{Y_2}{SL} < N_2 < \frac{Y_2}{SL}.$$

This may be always satisfied, once settled at the initial conditions, if the following relation exists;

$$G(N_2) = G(Y_2) - \bar{G}(SL) \quad \text{or} \quad G(N_2) = \frac{1}{\varepsilon}[\bar{G}(A_2) - \bar{G}(SL)].$$

Substituting (11) or (13) into this, we get

$$\frac{1}{1-W}[\bar{G}(L) - W\bar{G}(N_1)] = \frac{1}{\varepsilon}[\bar{G}(A_2) - \bar{G}(SL)]$$

or

$$\frac{1}{1-W}\Big\{\bar{G}(L) - \frac{W}{r}[\bar{G}(A_1) - (1-\beta)\bar{G}(SL)]\Big\} = \frac{1}{\varepsilon}[\bar{G}(A_2) - \bar{G}(SL)].[11]$$

On the other hand, if the growth rate of the labor force in sector II is comparatively low (owing to a moderate population increase or an insufficient demand for labor in sector I), or technological progress is rapid while subsistence wages are stationary in sector II i.e.,

---

[11] In the most simplified case, in which the levels of technology in sector II and subsistence level remain constant, it becomes
$$\bar{G}(L) = \frac{W}{r}\bar{G}(A_1).$$

$$\bar{G}(N_2) < \frac{1}{\varepsilon} \left[\bar{G}(A_2) - \bar{G}(SL) \right]$$

or

$$\frac{1}{1-W} \left[\bar{G}(L) - W \bar{G}(N_1) \right] < \frac{1}{\varepsilon} \left[\bar{G}(A_2) - \bar{G}(SL) \right]$$

or

$$\frac{1}{1-W} \left\{ \bar{G}(L) - \frac{W}{\gamma} \left[\bar{G}(A_1) - (1-\beta) \bar{G}(SL) \right] \right\} < \frac{1}{\varepsilon} \left[\bar{G}(A_2) - \bar{G}(SL) \right],$$

then the economy will move from this phase into the 'neo-classical' one in which real wage rates and the allocation of the labor force between the two sectors are determined in accordance with the principle that marginal productivity of labor should be equal in both sectors.

In the case of a high growth rate of the labor force, a moderate technological progress or a rapid increase in subsistence wages; i.e.,

$$\bar{G}(N_2) > \frac{1}{\varepsilon} \left[\bar{G}(A_2) - \bar{G}(SL) \right],$$

the phase will emerge in which real wage rates should be equal to the average productivity in sector *II*.

These examinations suggest the conditions of transition from the phase of unlimited supplies of labor to the phase of neo-classical system: moderate increases in population and subsistence level, a rapid technological progress and negligible output elasticities with respect to natural resources in both sectors, and a large share of labor force in the capitalists sector.[12]

Concluding Remarks

First, we support the thesis of unlimited supplies of labor in theory. The basic feature is, we believe, that the capitalists sector depends on wage rates determined outside this sector,

[12] The transition between these possible phases of economic development was discussed by Minami elsewhere [8] [9]. The mechanism of transition between phases in terms of the model developed in this paper would have required an extended elaboration. This deserves separate analysis.

that is in the subsistence sector. This feature will fit well with historical realities in countries or phases with surplus populations, if more flexible assumptions are duly made.

Second, in particular, the assumptions of an unchanged subsistence level and of no technological progress in the subsistence sector are too rigid to be applied to historical realities. Historical trends of increasing subsistence levels, together with technological progress, in our view, can be assumed consistently with the basic features of unlimited supplies of labor.

Third, such a generalized model, as examined under a simple assumption of a neutral technological shift in the production function of the Cobb-Douglas type, revealed in particular, among others, the following: the possibility of having stable solutions depends first upon the output elasticity of natural resources, and secondly, upon the relation between the rate of technological shift and the product of output elasticity of labor and the rate of increase in wage rates.

Fourth, the most significant case among those having a stable solution is that in which the output elasticity of natural resources is not negligible and the rate of technological shift is greater than the product of output elasticity of labor and the rate of increase in wage rates. In this case, the boundary condition for the phase of unlimited supplies of labor is definitely given in terms of respective rates of change in population, technology, subsistence level and of the sectoral shares of labor force employed.

Fifth, an empirical examination of the above theoretical conclusions is highly desirable. The Japanese historical experience, we believe, presents one of the best test cases. This, however, would be the subject of a separate paper.

REFERENCES

1. K. Ara, "A Model of Dual Economy," *Hitotsubashi Journal of Economics*, March 1962.
2. P.T. Bauer and B.S. Yamey, *The Economics of Under-Developed Countries*, London 1957.
3. S. Enke, "Economic Development with Unlimited and Limited Supplies of Labour," *Oxford Economic Papers*, June 1962.
4. N. Georgescu-Roegen, "Economic Theory and Agrarian Economics," *Oxford Economic Papers*, Feb. 1960.
5. W.A. Lewis, "Economic Development with Unlimited Supplies of Labour," *Manchester School of Economics and Social Studies*, May 1954. [Reprinted in *The Economics of Under-development* (ed. by A.N. Agarwara and S.P. Singh, London 1958)].
6. ——, "Unlimited Labour: Further Notes," *Manchester School of Economics and Social Studies*, Jan. 1958.
7. D. Mazumdar, "Underemployment in Agriculture and the Industrial Wage Rate," *Economica*, Nov. 1959.
8. R. Minami, "Economic Growth with Different Supply Functions of Labour," (in Japanese) *Kikan Riron Keizaigaku* (*Economic Studies Quarterly*), May 1963.
9. ——, "Economic Growth and Labour Supply," *Oxford Economic Papers*, July 1964.
10. K. Ohkawa and H. Rosovsky, "The Role of Agriculture in Modern Japanese Economic Development," *Economic Development and Cultural Changes*, April 1961.
11. K. Ohkawa, "The Pattern of Japanese Long-term Economic Growth," Presented to Hongkong Conference of Income and Wealth, 1960, published in V.K.R.V.Rao and K. Ohkawa (eds.) *Asian Studies in Income and Wealth*, Asia Publishing House, 1965.) [Containd in this volume].
12. G. Ranis and J.C.H.Fei, "A Theory of Economic Development," *American Economic Review*, Sept. 1961.
13. ——, "Innovation, Capital Accumulation, and Economic Development," *American Economic Review*, June 1963.
14. A. Smithies, "Productivity, Real Wages, and Economic Growth," *Quarterly Journal of Economics*, May 1960.

AGRICULTURE

AND THE TURNING-POINTS

IN ECONOMIC GROWTH

Introduction

The purpose of this paper is to describe the changes which have taken place in agriculture in the century of Japan's modern economic growth. For this purpose, the thesis of turning-point will be used. In using this concept, the central problem which confronts us is, I believe, that of finding consistency between "historical" turning-points and "theoretical" turning-points.

The concept of a turning-point in economic growth was first established by Arthur Lewis in his well-known article, "Unlimited Labour: Further Notes" [4]. It is the point at which the economy turns from the first stage of development with an unlimited supply of labor towards the second stage of development with a limited supply of labor. Agriculture was treated as a most important component of the "subsistence sector" (versus the "capitalists sector") in his two-sector model. He discussed the peasant economy in some detail as the source of an unlimited supply of labor during the first stage of economic development.

Reprinted (with some revision of the third section) by permission of the Institute of Asian Economic Affairs, Tokyo, Japan, from The Developing Economies, *Vol. III No. 4, December 1965, pp. 471–486.*

Since then, not a few authors have followed this line of thought and the concept of a turning-point has become popular in the field of development economics. An outstanding example of the use of this concept is found in the more sophisticated model presented by Fei and Ranis [1]. They developed not only an overall analysis of the economy but also a detailed scrutiny of agriculture. They no doubt contributed much to furthering the theoretical aspects of Lewis' original idea. In my view, however, the thesis of a turning-point seems to be inadequately used in applying their theoretical model to historical realities. This is particularly so with respect to agriculture in discussing the Japanese experience. In their analysis, the turning-point is demarcated at about 1917, implying that at that time Japanese agriculture entered into the process of modernization. One may intuitively cast doubts about this assertion, because from that time to the present the place of agriculture in the Japanese economy, as most Japanese economists believe, has remained extremely backward, and is far from being completely modernized. This may serve well to illustrate that there are difficulties in treating the changing place of agriculture in terms of the theory of turning-point.

In a model of this type it is assumed that the turning-point in economic growth *should* coincide with the turning-point in agriculture; during the first stage real wage rates will be equal to the subsistence level which is assumed to be kept unchanged with regard to agriculture, and at the turning-point this mechanism will cease to work and from then on real wage rates will rise in parallel with the trend of increase in the marginal productivity of labor, which must now be equal between agriculture and the non-agricultural sector. This is the simplest statement of what is implied in the theory of this type with regard to a process of equilibrium growth. The turning-point in agriculture is the commercialization point in Fei = Ranis terminology. The problem for us is that this point is assumed in theory to coincide with the point at which real wage rates begin to increase in the industrial sector, and that in reality this assumption is not warranted.

It is interesting to remind ourselves that Lewis himself had a much more flexible attitude in applying his thesis to the historical process of economic growth, and that he rightly admitted the possibility of wage rates rising even before the economy arrives at the turning-point. In fact, with respect to Japan, he suggested the turning-point to be somewhere in the 1950's despite recognizing an actual increase in real wage rates after World War I. Although he gave no explicit explanation concerning the turning-point in agriculture, Lewis' flexible attitude is suggestive for our approach. In my own view, it seems risky to apply theoretical models directly to the historical realities without "stylizing" them adequately. The *a priori* assumption of a coincidence between the turning-point of agriculture and that of the whole economy, I believe, requires further scrutiny in the light of the Japanese experience.

In the first section I will apply our phasiology in stylizing the historical complexities. Japan presents an Asian example of developed "traditional" countries with a long pre-modern history before its start to modern economic growth. Our operational hypothesis is that an interplay between the modern elements and the traditional elements brought forth basic changes in the growth pattern and economic structure of such a country. When these changes form identifiable and relatively unified periods, these periods are defined as *growth phases*. The dating, identification, and historical explanation of these phases were the major task which Henry Rosovsky and I attempted in a previous joint paper [5]. In it, agriculture was treated as the most important traditional sector. I believe it is useful to begin with the discussions that follow by referring to this phasing.

In the second section the discussions will be concentrated on agriculture. The possibility of defining a turning-point in this particular sector will be explored in some detail in the light of the historical facts of Japanese agriculture. In so doing, attention will be focussed in particular on three elements of the traditional features of agriculture: production organization, human behavior, and the type of technological advance.

Finally, in the last section what has taken place in the non-agricultural sector will be observed in a most simplified manner and the relation between the possible turning-point in general economic growth and that of agriculture will be discussed. In so doing, instead of treating the non-agricultural sector as a homogeneous modern sector, a division of this sector into two sub-sectors seems useful: the genuinely modern sector and the semi-modern sector. Along this line of thought, there will be suggested in conclusion the possibility of a coincidence between the historical turning-point and the *modified* theoretical turning-point, with both agriculture and non-agriculture consistently included.

Growth Phases and Discontinuity

The growth phases were identified historically in a previous paper cited above as follows: [5]

A. The First Phase of Modern Economic Growth, 1868–1905
   I. Transition, 1868–1885
   II. Initial Modern Economic Growth, 1886–1905
B. The Second Phase of Modern Economic Growth, 1906–1952
   III. Differential Structure: Creation, 1906–1930
   IV. Differential Structure: Economic and Political Consequences, 1931–1952
C. The Third Phase of Modern Economic Growth, 1953–?
   V. Post-war Growth, 1953–present.

A growth phase is not an arbitrarily selected interval of years; it must conform to certain analytical principles. Following Simon Kuznets' concept of modern economic growth with his criteria for identifying it, we tried to apply what he has called the minimum requirements for a "stage theory" [7]. In brief, what we have done can be stated as follows.

The years between 1868, the Meiji Restoration, and 1885, the end of the Matsukata Deflation, form the transition. It seemed to us that in 1868 modern economic growth became a national objective and that the actual beginning of such growth took place in 1886. Thus the transition is defined as an interval of a lag between the adoption of a national objective and the beginnng of its achievement. Leaving out discussion of the transition period, three major growth phases are relevant here. The first, lasting from 1886 to 1905, the end of the Russo-Japanese War, is characterized by the concurrent growth of the modern and traditional sectors. The modern growth was largely dependent upon the growth of the traditional sector, and agriculture constituted the core of the traditional economy. The second growth phase, lasting from 1906 to 1952, including the war and the subsequent post-war rehabilitation period, is characterized by the independent and vigorous growth of the modern sector, concentrating on "light" industries, while development in the traditional sectors lagged. Rapidly growing modern sectors and lagging traditional sectors created what we have called the "differential structure" and its first sub-phase (III) is identified as belonging to the years 1906–1930: around 1931 artificial heavy industrialization due to military mobilization began, and the subsequent years until around 1952 are demarcated as the second sub-phase of abnormal nature. The Japanese economy made a fresh start after World War II and the third growth phase began in about 1953, and will last for some years to come. It is characterized by a further expansion of the modern economy centering on "heavy" industries. A possibility was suggested in this previous paper that during the third phase the traditional elements will eventually be dissolved if the economy succeeds in growing further.

What concerns us most is an implicit recognition of a sort of "turning-point" from one phase to another in the years of 1885–1886, 1905–1906, 1930–1931, and 1952–1953. These I would like to call the *historical* turning-points in terms of growth phases as distinguished from turning-points theoretically defined. In the previous paper, the dating of these historical turning-points was first given from the broad historical aspect and then endorsed statistically in terms of the troughs which were identified with respect to the long-swings in the rate of output growth. If one agrees with us in recognizing that all these phases are distinctive enough in their characteristics and that they bear certain historical relationships between the preceding phase and the succeeding phase, then these historical turning-points will have proper meaning. It is beyond the scope of this paper to describe these in enough detail to clarify the historical meaning of each turning-point. However, I think it is desirable at least to answer the question of why these turning-points can actually be distinctly identified.

The endogenous relationships between the modern and the traditional sectors cannot necessarily be assumed to change in a discontinuous manner. If they appeared in a continuous way without making breaks over time, there could be no means of identifying the turning-points. In the Japanese case of modern economic growth, however, there actually is discontinuity and it is statistically reflected by the output pattern of long-swings. What are the underlying mechanisms which create alternations of upswings and downswings? This is a question very difficult to answer in full. But a central driving force is, we believe, the changes in the rate of capital formation. Statistical evidence is not lacking. The proportion of gross domestic fixed investment in GNP is a most convenient indicator for this. During the initial phase 1890–1905 (no data are available for the years before 1890), this proportion was kept almost unchanged at a level of 14–15%. From 1905–1906 it began to rise rapidly for the first time and reached some 19% in 1911. During the second phase the proportion fluctuated up and down, but not much, and it never substantially exceeded a level of 20% until the next turning-point in 1930—1931. From then on it again rose sharply, reaching 30% in 1937, the peak year. In the post-war phase it again started to increase from 25% in 1953, rose very sharply, and arrived at a record high of some 40; in 1960–1961. [These datings and figures all refer to the smoothed series of seven-year (five-year for post-war years) moving averages based on [9]. The intervals during which the rate of capital formation rises sharply are called investment spurts. Except for the first one in 1885–1886, all the historical turning-points mentioned above were the starting-points for each investment spurt.

Now, in the light of the historical pattern of economic growth described above, let us consider the problem of applying the theoretical concept of a turning-point to reality.

First, the theoretical models of long-term economic growth generally treat the time-path as a *continuous* process, so that the point of exhausting the unlimited supplies of labor is to be given on a uniform line of growth trend; there is assured no possibility of identifying such a point distinctly. The discontinuity to be found historically is therefore a prerequisite for providing such a possibility. This prerequisite cannot always be assumed to exist. The historical turning-points stated above are accordingly of great significance in suggesting that such a possibility can be expected in Japan's case.

Second, however, we have to note that the historical turning-point does not necessarily coincide with the theoretical one.

Moreover, there is a risk of confusing the two. For example, the first investment spurt which marked the beginnng of the second growth phase was followed by the World War I boom. During this period a shortage in the labor supply was felt temporarily; a shift in the labor force from agriculture to the rest of the economy was accelerated; and money wage rates tended to rise. The real wage rates thus showed a rise later on due to the downward rigidity, as commodity prices turned to fall after the end of the war. The turning-point around 1917 suggested by Fei = Ranis, in my view, seems to be derived from these *swing* phenomena. Actually, in each growth phase, the rate of increase in the demand for labor generally tends to be accelerated during the upswings, while it is decelerated during the downswings. The real difficulty therefore lies in the task of distinguishing the *trend* phenomena from the swing phenomena. We have to refer to the trend phenomena, meaning thereby the lasting structural changes which transcend the swing phenomena.

The Turning-Point in Agricultural Development

Among the historical turning-points mentioned above with respect to growth phases, let us pay particular attention to the post-war one. The reason for this is that from around 1952–1953 there began a distinct and sustained decrease in the labor force engaged in agriculture and such a phenomenon was never noticed in the preceding three turning-points. One may doubt whether the post-war change will be sustained even after the end of the spurt, because, as has previously been suggested, in a spurt period of the economy the rate of labor shift tends to be accelerated. In my view, based on an observation of trends, however, the recent decrease in the agricultural labor force will continue in the future as a basic tendency, though of course the tempo may fluctuate according to the possible swings of the economy.

The historical turning-point in agriculture can be defined in various ways according to different conceptual frames. In the light of the above-mentioned experience in Japan, I believe it is most reasonable to define this turning-point in terms of the labor force performance. I would like to identify it by the point from which the labor force engaged in agriculture begins to decline as a trend phenomenon. This implies that the growth of the non-agricultural sector arrives at a point at which the demand for labor in this sector can only be fully met by a labor shift out of agriculture. What is its significance with respect to the structural changes within agriculture? To answer this question is the major aim of this section.

First, let us describe the basic historical facts which Japanese agriculture manifested before arriving at a turning-point. They can be stated as follows:

(1) The numbers of the labor force engaged in agriculture were kept more or less unchanged (except for the abnormal period immediately following the last war).

(2) The acreage of arable land was maintained almost unchanged (except in Hokkaido where a considerable amount of reclamation took place), so that the factor-proportion with regard to land stock and labor remained almost constant in the aggregate.

(3) Within agriculture, the distribution pattern of farm size changed little. No sizeable shift from smaller to larger farms was witnessed; instead, a tendency of concentrating towards medium-size farms was largely seen during the second phase.

(4) Owner farmers remained the core of the land system, although tenancy extended to a considerable extent under the traditional landlordism, particularly during the first phase.

(5) Inputs of working capital increased considerably (and fixed capital to some extent) accompanying an increase in output and labor-productivity under the sustained production organization of the traditional type characterized by (3) and (4) above.

These five characteristics have been discussed in much detail and the reader is requested to refer to sources [3] and [6] if necessary. Here I want to discuss these characteristics in their relevance to the pattern of technological advance and human behavior. In a broad setting the type of technological progress in Japan's agriculture can basically be characterized by its *neutrality to scale of farming*, meaning thereby that the productivity of input differs little among farms of various scales, small and large. This type is naturally supposed to take place where and when the major input is of a perfectly divisible nature.

In terms of the growth phases stated in the previous section, the place of agriculture changed basically between the initial phase and the second phase. From the standpoint of technology in particular, the initial phase was characterized by a nation-wide diffusion of the traditional technology selected from the backlog inherited from the pre-modern Tokugawa period, while from the beginning of the second phase a new application of modern science appeared to have been effective in establishing a system of technology appropriate to Japanese agriculture. What concerns us here, however, is not the distinction as such between the two phases, but rather their similarities. It goes without saying that a renewed diffusion of the traditional technology was effective because it met the requirement of the unchanged production organization inherited from the pre-modern period. The later development of applying modern science was directed not along new lines but towards improving agricultural technology of the traditional nature—better methods of cultivation, improvements of seeds and fertilizers, etc., all of which were designed to fit the traditional farming system. Thus, from the present

130

point of view, Japan's agricultural technology up to the turning-point can be basically characterized by its perfect adaptation to the production organization of the traditional type.

The traditional production or system has often been called a remarkable example of the land-saving type. This is true. However, if we turn our eyes to the relation between the type of technology and the organization of production, the aspect in which it differs should, I believe, be emphasized. The previously-mentioned nature of scale-neutrality appears to be of most importance. The effect of inputs such as fertilizers, improved seeds, insecticides, etc., is supposed to bring forth no distinction between small-scale farming and large-scale, because these have almost perfect divisibility in their technical nature. Statistical evidence is not lacking. Measurements of production functions of the Cobb-Douglas type applied to such basic crops as rice, wheat, and barley for several years in the 1930's show almost without exception that the sum of output elasticities is very close to unity; that is, a prevalence of a production situation approximately equal to a constant return to scale [8].

Important is the interrelationship which is supposed to have been obtained between the traditional organization of production and the agricultural technology of this type. Almost the entire increase (but no more than this increase) in the agricultural labor force was absorbed by the development of the non-agricultural sector. With this given condition, technological advances of the neutral type in agriculture contributed to all classes of farmers almost uniformly with the effect that the traditional organization faced no substantial dissolving forces from technological innovations; owner-cultivated family farms—the core of Japan's land system—contributed much towards implementing and diffusing the advanced technology of this type, and thus maintained and even developed traditional small-scale farming.

Under such conditions, the attitude and behavior of the people must have been characterized by tradition. Even confining comments to the topics relevant to economics, there are too many to be discussed here. For the specific purpose of this paper, the points that follow are most important.

(1) The traditional household farming under a system of primogeniture was maintained almost unchanged within the realm of the traditional community; the head of the household and the dependent family members were clearly distinguished in status.

(2) The pattern and level of living was kept traditionally within this household system, and this constituted the means by which the "agrarian basis" of Japan's social structure was maintained.

(3) There was a social basis for accepting the "agrarian principle" as distinguished from the general economic principle in the people's mind and in Government policy; the law of technological advance must be different in agriculture from that of industry; small-scale family farming is the best form of organization for agriculture, etc.

The basic condition which maintained these behaviors and attitudes is, I believe, highly relevant to that which sustained the traditional production organization. In my view, this condition is the constancy of factor-proportion with respect to the land stock per unit of labor force as was provided to agriculture in a sustained manner in Japan's modern economic growth.

Our second topic concerns the post-war experience. Much has been said about the Land Reform which was carried out during the Occupation period. Traditional landlordism was dissolved with the effect that the status of owner farmers was greatly strengthened. It is also important to note that the traditional household system was legally and socially revised together with the legal abolition of primogeniture. I am ready full

132

to recognize the important effects which these institutional and social reforms brought forth in changing the place of post-war agriculture. However, what is more important for the present purpose is the fact that all these resulted to a considerable extent in sustaining small-scale farming. Up to the present, the aggregate decrease in the agricultural labor force seems to have accompanied only a slight sign of change in the distribution of farm size in favor of larger farms.

On the other hand, significant changes have taken place in the type of technological advance in post-war agriculture. There is empirical evidence for contending that a scale economy appeared in recent years; productivty of input tends to be larger as the size of farm increases. This must be highly relevant to the mechanization and diversification of post-war farming. Japan's agricultural machines are of a very small scale by international standards, but once they are effectively introduced into the system of farming technology a distinct economy of scale appears. Diversification towards livestock farming presents another factor which leads to producing an enconomy of scale. Again statistical evidence is not lacking: the annual *Survey of Farm Households* complied by the Ministry of Agriculture and Foresty can be used for this purpose. In a more sophisticated way, the measurement of agricultural production functions broadly indicates a possibility of increasing returns to scale [8]. Such a change in the type of technology is, I think, the most decisive factor in transforming Japanese agriculture for the future.

Can we give a reasonable explanation for a concurrent occurrence of such a change in technology and of the decline in the agricultural labor force? At first grance, it seems very easy to say "yes" in terms of the substitution of labor by capital. Actually, however, it is not so simple. The heavy industrialization of the Japanese economy, accompanied by a rapid rise in the income level of the people, no doubt brought in "induced effects" on agriculture in terms of technology and demand for output. With the unchanged scale of farming, therefore, mechanization and diversification did begin to take place as a path-breaking force. These cannot simply be interpreted as only the direct result of a labor shortage, although an accelerated outflow of the agricultural working force, especially among young workers, certainly encouraged the diffusion of mechanized farming.

A trend of decrease in the agricultural labor force has undoubtedly been caused by a rapid increase in the demand for labor in the non-agricultural sector. But it has certainly been encouraged by a reduced social rigidity in the new social environment of post-war Japan. In general, people's behavior in the rural community tended to change the long-sustained traditional patterns; their confidence in the agrarian principle seems to be fading away. The production organization based on traditional family farming began to show signs of transformation towards modernization, although with difficulties in adapting to the new situation due to institutional lags. A further change in the factor-proportion with respect to the man-land ratio, together with a further change in the type of farming technology which is already oriented towards enlarging the farm-size, will encourage farmers towards modernizing Japanese agriculture.

The shift performance of the labor force has previously been adopted in identifying the turning-point in agriculture. It is now clear that it implies for the most part the associated changes in the basic structure of agriculture concerning the production organization, human behavior and, in particular, the type of farming technology. During the first long phase before the turning-point, the technological advance characterized by scale neutrality was dominant and the second long phase which just recently started will be dominated by farming technology which advances scale economies.

Turning-Points: Historical And Theoretical

The turning-point previously defined with respect to agriculture is of a historical nature. Does it coincide with the theoretical one? The latter is the point at which agriculture ceases to be the source of an unlimited supply of labor. What the theory asserts can briefly be described as follows. Up to that point the supply price of labor is determined by the subsistence level prevailing in this sector, but now the increased marginal productivity of labor (due to a decrease in the labor force, assuming its decreasing returns) becomes equal to the subsistence level. From that point on the wage rates will not be determined by the subsistence level prevailing in the traditional sector, but will be seen to be equal to the marginal productivity of labor within the whole economic system. The peculiar place of agriculture will disappear because the marginal productivity of labor in agriculture will be equal in equilibrium to that of the non-agricultural sector. Considering these properties of the theoretical turning-point, one will intuitively decline to identify its coincidence with the historical one simply because of the previously recognized fact that the traditional organization of production changed little in the post-war years, even after the historical turning-point occurred. How can we form a bridge between the two?

The answer will be found in the fact that the non-agricultural sector is not homogeneously modern but rather heterogeneous, in containing both modern and traditional elements. There is ample evidence for this, both historical and current. The problem is therefore how one can modify the theoretical frame in order to fit Japanese reality.

To begin with discussing the empirical facts, let us remind ourselves of what has been described in the previous section in

135

discussing the growth phases. The dichotomy used there (traditional versus modern sectors) now deserves further consideration. For the initial phase of the concurrent growth of the modern and traditional sectors, the dependence of the modern sector upon the traditional economy was pointed out. This implies historical complexities which cannot be fully explained here. But what is essential in the present context is that the "modern" sector was actually composed of both the modern and traditional elements and was not genuinely modern. It depended upon a labor force, mostly young and single, unseparated from rural households. Technology was not fully mechanized, often depending much on material supplies from agriculture. Organization of production was close to that of the factory system but on a small scale, and capital intensity was not much higher than the traditional level. These properties can be categorically distinguished from the genuinely modern ones. For lack of adequate terminology, I would like to call them "semi-modern." As a matter of fact, the genuinely modern sector was merely an enclave, and the semi-modern sector was dominant during the initial growth phase. With respect to the relation between the traditional sector and the semi-modern sector, the notion of unlimited supplies of labor can be applied to the initial phase. Statistical evidence is not lacking; real wage rates increased at a very slow pace until around the time of the turning-point in 1905–1906.

The rate of increase of capital intensity—a basic indicator of modernization—marks a turn just around this time; although it rose at a very slow pace during the first phase, from this date it began to show a sharp rising trend corresponding in time to the first investment spurt mentioned in the first section. In that section the second growth phase was characterized by a differential structure, meaning thereby the independent and vigorous growth of the modern sector with the traditional sector lagging

136

rather far behind. Now, in our new framework, the *independent* growth is to be exclusively applied to the genuinely modern sector. Again the historical realities are complex, but it may be categorically allowable to characterize this sector by certain properties such as mechanized technology, a larger scale of production organization, dependence on the modern working force (including skilled labor) separated from the traditional household economy, and above all, a greater intensity of capital. Historically, the first investment spurt seems to imply a real inauguration of such a modern sector. In this sense, it marks a turning-point of great significance to Japan's modern economic growth. Following his original notion of the "initial big spurt," I would like to call it the "Gerschenkron's point" [2], although his notion is not exactly same as ours.

What concerns us further is the fact that the unlimited supply of labor did not cease at this point but rather continued to exist substantially in the subsequent years. The semi-modern sector developed further during this second phase, still depending much upon the traditional sector. In the twenties and thirties a major part of non-agricultural employment was still provided by the semi-modern sector, a close tie between agriculture and this sector was sustained and sometimes even strengthened. The retardation of agricultural growth was aggravated by increased food imports from Korea and Taiwan due to Japan's imperialistic expansion, and a further capital intensification in the modern sector, particularly in factory manufacturing, put pressure on the labor market which showed no sizable increase in employment during the twenties. These phenomena may be enough to give a broad picture of what we previously called the differential structure. It can be said that this was after all created and sustained by the condition of "an unlimited supply of labor", in the sense that the semi-modern sector depended upon the wage rates essentially determined by the subsistence level prevailed in the traditional sector.

Categorically, the differential structure thus implies a coexitence of three sectors: modern, semi-modern and traditional. An equilibrium analysis of the growth process of such an economy seems extremely difficult and no attempt will be made here to present it. The description that follows is merely intended to give an idea as to the background for formulating a model for such an analysis. First, there seems to exist no difficulty in applying the theoretical notion of an unlimited supply of labor to the part of the economy which is supposed to be composed of the two sectors: traditional and semi-modern. Secondly, the real difficulty lies in dealing with the genuinely modern sector. For the sake of simplicity, let us typify its nature by the type of technology embodied in its higher capital intensity. What concerns us most here is its creation of a higher wage rate which is independent of the traditional subsistence level. It goes without saying that for a "follower" country like Japan, the formation of the modern sector used to depend heavily on the so-called borrowed technologies from advanced countries. Adoption of such a technology usually requires a higher capital intensity and realizes a higher labor productivity as compared with the domestic level. A possibility of raising the wage rate for the labor employed in this sector is thus introduced. So far as the labor thus employed cannot be replaced easily by the labor force at large, an independent level of *modern* wage rates is established. Given severe international competition, the late-comers are always pressed to increase industrial productivity and the process of catching-up necessarily tends to adopt such increases in the wage rates as a *result* of the increased productivity. Needless to say, during the second phase of Japan's modern economic growth, a force of this kind was at work to a considerable extent. Accordingly, the demands for the labor force were, so to speak, dualistic: one modern and the other semi-modern; in theory the latter is supposed to expand its production to the point where its marginal productivity equals the wage rate determined by the traditional level of subsistence most prevalent in agriculture. Up until the time the post-war spurt took place, such a structure seems to have been basically maintained.

The post-war spurt for the first time brought forth a relative shortage of labor in the Japanese economy. It is interesting to note that this is reflected most distinctly by a phenomenon of narrowing the range of *wage differentials* which had previously existed between the young workers and the aged adult workers, and between small-scale enterprises and large-scale enterprises. This can be interpreted in terms of our categories as follows: a drastic change has taken place in the part of the economy in which a condition of an unlimited supply of labor had prevailed. The wage rates relevant to that part have increased relatively compared to those of the modern sector. This provides good evidence in retrospect for the fact that during the second growth phase the existence of surplus labor in this part of the economy was a major cause of its low wage level.

Now, the turning point of agriculture previously defined is reconsidered in relation to what has been described above. First, the phenomenon of narrowing the range of wage differentials, which is crucial to our analysis, took place, broadly speaking, concurrently with the occurrence of the turning point of agriculture: agricultural wage tended to increase sharply in relation to that of the semi-modern sector, so that the latter cannot be assumed to be determined by the subsistence wages in agriculture. It is possible to consider in essence a mechanism in which the wage rates will be equal to the marginal productivity of labor at a state of competitive equilibrium between agriculture and the semi-modern part of the non-agricultural sector.

Second, however, the peculiar place of agriculture seems not to disappear because the marginal productivity of labor in agriculture still remains to be lower than the prevailing wages in rural districts with respect to a considerable number of farmers. This important fact takes place because equality between wages and marginal productivity of labor in agriculture can only take place with respect to the upper class of farmers. After the turning point of agriculture, therefore, still we cannot apply the marginal principle fully to this sector.

Having recognized these points, I would like to say the following. It is possible and useful to apply the theory of an unlimited supply of labor to the Japanese economy but with an important modification. The postwar turning point of economic growth, which broadly coincides with the turning point previously defined with agriculture, can be recognized in its different nature as compared with the original theoretical definition. This I would like to call the *first* turning-point. In theory, this point marks the cease of subsistence wages but the subsequent phase cannot be characterized by a full operation of the marginal principle. It might be adequately characterized as a possible process of dissolving the traditional organization of agriculture together with the traditional elements involved in the semi-modern sector. This turning point does not mean directly the turn towards the maturity of modern economic growth, because traditional elements still remain in the economy for the subsequent years. This is why it is specifically called "the first" turning-point with expectations for a second to follow.

In order to give a more explicit bridge between the historical and the theoretical concepts, a few words will be needed. In this long phase to come, the marginal priciple will work even in agriculture as a basic behavior, and in this sense, this sector will become similar in nature to the semi-modern sector; in principle, competitive forces will work between them, implying that the semi-modern sector will be able to increase its employment by raising its demand price for labor. On the other hand, as a part of this sector becomes more modernized, it will become similar in nature to the modern sector, and an increased demand for the working force in the modern sector will be met by raising the level of wage rates. Thus as a whole, the labor supply will be limited to a certain extent, but not perfectly, so long as the possibility of shifting the labor force from the sector of lower productivity to the sector of higher productivity exists. In this sense, this might be labelled the phase of *semi-limited* supplies of labor as distinguished from the phase of a limited supply as well as the phase of an unlimited supply of labor. A complete modernization of agriculture is expected in theory to come after the economy passes through another turning-point which will demarcate the phase of semi-limited supplies of labor and the phase of limited supplies of labor. I would like to call this the *second* turning-point.

By way of conclusion, I would like to summarize the following major propositions and implications presented in the main text:

(1) In the light of Japan's record of modern economic growth, the changing place of agriculture can basically be grasped by the thesis of the turning-point, if the theoretical notion could be interpreted consistently with the historical turning-points.

(2) Several historical turning-points can actually be identified with regard to growth phases. Among them, the followings are specifically noted:

(i) What we call Gerschenkron's point is identified at around 1905–1906. This is the turning-point towards a genuine inauguration of the modern sector but has nothing to do with the inner structural changes in agriculture. The turning-point of agriculture is defined as the point at which the numbers of the agricultural labor force begin a sustained decrease. This is identified during the 1950's, which coincides with what we call the first turning-point.

(ii) Until the Japanese economy arrived at that turning-point, agriculture had maintained its traditional elements almost *in toto* and after that it began, for the first time, the process of modernization. This process is expected to continue during the coming long phase of a semi-limited supply of labor, until the economy is able to reach what we call the second turning-point.

(3) The implication for the economies of other Asian countries with surplus labor in agriculture is that the formation of a differential structure is unavoidable if the modern sector grows "successfully," and that it is highly desirable to make a sharp distinction between Gerschenkron's point and the first turning-point in Lewisian setting. And I want to suggest that the social implications of what a differential structure would bring forth in these countries might deserve much more attention than has usually been paid.

REFERENCES

1. Fei, John C.H. & Ranis, Gustav, *Development of the Labor Surplus Economy: Theory and Policy*, Illinois, Richard D. Irwin, 1964.

2. Gerschenkron, Alexander, *Economic Backwardness in Historical Perspective*, Cambridge, Mass,. The Belknop Press of Harvard University Press, 1962.

3. Johnston, Bruce F., "Agricultural Development and Economic Transformation: A Comparative Study of the Japanese Experience," *Food Research Institute Studies* (Standford University), Vol. III, No. 3 (Nov., 1962).

4. Lewis, W. Arthur, "Unlimited Labour: Further Notes," *Manchester School of Economics and Social Studies*, January, 1958.

5. Ohkawa, Kazushi & Rosovsky, Henry, "A Century of Japanese Economic Growth," in *The State and Economic Enterprise in Modern Japan*, edited by W. Lockwood, Princeton, Princeton University Press, 1965.

6. Ohkawa, Kazushi and Minami, Ryoshin, "The Phase of Unlimited Supplies of Labor," *Hitotsubashi Journal of Economics*, June, 1964. (Contained in this volume)

7. Kuznets, Simon, "Notes on the Take-off," in *The Economics of Take-off into Sustained Growth*, edited by W.W. Rostow, London, Macmillan 1963.

8. Yuize, Yasuhiko, "Nogyo ni okeru Kyoshiteki-Seisankansu no Keisoku (Aggregate Production Function of Agriculture)," *Nogyo Sogo Kenkyu*, October, 1964, and Ohkawa, Kazushi, *Shokuryo-keizai no Riron to Keisoku* (Theory and Measurement of Food Economy), Tokyo, Nihon Hyoron-sha, 1945.

9. Worksheets of the Hitostubashi Project of Japan's Long-term Economic Growth at the Institute of Economic Research, Tokyo. P.S. Later they were published with revision. See Kōichi Emi, *Shihon keisei* (Capital Formation), Vol. 4 of Long-Term Economic Statistics of Japan since 1868, Toyo Keizai Shinposha, Tokyo, 1971. The pattern of investment proportion during the initial phase comes out different from what was described in this paper.

THE PHASE OF

SEMI-LIMITED SUPPLIES

OF LABOR

Introduction

In pursuit of the long-term pattern of Japanese economic growth, we have been discussing in theory and history the problem of growth phases of economic development. The relation between changes in the demand for labor, associated with capital accumulation and technological progress and changes in the state of labor supply is, I believe, one of the most important aspects of the problem. It is the purpose of this paper to analyze the supply side of labor, focussing on a specific aspect, that is the phase of semi-limited supplies of labor.[1]

Following W.A. Lewis' pioneering work in this field, most authors retain his original two-stage theory: the phase of unlimited supplies and the phase of limited supplies of labor. I found this

---

[1] This idea was first mentioned but not developed enough in my paper, "*Seichoso-kudo to rodoryoku no bumonkan haibun* (Velocity of Growth and the Sectoral Allocation of Labor), 1960, contained in K. Ohkawa "*Nihon keizai bunseki*" (Analysis of Japanese Economy), Shunju-sha, 1962. A similar idea is found in S. Enke, "Economic Development with Unlimited and Limited Supplies of Labour", *Oxford Economic Papers*, June 1962.

A revised English version of "Rōdō kyōkyu ga hanseigenteki na keizai" *in* Keizai Kenkyu, *Vol.* 15, *No.* 3, *July* 1964, *pp.* 254–257.

dichotomy inappropriate in the light of Japanese experience, and would like to propose another phase of "semi-limited supplies of labor" which should exist between the two. Why is this needed? The Lewisian model is theoretical in its original conception and it is quite natural that it should not fit the historical reality of any individual country in a ready-made fashion, as any theory does not. My dissatisfaction with this model is not for such a general reason in application. The characteristics of the proposed phase seem different in theoretical nature from those of other two phases and it is, I believe, desirable to distinguish it from the other two.

In the first section the characteristics of the phase of semi-limited supplies of labor will be discussed in comparison with those of other phases. In the second section, a very simplified model will be developed in order to explain the significance of the proposed phase. Finally, in the last section, a problem of application of this model to the Japanese pattern of growth will be tested.

Characteristics of Semi-Limited Supplies of Labor

First, let us classify the varied state of labor supply into three types: S_1, S_2, and S_3 in Chart 1 represent labor supply curves respectively. S_1 shows a state of increasing labor supply with constant wage rates; S_3 shows a state of unchanged supply of labor irrespective of the level of wage rates; and S_2 shows a state of increasing labor supply associated with an increase in wage rates. The first one describes unlimited supplies of labor whereas the second one represents limited supplies of labor. The Lewisian model assumes that the shift from S_1 to S_3 will take place at the turning point, demarcating the phase of unlimited from the phase of limited supplies of labor. Our scheme differs from this in that as capital accumulation goes on first a shift from S_1 to S_2 will take

146

Chart 1.   Labor Supply Curves

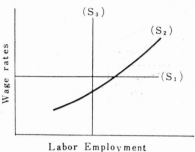

Labor Employment

place at the first turning point and if capital accumulation goes on further beyond this point then another shift from S_2 to S_3 will eventually take place at the second turning point.   The phase of unlimited supplies of labor is defined by the boundary demarcated by the initial point from where modern economic growth starts and the first turning point, whereas the phase of semi-limited supplies of labor is defined by the boundary demarcated by the first turning point and the second turning point.[2]   Limited supply of labor of course characterizes the third phase.

Second, the classification defined above will be applied to the economic growth of a two-sector structure: capitalists sector and subsistence sector.   Hereafter the former is called Sector *I* and the latter Sector *II*.   According to the Lewisian model, capital accumulation goes on in Sector *I* depending upon the unlimited supplies of labor from Sector *II* until the economy reaches the turning point.   After the turning point, Sector *II* should disappear

[2]   The term "semi-limited" is intended to express a state of labor supply which is flexible or elastic to a certain extent with respect to wage rates.   In other words, a labor supply can be increased by a rise of wage rates whereas this is impossible in the case of limited supply.   As capital accumulation goes on throughout the second phase, the flexibility of labor supply will actually decrease overtime.   Therefore, we cannot assume a constant elasticity of supply with respect to labor.   Neither unlimited nor limited supplies of labor can exist actually as a perfect state.   These do not matter, however, in order to grasp the essence of the mechanism.

Chart 2. Unlimited and Semi-limited Labor Supply (Sector II)

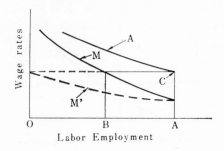

Labor Employment

because the marginal principle will work homogeneously all over the economy. Against this, in my view, the end of unlimited supplies of labor at the first turning point is not necessarily accompanied by complete dissolution of Sector *II*. Instead, this sector will continue to exist for the subsequent phase and will be the source of flexible supply of labor (labor supply curve S_2).

Chart 2 shows a state of Sector *II* following the conventional way of illustrating the Lewisian model. The phase of unlimited supplies of labor is demarcated by two points *A* and *B* on the horizontal axis. While the economy stays in this phase the marginal product of labor (M) is lower than the subsistence level (C) so that the supply price of labor to Sector *I* is given by *C* instead of *M*. At point *A* average productivity of labor is equal to *C* and this is intended to indicate the minimum boundary. Point *B* indicates the turning point, where *M* becomes equal to *C*. As capital accumulation goes on, a movement $A \rightarrow B$ is supposed to take place, accompanying an increase in the level of *M* and eventually the economy reaches point *B*. After the economy passes through this point, *M* will be bigger than the level of *C* and the latter will no longer be relevant. This is the simplest explanation of the Lewisian model. The chart is intended to draw particular attention to the fact that it still appears to be labor employment in

"Sector *II*" (indicated by the range *OB* on the horizontal axis) even after the economy passes through the turning point. Complete disappearance of Sector *II* is indicated by point *O*. Another curve of marginal productivity of labor (*M'*) is drawn in the chart to indicate a special case of concurrent occurrence of an equality *M=C* and disappearance of Sector *II*. There is no contradiction in this particular case with respect to the Lewisian model since it implies that the existence of Sector *II* depends upon the sustainance of the inequality *M<C*. What this model does not allow for, in theory, is the existence of Sector *II* indicated by a range of employment *OB*.

Let us turn to Sector *I*. As previously mentioned, the first phase has S_1 as its labor supply schedule whereas S_3 represents the labor supply schedule for the second phase of the Lewisian model. In the former the wage rates are given from outside the system of Sector *I*, while in the latter the labor force is given from outside the system of Sector *I*, corresponding to the classical and neo-classical system respectively. The phase of semi-limited supplies of labor seems to belong to neither the classical nor the neo-classical system: the wage rates cease to be given from outside and are to be determined endogenously within the system and in this sense it is similar to the phase of limited supplies of labor. But on the other hand, a rise of wage rate will increase labor supply to Sector *I* and in this sense it differs from the phase of limited supplies of labor.

For simplicity, let us assume no increase in the labor force due to population growth and look again at Chart 2. After passing through point *B*, the continued growth of Sector *I* will only be possible by absorbing labor from Sector *II*. A continued shift of labor from Sector *II* to Sector *I* will be the indispensable condition for sustaining capital accumulation. This shift will raise the level of marginal productivity of labor in Sector *II* as curve *M* shows. The equilibrium wage rate determined endogenously can be indicated by this curve *M*. The supply price of labor thus, unlike

149

the case of unlimited supplies of labor, is not independent of the labor demand of Sector *I*. As seen from the side of Sector *I*, an increase in its labor employment is now only possible through raising the demand price of labor, corresponding to the increase in marginal productivity of labor in Sector *II*. This is the interpretation of the system in which supply curve of labor S_2 will work. This interpretation is basically different from the Lewisian model in that source of labor shift is still assumed to come from "Sector *II*" despite the fact that the marginal principle is assumed to operate endogenously within the system.

A Three-Sector Model

It has been confirmed that seen either from Sector *II* or from Sector *I* the proposed phase of semi-limited supplies of labor cannot be drived from the Lewisian model. And yet, the historical reality of capitalistic development convinced us that the shift of labor from a low-productivity sector to a high -productivity sector has been one of its major conditions. This phenomenon seems to be too important to be treated merely as a product of a transition from the phase of unlimited to the phase of limited supplies of labor because economic history shows that the labor shift from a low-productivity sector to a high productivity sector continued for a long time to be the major source of labor supply to modern economic growth.

It is my view that a three-sector instead of two-sector model is most appropriate to treat the phase of semi-limited supplies of labor. Let us divide Sector *I* into two sub-sectors: Sector *Ia* and Sector *Ib*. The marginal productivity of labor is assumed higher in the former than in the latter and accordingly the equilibrium wage rate is higher in the former than in the latter. This division is made based on Japan's experience which presents wage differentials between large-scale and small-scale enterprises. Quality difference of workers is of course partly responsible for these differentials. But we have empirical data enough to assume that even for workers of the same quality wage differentials do exist in a normal and sustained state. This is the very basis of our concept of differential structure. For simplicity, Sector *Ia* represents modern, large-scale enterprises and Sector *Ib* semi-modern, small-scale enterprises.

For the phase of unlimited supplies of labor, we now have

$$M_2 < C = w_{1b} = M_{1b} < w_{1a} = M_{1a}, \tag{1}$$

where M, w and C stand respectively for marginal productivity of labor, wage rate and the subsistence level in Sector *II*. The shift of labor from Sector *II* to Sector *Ib* implies, on a path of competitive equilibrium, an equality between the subsistence level (C) and wage rate in sector *Ib* (w_{1b}), while the labor shift from Sector *Ib* to Sector *Ia* is produced by the wage differential $w_{1b} < w_{1a}$. The state of unlimited supplies of labor is retained as before. If the role of Sector *Ia* is still minor as in the case of the early phase of modern economic growth, Sector *Ia* can be dropped and equation (1) will be reduced to the same as in the Lewisian model.

At the first turning point, the marginal productivity of labor in Sector *II* (M_2) becomes equal to that of Sector *Ib* (M_{1b}), so that we have

$$w_2(M_2) = w_{1b}(M_{1b}) < w_{1a}(M_{1a}). \tag{2}$$

Between Sector *II* and Sector *Ib* we now have no discrimination to make and substantially the economy can be dealt with by a two-sector model. During the second phase equation (2) will operate. The labor shift will continue from the now combined Sectors *II* and *Ib* to Sector *Ia*. This is the phase of semi-limited supplies of labor: the marginal principle works fully for the entire economy but because of the existence of wage differentials an expansion of Sector *Ia* is possible by a shift of labor from the sector of lower productivity. It goes without saying that at the second turning point the latter sector will disappear and the economy will

151

become completely homogeneous, and it can then be represented by a one-sector model. This is a state of maturity.

A crucial point of the above model depends on the possibility of giving a reasonable explanation of the equilibrium co-existence of the two sub-sectors. Suppose an equilibrium state of equal rates of capital return for both sub-sectors. Under the existence of wage differentials, we believe, technology must be different between the two sub-sectors: technology of Sector Ia is capital-intensive whereas technology of Sector Ib is labor-intensive. Before giving a proof of this specific proposition, however, I would like to discuss in general the characteristics of co-existence of different technologies in a very simple way.

Assuming production functions of the Cobb-Douglas type with constant returns to scale, let us examine the implication of the co-existence of two sub-sectors, which has hitherto been indicated by the difference of productivity level, that is $Y_a/L_a > Y_b/L_b$ (Y and L stand for output and labor; suffix a and b for Sub-sectors Ia and Ib respectively). At an equilibrium condition with respect to labor we have

$$w_a = \beta_a \cdot Y_a/L_a \quad \text{and} \quad w_b = \beta_b \cdot Y_b/L_b,$$

where w and β stand for wage rate and labor's relative income share (in this case at the same time, output elasticity with respect to labor). If there is no wage differential ($w_a = w_b$), we have $\beta_a < \beta_b$, that is a differential of output elasticities with respect to labor between the two sub-sectors. Likewise, we have

$$\pi_a = \alpha_a \cdot Y_a/K_a \quad \text{and} \quad \pi_b = \alpha_b \cdot Y_b/K_b,$$

where, π, α and K stand for rate of return on capital, capital's relative income share (output elasticity with respect to capital) and capital respectively. Because of our assumption of $\alpha + \beta = 1$ for both sectors, at a state of equal rates of capital return, we have $\alpha_a > \alpha_b$ and $\dfrac{Y_a}{K_a} < \dfrac{Y_b}{K_b}$. The output elasticity with respect to capital has a differential between the two sectors and capital pro-

152

ductivity (the reciprocal of the capital-output ratio) is bigger in Sector *Ia* than in Sector *Ib*.

Thus at a competitive equilibrium state for both capital and labor market, the co-existence of a high productivity sector and a low productivity sector implies a technological difference in terms of output elasticities of production factors: the former is capital-intensive and the latter labor-intensive. At the same time capital intensity (K/L) is higher in Sector *Ia* than in Sector *Ib*. This is easily drawn from the two inequalities regarding Y/L and Y/K above. Our interpretation is that if different technologies are available in terms of output elasticities the difference of factor productivities $(Y/L, Y/K)$ is an equilibrium phenomenon and does not necessarily imply the differential structure of factor prices.

The differential structure of factor prices can be examined in terms of either labor or capital based on the recognition confirmed above. The present discussion directly concerns the case of labor.[3] What will be the effect of wage differentials $(w_a > w_b)$?

For simplicity, let us assume that equal rates of capital return prevail in both sectors $(\pi_a = \pi_b)$. From the equation $\omega = \beta \cdot Y/L$, we can intuitively say that there are two cases:first, if the output elasticity with respect to labor, β, is technologically given the gap in average productivity, Y/L, will be wider than in the case of no wage differentials and second, that to the extent that β is flexible, existence of a wage differential will manifest itself in a smaller difference of β (and hence α) between the two sectors as compared to the case of no wage differentials. A more general relation can be given as follows.

Our previous assumption of equilibrium states for both sectors can give

$$\frac{K_a}{L_a} = \frac{\alpha_a}{\beta_a} \cdot \frac{\omega_a}{\pi_a}, \quad \frac{K_b}{L_b} = \frac{\alpha_b}{\beta_b} \cdot \frac{\omega_b}{\pi_b},$$

---

[3] In the original paper, the case of capital was developed. In light of Japanese experience, it is reasonable to assume that sustained differentials exist between the semi-modern and modern sectors with respect to the rates of return on capital.

and considering $\pi_a = \pi_b$, we have

$$\omega_a/\omega_b = \left(\frac{K_a}{L_a} \middle/ \frac{K_b}{L_b}\right) \cdot \left(\frac{\alpha_b}{\alpha_a} \middle/ \frac{\beta_b}{\beta_a}\right).$$

The equilibrium wage differential is expressed by two ratios: capital intensity ratio and output elasticity ratio. The former is greater than unity and the latter is smaller than unity — these are derived from our previous assumptions. The wage differential can be associated with either a bigger ratio of K/L or a bigger ratio of output elasticities as compared to the case of no wage differentials. We cannot say *a priori* which ratio will be affected more, but at any rate even such a simple treatment could give an interpretation of what the existence of differentials with regard to wage rate and accordingly marginal productivity of labor implies. From an empirical point of view, I am much inclined to say that a bigger difference of capital intensity between the semi-modern and modern sectors is much more relevant to the present discussion because there is actually a relatively narrow limit for the variance of output elasticities. In this sense, we may be able to say the following.

As capital accumulation goes on, capital intensity will become higher in Sector I as a whole, but in particular in Sector Ia, resulting in a bigger difference of capital intensity between this sector and Sector Ib. In a country of economic backwardness where technology borrowed from advanced countries is influential, it is technologically imperative to raise K/L, so that there must a strong tendency for a wide capital intensity gap. The wage differential seems to correspond to this phenomenon. From the viewpoint of enterprisers in the modern sector, it is possible to raise the wage rates higher than the prevailing level in the semi-modern sector in a quite competitive way.

In the above-mentioned model, the differential structure of employment has been highly simplified. In reality, differential wage rates do exist not only between sectors but also within each

Chart 3.   Differentials of Marginal Productivity of Labor in Sector II

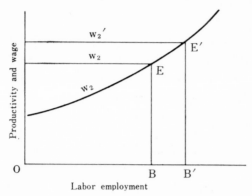

sector.   This poses no serious problems for Sectors *Ia* and *Ib* where use of an average concept raises no difficulty.   For Sector *II*, however, the simplification ignoring the differentials within that sector does raise a substantial problem which needs to be discussed further. In Sector *II* there is a wide range of variation with regard to the production efficiency of operation units.   Essentially this is the sector of the self-employed and yet the differential of production efficiency can be represented by the marginal productivity of labor (M_2) as illustrated in Chart 3.

Suppose the economy is at the first turning point.   Previously we defined $M_2 = M_{1b}$ between Sectors *II* and *Ib*.   This was a great simplification and in fact this equality does not necessarily fit for all the units of production in the self-employed sector.   For example, suppose that the equality is seen at point *E* in the chart. At this point, by definition wage rates should be equal between the two sectors $(w_2 = w_{1b})$.   In the chart, a straight line of w_2 drawn parallel to the horizontal line passing through point *E*, is intended to indicate the level of prevailing wage rates in this sector.   Even self-employed unit of production temporarily employ workers: for example in small-scale farming, peasants hire workers during the busy season as the marginal productivity of labor is

155

high enough to pay the prevailing wage rates. Larger-scale farmers hire permanent workers by paying the prevailing wages, although their number must be minor. At any rate, against this background we can think of the prevailing wage rate in this sector, which now becomes equal to that of Sector *Ib*. What is different from the first phase is that w_2 is not determined by C within this sector. Thus it is clarified that even at the first turning point there is a section of labor (self-employed and family labor) whose marginal productivity is lower than the prevailing wage rates ($M_2 < w_2$) in Sector *II*. What distinguishes this model from the Lewisian one is that the operation of marginal principles does not necessarily wipe out the so-called underemployment. As capital accumulation goes on further during the second phase the under-employed labor in Sector *II* will be a continued source of labor supply to Sector *Ib*.

Having said this, 1 would like to re-consider a problem— what is the real difference we can recognize between the phase of unlimited supplies of labor and the phase of semi-limited supplies of labor? With respect to the pattern of labor shift from Sector *II* to Sector *I* and from Sector *Ib* to Sector *Ia*, there seems no difference between the two phases: during both phases the labor force continues to shift from a sector of low productivity to a sector of high productivity. As capital accumulation goes on in the latter sector, this process of sectoral re-allocation of labor will continue without interruption so long as the sectoral differential of marginal productivity of labor and hence wage rate exists. What makes the difference is the mechanism of wage determination. The theory assumes that in the first phase capital accumulation in Sector *I* has no effects on the wage level whereas in the second phase it does have effects—a very simple but basic proposition.

Some amplification will be needed on this last point. In Chart 3, if we consider the first phase, under the assumption $w_b = C$, the relation between wage level and the curve of marginal product-

156

ivity of labor, M_2, is the same for the second phase. What makes the difference is the following. Let us assume that the wage rates increase from w_2 to w_2' in the latter phase. The range of underemployment in this sector will increase from OB to OB' on the horizontal line. The source of labor supply to Sector I will increase. During the first phase this will not occur so long as the level of C is assumed unchanged.[4] The labor supply is elastic with respect to wage changes. It seems to me that without the assumption of the differentials of marginal productivity of labor such an interpretation cannot be possible.

Empirical Application

I have no intention of discussing all the problems which may arise in applying a simple thesis of this kind to the historical experiences of modern economic growth. What is intended here is to make some comments on the particular problems which, I believe, are important in the light of Japanese experience.

First, on the performance of Sector II. According to the usual interpretation of the Lewisian model, the historical process of the first phase has been explained by a trend of decrease in the labor force in Sector II and we followed the same way illustrating it by Chart 2. However, historically modern economic growth appears to have a long period in which the subsistence sector does not contract in terms of labor force. For example, in Japan it was only in 1955 that the labor force in Sector II, represented by the sum of proprietors and family workers, began to decrease. Domographic increase in the labor force had been the major source of

---

[4] It is possible and even more useful to assume an increase in the subsistence wage level. For simplicity, we do not adopt such a flexible assumption. If it increases from C to C' $(=w_2')$ in Chart 3, what has been said for the second phase in the main text can also be applied to the first phase. The difference between the two phases in this case is simply that the cause of change takes place endogenously within sector II in the first phase while in the second phase it does not.

labor supply to Sector *I* until around that year and this fact has been ignored in the theory described above. Without giving an appropriate interpretation of this important fact, therefore, the thesis cannot be useful.

Let us assume that the number of labor force occupied in Sector *II* is held unchanged while capital accumulation goes on in Sector *I*. In Chart 2, instead of moving from point *A* to point *B* on the horizontal axis, the labor force in Sector *II* will continue to remain at point *A*. All the increased labor force due to demographic causes in this sector is assumed to be supplied to Sector *I*. There is no problem in making this assumption so far as labor supply of this kind takes place at subsistence wages and no modification is needed for defining the phase of unlimited supplies of labor. However, it is to be noted not in theory but in practice that the economy will retain point *A* of Sector *II* for the major part of the first phase. This raises a problem that the interpretation of the mechanism of the first phase as being merely a movement from point *A* to point *B*, as we did previously, cannot be realistic.

Second, on the change in the mechanism of wage determination. As has previously been summarized, the core of the Lewisian theory is that the capital accumulation in Sector *I* will affect wage rates in the second phase while it does not in the first phase. It is difficult to identify empirically the turning point between the two phases in terms of this proposition. The most relevant phenomenon in this respect in Japan's experience is the distinct tendency for wage differentials to narrow and I believe this is perhaps the best indicator of the turning point, although it is an indirect one. During the first half of the 1960's in Japan, between agriculture and non-agriculture, between small-scale and large-scale enterprises and between unincorporate and corporate sectors etc., the long-standing wage differentials narrowed distinctly. This suggests that the wage level in Sector *II* is raised from outside to the level of the wage rates prevailing in Sub-sector *Ib* in our terminology, together with a less pronounced tendency for wage differentials to narrow as between Sub-sectors *Ib* and *Ia*. If we can assume the operation of marginal principle basically for Sector *I*, this begins to narrow wage differentials prevail to Sector *II* through raising the wage rates there.

Third, let us pay particular attention to the fact that these two turning points—the point at which the labor force decreased in Sector *II* and the point at which wage differentials, began to narrow, occurred rather close together in time. This appears to be rather natural because both phenomena are caused by a common factor—a basic change in the supply-demand relationship of the labor market. Therefore, in theory, it would be possible to ignore a process of movement from point *A* to point *B* in Chart 2 as far as the first phase is concerned and consider it as taking place solely in the second phase—that is the phase of semi-limited supplies of labor. The shift of labor force from Sector *II* to Sector *I* will increase the marginal productivity of labor in the former sector and this can be said to be the characteristics of this phase as distinguished from the first phase.

By way of conclusion, I would like to say that the phase of semi-limited supplies of labor can be distinctly identified empirically at least as far as the Japanese experience is concerned.

Appendix

(A) *Illustration of Chart 3 in the main text.*

The differentials of marginal productivity of labor and its relation to the prevailing wage rates in Sector *II* are illustrated by agriculture—the major sector of the self-employed.

In Table 1, the average productivity, Y/L, rises as the scale of farm operation ncreases while wages prevail evenly; the wage-productivity ratio declines as the scale increases. It is 78% on the average. The output elasticity with respect to labor measured by several authors ranges from 0.43 to 0.67 . A comparison of the wage-productivity ratio in the table and these figures of output elasticity gives an evidence that a great number of workers in agriculture are "over-

Table 1. Productivity-Wage Relations in Farm-households by Farm Operation Scale, 1964

Farm scale of operation	Net product per worker (Y/L)	Wages (w)* earned	Ratio $\left(w \middle/ \dfrac{Y}{L} \right)$
	hectare	yen	yen	%
(1) Under 0.5	638	743	116.2
(2) 0.5 − 1.0	827	787	96.9
(3) 1.0 − 1.5	945	777	81.4
(4) 1.5 − 2.0	1,067	778	72.9
(5) 2.0 − 2.5	1,229	755	61.4
(6) 2.5 − 3.0	1,367	744	54.4
(7) Over 3.0	1.760	749	42.5
Average	989	762	77.5

Source: Ministry of Agriculture & Forestry, *Noka keizai chosa* (Farm Economy Survey): the 1964 Survey excluding part-time farmers.

Remarks: * daily wages paid for both farm and off-farm jobs of family members, belonging to each scale-class.

Table 2. Changes in Wage Differentials, 1953–63.

	Ratios of daily agricultural wages to non-agricultural wages, 1953=100		Ratio of unincorporated to incorporated wages
	Unincorporated	Incorporated	%
1953	100	100	60.6
1954	108	107	60.1
1955	109	103	58.6
1956	110	109	57.8
1957	103	105	62.1
1958	95	99	63.6
1959	101	105	62.9
1960	102	109	65.1
1961	120	129	65.6
1962	142	149	64.0
1963	177	211	64.6

Source: Agricultural wages from M. Umemura and Others, *Noringyo* (Agriculture and Forestry), Vol.9 of *Choki keizai tokei* (Long-term Economic Statistics of Japan since 1868), 1966, Toyo Kekizai Shinposha, Tokyo, Table 34, pp. 220–221. Unincorporated and incorporated wages are estimated by the author from the unpublished data provided by Economic Research Institute, Economic Planning Agency.

Table 3.   Number of Gainfully Occupied People, 1872–1963
(million)

	Employed workers	Proprietors and family workers
1872	1.6	17.4
1920	7.8	19.1
1930	9.4	19.9
1940	13.4	18.8
1950	14.0	22.6
1955	17.8	21.4
1960	22.7	21.8
1963	25.8	20.3

Source: for 1872–1955 from W*agakuni kanzen koyo no igi to taisaku* (Significance and Policy of Full Employment) Showa Dojinkai, 1957, p. 689 (T. Ishizaki estimation). For 1960 and 1963 from the *Labor Force Survey*. These are roughly comparable with the census data for the earlier years.

occupied" or under-employed: their marginal product is lower than the prevailing wages.

(B)   *A tendency for wage differentials to narrow.*

The wage data are not available by the three-sector classification of our model. Rough approximations can be given, however, by the wage series for agriculture, unincorporated and incorporated non-agricultural sector.

The figures in Table 2 show that i) agricultural wages tended to increase rapidly in relation to the non-agricultural wages since around 1960 and ii) unincorporated wages also tended to increase in relation to the incorporated wages, although the pace was much less pronounced.

(C)   *The number of labor force occupied in the self-employed sector.*

In Table 3, the sum of proprietors and family workers approximates the labor force employed in Sector *II*. In contrast to a rapid increase in the employed workers, its number changed a little: until 1950 a slight increase and then a slight decrease are seen. It is only in 1960 that its number became smaller than the number of employed workers.

161

Part III
Agriculture and Economic Growth

CONCURRENT

GROWTH OF AGRICULTURE

WITH INDUSTRY*

Agriculture's role, its contribution, its function—whatever we may call it—(no one would deny its importance) in economic development is the subject of this chapter.

We shall not describe the details of the historical development of Japanese agriculture;[1] rather we shall attempt first to discuss conceptual problems which, we believe, require clarification. Second, in terms of our specified concepts, some factors crucial in attaining the concurrent growth of agriculture with industry will be discussed. In so doing, the Japanese experience will be examined in terms of concise presentations as one of the typical cases of economically backward countries.

* I should like to aknowledge my great indebtedness to Professor Henry Rosovsky, University of California, Berkeley, my collaborator in a research project on Japan's modern economic growth. The basic idea of this chapter came from discussions we enjoyed together in the course of working on this project.

[1] See: Kazushi Ohkawa and Henry Rosovsky, "The Role of Agriculture in Modern Japanese Economic Development," *Economic Development and Cultural Change*, Vol. IX, No. 1, Part II, Oct. 1960.

Kazushi Ohkawa, "Significant Changes in Japanese Agriculture since 1945," *Journal of Farm Economics*, Dec. 1961 (contained in this volume).

Bruce F. Johnston, "Agricultural Development and Economic Transformation: A Comparative Study of the Japanese Experience," *Food Research Institute Studies*, (Stanford University) Vol. III, No. 3, Nov. 1962.

Reprinted by permission of the Iowa State University Press, from Roger N. Dixey, ed., International Explorations of Agricultural Economics, *1964, pp. 201–212.*

The Notion of "Prerequisites"

We choose 1868, the year of the Meiji Restoration, as the point of departure for modern economic growth in Japan. We do so, as it can be claimed that at this point modern economic growth became a national objective. Japan's given conditions—the inherited conditions from which modern economic growth started—are characterized by a typical pre-modern economic level and structure of the Asian type. Though the available data are not reliable enough with regard to the current conditions, we can make the following points. Both productivity and income per capita were very close to the present average low level of most countries in South-east Asia (rice yield, about 60 bushels per hectare; per capita national product, about $60 at the present rate of exchange). The industrial and occupational structure was of the typical pre-modern type (agricultural population, 75–80 per cent). Production organization of agriculture was extremely small scale (one hectare of farm land per household). Nevertheless a high rate of surplus existed, based on the inherited pattern of feudal income distribution (rent in kind, more than 50 per cent of rice yields).

None of the above should give the impression that Japan's economic structure was completely static in the period before 1868. Actually, a number of factors are often cited by some economic historians as evidence of changes in the economic structure for the later part of the pre-modern period. Among them, growth of output and commercialization of agriculture in particular are relevant here. Based on these facts they tend to emphasize a noticeable development of agriculture before Japan's start in industrialization. But we think these were limited regional phenomena and accordingly disagree with this argument. We take the view that the industrial revolution in Japan was not preceded by nationwide agricultural development but that agricultural development started simultaneously with industrial development.

There is a historical line of thought which assumes that the order or sequence of industrial development in advanced countries must be repeated in a more or less similar way in backward countries. In Britain the industrial revolution was preceded by the agricultural revolution, so that the development of agriculture may be considered a historical *prerequisite* for industrial development. I am afraid that this may be a too simplified presentation. But any sophisticated version may not alter the core of its thought. We see its integrated concept in the notion of *necessary prerequisites*. According to this notion, there are a number of necessary prerequisites or preconditions for industrial growth, without which it could not begin. Rostow's thesis of stages of economic growth is an outstanding example.

So far as agriculture is concerned, this notion seems to be not applicable to the Japanese case. As noted above, industrial development in this country may have begun without the precondition of agricultural development. In its basic contents, we believe, there is no doubt of this. With respect to its detailed implications, however, further explanations may be needed. Among them the following two points are indispensable.

First, we have to make a distinction between the abolition of a pre-modern institutional framework and the existence of an increase in the productivity of agriculture, although actually these two are closely interrelated. In our earlier discussions, the development of agriculture meant simply the latter—an increase in the productivity of agriculture, irrespective of the patterns of accompanying institutional changes. But the discussion of prerequisites usually contains both the former and the latter. Immediately after the Restoration the new Meiji Government, quickly and on a national basis, denounced all feudal regulations

167

controlling such things as planting crops, private ownership and sale of land, as well as changes of occupation and residence. These revisions were indispensable to the subsequent modern economic growth. Therefore we do not object to the assertion that abolition of these pre-modern regulations was the necessary precondition for modern economic growth. There is no vagueness in this as far as the Japanese case is concerned, because the legal emancipation was a clear-cut phenomenon. However, for the countries whose pre-modern restraints on peasant farming have been maintained to some extent into later periods, our conceptual distinction cannot be applied so clearly. Industrialization could begin with some pre-modern restraints. Even in Japan's case some economic historians claim the actual remnants of feudal restraints after 1868. Nevertheless, in principle we are much inclined to made a distinction between the two and to disagree with the notion of preconditions in terms of productivity development.

Secondly, we have an impression that there has often been confusion between *pre*conditions and conditions, and that these two different concepts have sometimes been used interchangeably without distinction. For example, there is an argument that the increase in labor productivity of agriculture is a necessary condition for industrial development, because industry cannot draw the required labor force away from the land if agriculture does not raise its productivity. This is simple logic and no one would deny it to the extent that the agricultural surplus produced by its increased productivity is the source of development of the non-agricultural sectors. However, such an argument often has been erroneously used in association with the thesis of preconditions of agriculture for industrialization. Such a line of thought seems to be strengthened by a feeling that the present level of productivity of agriculture in most countries in Asia is too low to be the required precondition for industrial development, in association with a recognition of a conspicuous gap between the present low level of productivity in these countries and the European level at the eve of industrialization.

This is misleading. There was an agricultural surplus even in the pre-modern era of every country—without exception. As previously noted with respect to the given conditions in Japan at the time of embarking on modern economic growth, there was a high rate of surplus produced in agriculture. We have noted that this was possible not because of a high or an increased productivity of agriculture but because of the inherited pattern of pre-modern income distribution. The actual surplus tends to be much more influenced by the distribution pattern than by technical productivity. It is therefore risky to insist on a certain level of productivity of agriculture as a necessary precondition for industrialization.

The Contribution of Agriculture and the Pattern of Sectoral Interdependence

Throughout the entire subsequent period of economic growth in Japan, there has been a continuing growth of agriculture. Though it was faster in favourable conditions and slower when conditions were unfavorable, its average high rate of growth was pronounced. It is hazardous to expect the measurement of growth rates to allow for reliable international comparisons. However, consulting such data as are available, we believe that Japan's rate of growth of agricultural output was comparable at least to the most speedy rates realized in advanced Western countries. For example, in terms of real G.D.P. produced in agriculture, the annual rate of growth was 1.8 per cent in the pre-war period. The fastest rates in Europe hardly ever exceeded 1.5 to 2 per cent according to our estimates. The rate of industrial growth was much faster, of course, than that of agriculture,

169

recording around 5 per cent by corresponding measurements, but the gap between them is not our point here. The point is that Japanese agriculture developed not before but side by side with the process of speedy industrialization—a *concurrent* growth of industry and agriculture. What kind of conceptual framework is desirable to analyze this process?

The conventional approach has been given mostly in terms of a notion of *contribution* and the like. We have often heard the following: agriculture contributed to economic development by supplying food for increased demand and the labor force required for industrial development; it contributed by expanding the domestic market for industrial goods; the increase of its output-exports contributed by making it possible to promote the necessary imports of capital goods; the outflow of a surplus created in agriculture and directed to the rest of the economy was a contribution to the making of necessary investments and public expenditure for modernization. If we confine our discussion to the initial phase of modern economic growth, 1868 to 1905, all these versions in themselves are valid. There is no reason to doubt these historical facts. What puzzles us, however, is the vagueness of the notion of the so-called contribution. In a network of a concurrent growth process, is it really possible without difficulty to identify one sector's contribution to the growth of other sectors or of the economy as a whole? If it is, in what sense is it possible?

Let us begin with a simple fact. No one would deny that in the course of Japanese economic growth, industrial development also contributed to the growth of agriculture, especially if we were asked to use the notion of contribution: it gave a stimulus to agriculture by increasing and diversifying the demand for agricultural outputs; it contributed to the development of agriculture by absorbing the increased labor force in agriculture, thus preventing aggravated over-population on the land; it con-

170

tributed to the development of agriculture by increasing the supply of improved inputs (fertilizers, etc.); the progress of technology in industry could bring forth an induced progress of related technology in agriculture. Again all these facts we can recognize without hesitation.

It is evident, therefore, that the notion of sectoral contribution cannot be entirely independent; to a large extent it must be a reciprocal concept. We see a good example of sectoral interdependence in the case of the labor force outflow from agriculture to the rest of the economy. One can certainly recognize its sectoral contribution from either side: agriculture contributed to industry by supplying the labor force required by that sector, while industry contributed to agriculture by absorbing the increased labor force in that sector and preventing aggravated over-population on the land. One may still argue that the labor transferred from agriculture to the rest of the economy was produced in farm-households, so that from the view-point of the production costs of human elements, agriculture contributed to the non-agricultural sector and not the reverse. But, one can also point out that an over-supply of labor on the land would lead to a diminishing return of agricultural production and/or prevent the introduction of technological innovations. This negative effect was removed when the expansion of industry created jobs away from the land, so that industry contributed to agricutlure.

In general, the process of economic growth contains, as one of its major characteristics, the interdependence between various sectors of the economy: the growth (or retardation) of a particular sector influences, and in turn is influenced by, the growth (or retardation) of the other sectors. We call this relationship "sectoral interdependence." Economic growth usually leads to an increasingly close sectoral interdependence of the economy. Agriculture and industry would follow this general trend, but

171

with a variety of patterns from one country to another and from one phase to another within a single country. Therefore our task is to re-examine one by one the individual factors of contribution previously noted with respect to Japanese agriculture in order to answer the two questions:

1. What factors can really be identified as making a genuine sectoral contribution?
2. What was the specific pattern of sectoral interdependence?

Let us begin by discussing the former question. We previously referred to a well-known fact that the outflow of a surplus created in agriculture and directed to the rest of the economy was a contribution by making necessary investment and public expenditure for modernization. In Japan this was done mainly through the land-tax system. Its features were as follows: First, it fixed the land-tax rate as high as 30 per cent of rice yields at the beginning, a rate almost inherited from the pre-modern system; and second, in the subsequent period of economic growth, because of its fixed cash amount per area, its proportion gradually decreased as both productivity and the price of rice increased. This was economically rational for two reasons: possible decreases in the land-tax proportion acted as an incentive for developing agriculture; and other taxes based on the subsequent development of the non-agricultural sector substituted for it in later years.

We want to discuss this problem in theory apart from its practical means of transferring surplus. In a country where a concurrent growth of agriculture and industry is required, the possibility of transferring the agricultural surplus to the other sectors of the economy must be a decisive factor. By its very nature this cannot effectively be carried out by free market mechanism and therefore requires government intervention of one kind or other. Japan's case presented an orthodox action of government

172

in this general context apart from its actual means of implementation. This was a process of *forced* income transfer, unlike the case of demand-supply interdependence, which will be discussed in subsequent pages. The sectoral transfer of resources in this sense is the only case which we can really call the sectoral "contribution" without conceptual vagueness.

In answer to the second question, it is convenient to discuss two aspects separately.

The Pattern of Labor Supply

Let us begin with the specific pattern of the labor market during the initial phase of modern economic growth. The main facts were as follows: (1) The labor force engaged in agriculture was almost unchanged or even slightly decreased, so that its net increase was all absorbed by the non-agricultural sector. In European countries the labor force in agriculture increased until almost the 1920's, so that Japan's pattern is worth noticing. (2) The rate of increase in the total population in Japan was 0.7 to 1.0 per cent annum during the initial phase of modern economic growth and reached its maximum rate, 1.5 per cent around 1930. This is similar to the British pattern of population growth and implies a moderate rate close to the norm in Europe. We can assume that this was more or less the same with regard to the labor force growth, though the data are less reliable. (3) There was a pronounced difference, however, in the initial condition of industrial distribution of the labor force. As noted previously, in Japan the labor force engaged in agriculture was overwhelmingly large in proportion, while in advanced countries in Europe on the eve of industrialization it was much less, though again exact data are scanty. It is clear that, other things being equal, industry in Japan had to grow fast enough to absorb much more labor from agriculture if the agricultural population were to be unchanged. Population pressure of this kind, not that of the natural increase of the total population, was crucial in Japan's case.

A combined consideration of the above three facts would lead us to a valid question: How could Japan succeed in avoiding a much more aggravated population pressure on the land? Another question has often been raised: Why could not Japan reduce the farm population? This ignores facts 2 and 3 above, as well as the exceedingly high rate of growth of Japanese industry. To answer the former question, we have to mention the specific pattern of growth of the non-agricultural sector in particular, which growth was characterized by an application of relatively labor-intensive technology of production. This was particularly pronounced during the initial phase of industrialization. The rate of increase in employment amounted to two thirds of its rate of output growth. Although capital-intensive technology came into prominence later, small-scale enterprises based on labor-intensive technology did not lose their importance in the post-war industrial spurt.

What was the mechanism of these interrelated phenomena? In a broad sense, it was "a labor market with an unlimited supply of labor," in Arthur Lewis' terminology. The supply price of labor was basically determined by the level of subsistence of the people on the land. With real wage rates determined correspondingly by it, the enterprisers in the non-agricultural sector could employ their required labor force in an almost perfectly elastic manner. A salient feature of this mechanism, however, was the fact that both the labor productivity of agriculture and industrial real wage rates did increase *pari passu* at least until 1905–10 (annual rates, roughly 1.0 to 1.5 per cent). This is worth noticing, because of its difference from classical models (for instance A. Lewis's), where no increase in real wage rates is assumed in principle. We believe that the notion of an unlimited supply of labor can still be applied in this case on the assumption of a trend line of an increasing supply price of labor at a certain rate.

174

Output-Input Relationships and Commercialization

The supply of food and materials for industrial use, the production of goods for exports, and the demand for industrial products —these previously noted functions of agriculture can all be discussed in an integrated form of the conventional input-output relationship between sectors of the economy. Despite a lack of systematized statistical tables except for recent years, we can point out verbally the features of the Japanese pattern as follows.

1. Despite some partial commercialization of agriculture towards the end of the pre-modern period, industrialization started with typical subsistence farming. Because of the subsequent rapid changes in the institutional and economic structure and of the fast growth of industry, agriculture was integrated very rapidly into a monetized economy. Hence, the rapid response of agriculture to this drastic change contrasts with the slow, moderate response in advanced countries.

2. Ironically enough, Japanese agriculture changed its output structure not drastically but rather moderately through the subsequent years of rapid economic growth. The heavy yield of rice has long been maintained, forming the backbone of the traditional farm economy; diversification (especially into livestock farming) started on a significant scale only after World War II; structural change occurred only in the field of cash crops; even there the major line was an expansion of traditional sericulture, which during the initial phase was substituted for other traditional cash crops, especially cotton.

3. The moderate changes in the structure of output supply had their counterparts on the demand side. The people's pattern of food consumption changed little throughout the pre-war period, centering on rice, fish and traditional vegetables. Agriculture (and fishery) succeeded in increasing the supplies of these tradi-

tional crops to meet their increases in demand at least until around the time of World war I. This is proved by the *pari passu* trend of prices of agricultural commodities with that of the general price movement. The situation of an unlimited supply of labor was made possible by this equilibrium growth process of food supply-demand.

4. Expansion of the supply of agricultural material for industrial use was focused on sericulture and tea cultivation, which made possible an expansion of the exports of silk and tea. It is to be noted, however, that these products, and especially silk, differed from most export-orientated primary products in presently developing countries. They were combined products of domestic agriculture and domestic manufacturing and had a fairly extensive domestic market. Silk manufacturing especially was far from being a satellite of agriculture, unlike traditional food-processing industries, but had a noticeable effect in inducing the development of sericulture.

5. The failure to expand the cotton supply for the cotton-spinning industry, another major export sector in Japan, needs a brief explanation. In terms of comparative advantage of raising income per unit area, cocoons became increasingly superior to cotton, mainly because of giving many more opportunities of increasing labor input and value output per unit area. A very unfavorable man-land ratio, which was one of the given conditions at the start of Japan's economic modernization, was the basic factor for determinimg the direction of such a cash crop structure.

6. With respect to the function of expanding the domestic market for industrial products, there is only one point to which we would like to draw attention. Both the input of intermediate goods for farm production and the purchase of consumption goods for farm households increased very moderately throughout the pre-war period, although a post-war increase is noticeable. In terms of individual items, a drastic increase in the input of com-

176

mercial fertilizer was the only exception. But on an average, the proportion of inputs of intermediate goods of industrial origin to gross outputs amounted to barely 20 per cent in the pre-war period. Despite this moderate share of inputs in agriculture, it brought forth a significant increase in the demand for industrial goods, both intermediate and final. This was because the relative share of agriculture in the economy had been exceedingly high (in 1903 to 1907 the share of income produced in the primary sector was still some 40 per cent).

Through all these six patterns, we see the underlying salient feature that a growth process with balanced input-output relationships was more or less maintained despite the drastic structural changes and differential growth rates between agriculture and industry, and that this was made possible by the dominant place of agriculture based on a moderate change in the traditional output structure of the economy.

Type of Technological Progress and Economic Backwardness

The functions of agriculture discussed above were all made possible basically by the rapid progress of technology in increasing labor productivity. We noted that the behavior of real wage rates was characterized by a sustained increase in the labor productivity of agriculture. Supply of agricultural outputs with almost unchanged relative prices implies shifts of supply functions corresponding to the rest of the economy. Enlarging the market for industrial goods, outflow of savings of agriculture to the rest of the economy—both were continuously possible only by an increase in productivity. There is no doubt that technological progress in agriculture was the crucial factor in the sense that without it any one of its functions previously noted could not be realized.

What type of technological progress? Under a sustained condi-

177

tion of small-scale individual farming of an almost unchanged labor force and area of farm land in the aggregate, the output per worker increased at an annual rate close to 2 per cent on average in the prewar and at 3 per cent in the post-war period. Mechanization is quite a recent phenomenon and private investment for fixed capital was moderate. These facts suggest that the technological progress of Japanese agriculture was characterized by the land-and labor-saving type with a moderate increase of capital per unit of output. This pattern is defined, of course, in terms of changes over time. In the process of concurrent growth with industry, agricultural technology required a certain rate of progress in labor-saving in order to follow the technological progress of this type in industry. In addition, this required an accompanying progress of land-saving technology because of the severe limitation of an unchanged labor-land ratio. Furthermore, this twofold requirement could be met economically only with a moderate increase of capital. How to meet these severe triple requirements at the same time was a basic problem for the technological development of Japanese agriculture. And to a considerable extent they were met.

It has been widely recognized that within an interrelated system of agricultural technology, each component can make progress only in complementary relationships with other related components. We know the difficulty of squeezing certain key factors out of this interrelated system. Nevertheless, in the light of the unchanged production organizaiton of Japanese agriculture over a long time, it would not be illegitimate to point out the crucial factor. It was the progress of cultivating techniques in a broad sense, including seed improvement as a most important factor.

In this kind of technical progress by trial and error, we can see two distinct elements which made them possible: fuller utilization of indigenous techniques and borrowing foreign science and technology. In the initial stage the government tried to borrow

Western methods of large-scale farming. Since this ended in near failures the government started to encourage fuller utilization of indigenous techniques, and in fact this was successful. At the same time, however, the government extended a programme of technical-assistance activities so as to borrow foreign technology in a more appropriate way. This facilitated the application of the then newly developed agricultural sciences and technology to Japanese techniques of cultivation. During the initial phase of economic growth, the indigenous element played an important role, but foreign elements nonetheless contributed by bringing cumulative rewards in later periods.

What significant features does technological progress in Japanese agriculture suggest? We shall discuss this in terms of the notion of economic backwardness. However difficult it may be to quantify the degree of economic backwardness, whatever definition one may give to its concept, no one would deny the fact that Japan started economic modernization as a latecomer. Externally, by the 1870's the major Western countries were already in a stage of severe competition of imperialistic expansion. Internally, Japan's conditions were typically premodern.

Following the discussion of various patterns of agricultural development in Japan under the concept of sectoral interdependence, we wish to associate these patterns with the type of technological progress in the light of the general notion of economic backwardness.

An exceedingly fast rate of industrial growth implies various important patterns which can be understood in terms of this factor of economic backwardness. Most relevant here is borrowing modern technology from advanced countries. No one will doubt the fact that this was one of the major factors which were responsible for a fast rate of industrial growth.

In the case of concurrent growth, was this also true of agriculture? The answer to this, a natural question, is, "the same was true in agriculture." Irrespective of different types and degrees of borrowing advanced technology, we believe it is important to recognize the common element between the two major sectors of the economy. This is particularly so because it is widely recognized that backward countries in general have possible advantages in borrowing a backlog of advanced technology. Why has this been agreed to only with regard to manufacture? How about agriculture? One often has an impression that it is much more difficult in agriculture. Why? Various factors such as natural endowments (climate, soil, etc.), scale and organization of farming, institutional set-ups—the differences of these factors between advanced and backward countries, one may argue, are decisive in preventing the utilization of this possible advantage. Furthermore one would say this is still more difficult because of being combined with the non-mechanical, biological nature of agricultural technology.

We would say, however, that most of these do not prevent, they only modify, the factors of borrowing advanced technology. Japan's experience suggests the direction and type of modifications which were required to fit into its pattern of agricultural growth. Unlike the situation in manufacture, it suggests that it is not possible to borrow ready-made technology of foreign origin. A certain time interval is required before foreign elements can be used effectively to establish a country's own system of technology. In contrast to this handicap, the flexible nature of agricultural production in terms of factor-proportions and divisibility can count as a favorable element in agriculture as compared with manufacture. In manufacture, technological requirements often operate as a decisive factor in changing the scale and organization of production, which sometimes is out of keeping with the economic situation of backward countries. But in the case of agriculture, inputs such as seeds, fertilizers, and insecticides are all highly divisible and they can be used with different farm scales. In fact the fast progress of technology in Japanese agriculture, centering on the improvement of techniques of cultivation as noted previously, is highly characterized by the intensive use of this feature of agricultural technology: input divisibility and scale neutrality.

By way of conclusion, out of the various patterns of Japanese experience noted here, we would like to have the following points specifically high-lighted:

1. The nature of the problem of how to regard the functions of agriculture in economic development tends to differ according to the degree of economic backwardness of the country at issue.

2. Therefore, it is more useful to discover patterns of concurrent growth of agriculture and industry rather than to rely upon the conventional, rigid concept.

3. However, for economically backward countries in general it may not be illegitimate to say, first, that the nature of the problem for each country can most systematically be ascertained by applying a conceptual framework of sectoral interdependence. Secondly, with respect to agriculture specifically, the problem can be answered most effectively by examining the possible speed at which advanced technology in this sector may be borrowed in comparison with the corresponding speed in the case of manufacture.

ECONOMIC GROWTH

AND

AGRICULTURE

Introduction

The main purpose of this paper is to analyze the problem of agriculture which arises in the process of economic growth with special reference to the productivity-employment aspect. I will have in mind the Japanese experience in making theoretical approaches that follow, so that it may be helpful for foreign readers to describe first briefly the actual situation of the Japanese economy and agriculture.

The circumstances surrounding post-war Japanese agriculture have drastically changed in three respects: international prices and products can no longer be ignored; population pressure weighs heavily not only on Japan's food resources, but on her employment problem; and the land reform has profoundly affected the economic and social status of farmers.

First, losing two rice-growing territories, Korea and Taiwan, Japan suddenly became one of the world's great grain importing countries after the last war. Her position up to that time had

A revised and condensed version of "Economic Growth and Agriculture" in The Annals of the Hitotsubashi Academy, *Vol. VII, No. 1, October* 1956, *Hitostubashi University, Tokyo, pp.* 45–60.

been one of near food self-sufficiency in her economic bloc. In recent years the average import percentage of principal food commodities consumed has become as follows: rice 10, wheat 50, barley 40, soybeans 25 and raw sugar 95. The normal total value of food imports is 600 million dollars annually, which composes about thirty per cent of the total value of imports. This naturally constitutes quite a heavy drain on Japan's foreign exchange reserves. Because of the heavy food imports, moreover, Japanese agriculture has increasingly become subject to changes in the international grain market. Specifically the recent trend toward an over-supply of agricultural products in the world has exerted a strong pressure on the domestic price level of agricultural products.

Second, Japanese agriculture has had to absorb a considerable portion of the post-war increase in population and labor force, resulting from natural population growth and the repatriates from the overseas Empire. During the two decades 1915–1935, the population gainfully occupied in agriculture remained almost unchanged amounting to 13.6–13.7 million, which in 1935 composed 44 per cent of the total gainfully occupied population. Since emigration during that period was very small, the net increase in rural labor force was absorbed almost entirely by non-agricultural industries. This situation changed suddenly after the war. The population gainfully occupied in agriculture amounted to 16.5 million in 1955, 2.8 million bigger than the normal pre-war level. The arable land area, on the other hand, has decreased after the war, despite the Government's encouragement to increase arable land. The average arable land per farm household has decreased to 0.85 hectare from the pre-war one hectare level. The land-labor ratio in post-war Japanese agriculture has thus become even worse than the pre-war one, which had been widely known as one of the most unfavorable in the world. Furthermore, since the high rate of increase in the labor force (2 per cent a year) is expected to continue during the next ten or fifteen years, the situation in the rural area is expected to worsen in the near future.

Third, however, the post-war land reform has reduced the area of tenanted arable land to less than ten per cent of the total arable land, so that almost all the farmers now cultivate their own land without paying high rent to landlords. Before the reform about 46 per cent of the total arable land was tenanted and the landholders got a considerable portion of the production as rent in kind from tenant farmers. This drastic change has had a very favorable effect on the economic and social status of farmers. Most of them have become independent economic units cultivating their own land, and their earned income has risen considerably above the low pre-war level. Up to the present, the larger portion of the increased income has been spent on raising their level of living (the propensity to consume has been very large), so that the productivity effect of this reform is not yet sizable. Their standard of living has risen to the extent that their real income is almost equivalent to that of the urban working class. Thus a new social consciousness or notion that income parity should exist between farmers and urban workers has been introduced since the reform. This new situation makes it politically difficult to abolish the support measures of farm prices, allowing the international competition determine the domestic price level: the government's income support policy for the farmers becomes indispensable.

Confronting with these problems, the *five-year plan* adopted last year by the Government set two major objectives: the attainment of self-support or of balancing the foreign exchanges and the achievement of full employment by 1960. In its general programme, the two targets concerning agriculture are to be noted: one is that the future increase in the demand for main food is to be entirely supplied by increasing the domestic produc-

185

tion and the other is that agriculture is expected to aborsb 760 thousand additional labor force by 1960. The average growth rate of GNP is projected to be 5 per cent and that of the labor force 2 per cent, so that the annual rate of increase in labor productivity is expected to be 3 per cent. In comparison with it, the annual rate of increase in agricultural productivity is estimated to be 2.4–2.5 per cent. It is clear that the productivity difference between agriculture and non-agriculture is expected to be widened.

The *plan* has been described briefly in order to illustrate the basic problem with which Japanese agriculture will confront in the coming process of economic growth.

Output Equilibrium and Factor Disequilibrium

It stands out clear from the above description that the output equilibrium (balance between the demand for and supply of farm product) does not necessarily accompany the factor equilibrium (roughly, income or productivity parity between agriculture and non-agriculture). It is suggested also that the factor equilibrium does not necessarily bring forth the output equilibrium. Generally speaking, it is my view that in the growth path of a country like Japan there is a basic problem of *fundamental disequilibrium* concerning agriculture. The significance and implication of this concept will be explained later. Let us here reconsider the classical treatment of the relevant subject in comparison.

In the classical theory of economic growth the assumption of the so-called decreasing return tendency in the agricultural sector composes the essential core of the system. In our terminology, the decreasing return tendency may be expressed as follows: the rate of increasing labor productivity of agricultural sector is always apt to become smaller than that of non-agricultural sector or in other words, the unequal rate of increasing labor productivity between the two sectors is assumed to continue throughout the growth path. The effect of this un-equality is entirely considered in terms of the ever-rising tendency of the relative prices of agricultural products. This was natural and reasonable, because in that period the practical aim of the theory was to make clear the advantages of adopting free trade policy and of depending more and more on the foreign supply of agricultural products in order to meet the increasing domestic demand.

Most of the capitalistic developments in the western world have more or less followed along this line. As the results of this sort of policy and of the agricultural development in the new continents, the relative price of agricultural products has actually not risen so much, but remained nearly unchanged in the secular trend. In other words, the "agricultural problem" in the meaning of the classical school has been solved by developing international trade in the world. However, it is to be noted that in the classical model there is no room to appear the factor disequilibrium problem between the two sectors: agriculture and non-agriculture. In that system, it is entirely assumed that the effect of increasing cost in the agricultural production is to be paid from the total profits of capitalists in the closed economy, as the results of the increasing tendency of rent on the one hand and of the rising trend of money wage rates on the other. It is obvious that the perfect equilibrium of production factors (capital and labor) between the two sectors is fundamentally assumed in this model. Therefore, the classical thought can be understood as relying entirely upon the open system in regard to the means of solving the problem of unequal rate of increasing agricultural productivity behind that of the non-agricultural sector. The situation seems basically different in our case.

187

I would like to develop an analysis by use of simple models in order to clarify the nature of the problem, assuming that the economy is composed of two sectors: agriculture and non-agriculture. The three kinds of equilibrium growth, which concern output, capital and labor will be separately discussed.

First, an equilibrium growth of demand for and supply of agricultural output is simply described as a path which brings forth no changes in its relative prices. We can treat this path as if it were a real term model so long as the output price of non-agriculture is assumed unchanged. A long-term shift of demand for agricultural output is caused by changes in the size of population, real income per head and tastes, etc. The growth rate of demand (D) is expressed here simply by $p+\eta g$, where p and g stand respectively for the growth rate of population and that of real income per head and η denotes income elasticity of demand for agricultural output. The growth rate of net output (G_a) is assumed to be equal to that of the product gross of intermediate goods, the supply, (S), that is $G_a=S$, and we have $G_a=\eta g+p$ for an output equilibrium path under a closed system. On the other hand, letting g denotes the growth rate of labor productivity and p that of the labor force, for simplicity, we have $G=g+p$, where G stands for the growth rate of national income. Combining these two equations, we have another simple one, $G-G_a=(1-\eta)g$. This is transformed into

$$G_n-G_a=\frac{1-\eta}{1-\omega}\,g, \tag{1}$$

where G_n stands for the growth rate of products of the non-agricultural sector and ω for the weight of agricultural output to the national product, that is $G=G_a\omega+G_n(1-\omega)$. Equation (1) shows the necessary relationship between the growth rates of the two sectors in the process of products-equilibrium growth under the assumptions mentioned above. The difference between the two sectors' growth rates (G_n-G_a), which is expressed by δ hereafter, is important. Under normal conditions the value of δ is plus, since we know that $0<\eta<1$, $0<\omega<1$ and $0<g$.

On the supply-production side, the growth rate of agricultural output is treated as being composed of two factors, the rate of changes in labor employment (n_a) and that of labor productivity (g_a), that is $S=g_a+n_a$. The output equilibrium path is

$$g_a+n_a=p+\eta g. \tag{2}$$

In the prewar period, the labor force occupied in agriculture had been almost constant, so that n_a was approximately zero, and g_a had averaged around 2 per cent in the early period and 1 per cent after W.W.I.. In the former period the condition of $S=D$ had been nearly satisfied, whereas in the latter period it became a situation of $S<D$, implying a disequilibrium of production factors.

Second, by a factor equilibrium path I mean a sustained maintenance of equality of marginal productivity of production factors between the two sectors. To begin with capital allocation, the economy as a whole is assumed to be growing along the equilibrium path regarding investment-savings. If we denote the capital-output-ratio of agriculture and non-agriculture respectively by C_a and C_n, it will be possible to give the amount of investment required to maintain a given growth rate in each sector $(G_a$ and $G_n)$ respectively, which will be expressed by the terms G_aC_a and G_nC_n. If the average savings ratio in each sector is denoted by s_a and s_n respectively, the following relationships develop:

$$G_aC_a=s_a+\alpha, \quad G_nC_n=s_n+\beta \tag{3}$$

In this equilibrium growth process, the relation $GC=s$ of the economy as a whole is always maintained according to the assumption given above. (C is the aggregate capital-output ratio). It does not follow that $G_aC_a=S_a$ or that $G_nC_n=s_n$ as a necessary result. Thus α and β are introduced to account for the disequilibrium between investment and savings which normally appears in each sector. The relation $\alpha\omega=\beta(1-\omega)$ follows between the two terms α and β. If $\alpha>0$ then necessarily $\beta>0$, and *vice versa*. In the former case, the amount of savings is insufficient to maintain that rate of investment required to maintain the growth rate G_a in the agricultural sector, and amount of savings realized in the non-agricultural sector is partially transmitted into the former sector, and in the latter case the reverse will be true. It is a simple matter to arrange the above relations into another set of relations, deleting α and β, as follows:

$$\frac{s_a}{C_a} - G_a = \left(\frac{G_n C_n - s_n}{C_a}\right)\frac{1-\omega}{\omega}, \quad \text{and}$$

$$G_n - \frac{s_n}{C_n} = \left(\frac{s_a - G_a C_a}{C_n}\right)\frac{\omega}{1-\omega}. \tag{5}$$

The numerical values of these relations will be determined by the behavior of investment and savings. If the expected return of investment is smaller in agricultural than in non-agricultural sector a part of the savings in the former sector will flow out to the latter sector to be invested there, even though it may induce a product-disequilibrium. In general, a capital-equilibrium does not necessarily guarantee a product-equilibrium. It may be useful to point out the following.

It has been already made clear that $G_a < G_n$ (or a plus δ) is necessary in the products-equilibrium process. Hence on the simple assumptions of $C_n = C_a$ and $s_n = s_a$, the investment rate required to maintain the product-equilibrium process in agricultural sector $(G_a C_a)$ is necessarily smaller than that of non-agricultural sector $(G_n C_n)$, and savings in the agricultural sector can flow out to the non-agricultural sector. In such a case, agriculture may be called the sector which is playing a positive role in economic growth. When the value of capital-output-ratio of agriculture is smaller than that of non-agricultural sector, the outflow will naturally become more remarkable. In the early period of economic development of Japan, agriculture did certainly play such a positive role. The reverse case in which agriculture plays a negative role can take place depending on the numerical relationships between the three terms mentioned above. Japanese agriculture at present is an actual example.

Next, to discuss the labor allocation between the two sectors, a simple proposition is that the marginal productivity of labor is equal to the prevailing wage rate under a perfect competitive condition and that this equality will be maintained between the two sectors through the equilibrium growth path. I bring in the concept of equal rates of productivity growth between the two sectors, which satisfies the above condition. Previously we derived $G_a=g_a+n_a$ for agriculture. Correspondingly, we can have $G_n=g_n+n_n$ for the non-agricultural sector. In the path of equal rates of productivity growth, g_a must equal to g_n, so that we have

$$G_n-G_a=n_n-n_a, \tag{4}$$

which shows the required relationship between the two sectors in order to maintain a path of equal productivity growth rates. Under the above assumption of competitive labor market, equation (4) implies a path of equal rates of wage income growth between the two sectors. Because of $G_n>G_a$ in the output equilibrium, it means $n_n>n_a$ to that extent. In a special case of $n_n=0$, previously mentioned, the rate of increase in the labor employment in the non-agricultural sector is equal to the right hand term in equation (1).

Now, my particular concern is a sustained path of dis-equilibrium with respect to the labor allocation. The Japanese experience presents two facts in this respect: one is that the marginal productivity of labor in agriculture is lower than that of non-agricultural sector and the other is that the rate of productivity growth over time tends to be unfavorable to agriculture. In my view, this disequilibrium is basically caused by a state of "over-occupied" of labor (a state of excess-employment) in agriculture—the main subject to be discussed in the section that follows.

Here, in comparison with the model of classical school mentioned previously, let us draw attention to the following two points. First, the output-equilibrium is not needed if the economy is able to develop an open system favorably. If a growing economy is inclined to depend more and more upon foreign supply to meet the increasing demand for agricultural product, its growth rate would be higher than in the case of closed system. The equilibrium difference of the rates of changes in the labor force employed between the two sectors should be larger than that of the closed system, other things being equal. Hence, let us write

$$G_n{}'-G_a{}'=n_n{}'-n_a{}',\tag{4'}$$

where, each prime stands for the case of open system. In doing so, it is possible to diminish the over-occupied labor in agricultural sector to a certain extent. However, it is impossible to wipe out the dis-equilibrium of labor allocation in the light of Japanese experience: its rate of exports growth was much higher than the international level and yet the population gainfully occupied in agriculture could not decrease sizably.

Second, a sustained state of disequilibrium of labor allocation would lead to a trend increase of relative prices of agricultural output, as one may expect due to the relative cost increase in agricultural production. Essentially this was not the case in prewar Japan because the labor compensation in agriculture had been kept low due to the lack of alternative employment. Thus the sustained path of unequal rates of productivity growth did not materially reflect itself in a trend of rising agricultural prices.

"Over-Occupied" and "Disguised" Equilibrium

In general, when the marginal productivity of labor in any one sector is always lower than its normal level of the economy, this sector is defined as being in the over-occupied condition with regard to labor. The *"over-occupied"* (Kajō syūgyō) condition means that the lower marginal productivity of labor is caused by too-much occupation of labor force in this sector under the condition of decreasing marginal productivity curve. If the labor force occupied in this sector is reduced to a certain extent with no radical changes of production technique, the marginal productivity of labor will rise correspondingly to a certain extent. I said "always" in the above definition. This means that the phenomenon is not of cyclical, but of structural nature, or in other words that it will exist even in the case of full utilisation of capital stock in a most prosperous time.

The well-known concept "disguised unemployment" has generally been used in a similar meaning. However, it may be better to distinguish the concept defined above from this one. The former means the structural fact caused by the fundamental dis-equilibrium of the labor employment, while the latter does not necessarily so and has usually been used in relation to the Keynesian concept of unemployment. Another term of under-employment might be defined to be quite equal to the concept of over-occupation defined above and these two expressions might be used interchangeably. It is convenient, however, to use the latter to express exactly the nature of the problem we face mainly by two reasons; first, under-employment has often been used as quite a different meaning in the Keynsian terminology in order to express the condition of under-full employment of the economy as a whole, and second, in our case most of the labor forces in agricutural sector are not employed by enterprisers, but occupy themselves in their own farm work, showing quite a different characteristics of demand-supply behavior of labor from the modern type of employment.

Now let us return to our two-sector model. If the condition of equal rate of increasing labor productivity is not satisfied and $g_n > g_a$ takes place we certainly have the over-occupied condition in agricultural sector. In this case, the above defined "normal level" of marginal productivity of labor should be that of non-agricultural sector, because in the over-populated countries like Japan the capitalistic productions have been introduced mainly in the non-agricultural sector and we are naturally used to have the standards of economic comparisons in this sector. The modern type of employment is only prevailing in non-agricultural sector, while in agricultural sector the so-called self-employment is prevailing. In the situation like this, the incremental increase of demand for labor is determined by the capitalistic behavior in non-agricultural sector. When the amount of this demand is not sufficient to absorb the increasing supply of labor, the residual labor force is obliged to remain in the household-production work in agricultural sector. Thus the over-occupied condition in this sector is a residual phenomenon.

The following two are relevant: first, the factor proportion and second, the minimum level of marginal productivity of labor. The modern type of capitalistic production has relatively rigid factor proportion relationship, while the type of agricultural production has elastic factor proportion, so that the incremental increase of demand for labor in non-agricultural sector is apt to be limited on the process of modernization, while the residual labor mentioned above is apt to be absorbed by agricultural sector. But, there is, of course, a certain limit. If the over-occupied condition goes on over that limit, there will appear an unstable situation because of resulting a too-poor level of income of farmer's family.

In the latter context, I would like to develop another aspect of this subject. There are only a small number of hired workers in Japanese agriculture, while the most typical are the independent farmers whose income is composed of wages and non-wages (rent and profit, if any), functionally speaking—the so-called mixed income. Subjectively, they make no distinction between the two in comparing their income level with the workers' wage earnings in the non-agricultural sector. The consciousness or notion of income parity, mentioned in the Introduction, is at issue here. Let us simply assume an equilibrium state of labor allocation between the two sectors in that the parity is maintained between the average productivity of labor in agriculture and the marginal productivity of labor (hence wages) in non-agriculture. Regarding this sort of equilibrium, we recognize the following two points: first, from the viewpoint of optimum resource allocation, it is dis-equilibrium because the marginal productivity of labor is lower in agriculture as compared to that of non-agriculture; and second, from the viewpoint of labor market, however, we can see a sort of equilibrium condition, so that this situation should be understood as being of twofold character. I would like to define this a condition of *"disguised equilibrium"* for the reason that the situation should be considered as disguising the productivity dis-equilibrium behind the income equilibrium.

In the process of capitalistic development in a country like Japan, there remains still a lot of small proprietors who and whose family members are working by themselves, holding small amounts of production means of their own. Farmers holding a bit of land of their own are the most typical of these small proprietors. Their economic status are not uniform, ranging from relatively higher ones to lower ones. It is, however, not unrealistic to assume that they are almost competing with normal workers at large in earning their income. And particularly, the post-war improved status of farmers gives the realistic background on which the above-defined concept of disguised equilibrium stands.

These considerations may furthermore reveal that the conventional concepts are not appropriately applied to the phenomena we call attention here, because it is clear that the under-normal productivity of labor does not necessarily mean the existence of any sort of unemployment or of the condition to be remedied within a short period by particular measures. It is impossible to get an equal productivity condition between the two sectors by short period measures such as counter-cycle policies, because of the existence of fundamental dis-equilibrium. Therefore from the practical point of view, the sustained maintenance of the disguised equilibrium state should be a reasonable objective to be contained in the so-called "full employment" policy.

By way of conclusion, I would like to mention the following four points.

(1) The over-occupied condition of labor in agricultural sector is inevitable, because the required growth rate of the economy and the required rate of increasing employment demand in the non-agricultural sector in order to attain the factor-equilibrium condition is too big to be realized. This state is called a fundamental dis-equilibrium in the sense that the differential of marginal productivity of labor (and perhaps of capital) continue to exist as a basic structure.

(2) This structure contains a condition of over-occupied labor excess employment in agriculture and this is to be distinguished from the phenomenon conventionally understood in terms of disguised unemployment or the like. A concept of disguised equilibrium is useful in analysing the place of farmers in the growth path with a fundamental dis-equilibrium.

(3) A state of disguised equilibrium cannot necessarily be attained automatically with a free operation of the market

mechanism, so that the government intervention is logically indispensable for agricultural development, in order to maintain its rate of productivity growth *pari pasu* with that of the non-agricultural sector.

(4) Three measures are most important among others— a) a speeding up of the growth rate of non-agricultural sector at least to the extent that the population occupied in agriculture will begin and continue to decrease, b) introduction of improved production techniques into the agricultural sector to raise its labor productivity, and c) an inducement of more investments to agriculture, even if this sector becomes to play a "negative role" in the investment-savings relation.

SIGNIFICANT CHANGES

IN JAPANESE AGRICULTURE

SINCE 1945

The small size farm system of the Asian type and its place in an economy of rapid industralization of the modern type —these two features of Japanese agriculture make problems of "balanced growth" particularly important. Among many relevant factors, the following are the most influential in determining possibilities of "balanced growth:" Factor proportions (in particular, the man-land ratio); institutional framework (in particular, land tenure system); human elements (the mentality of farmers), the possibilities of technical progress, and the functions of the rest of the economy, including role of the government.

Balanced growth between agriculture and the rest of the economy can be treated simply in terms of two aspects: the balance of supply of and demand for agricultural output; and that of per-head real income between farmers and working population in the nonagricultural sector.

Viewed from the standpoint of balanced growth thus defined, the history of Japanese agriculture marked two distinct periods before World War II. The first, a period of balanced growth, continued from the initial stage of modernization in 1868 until the years just before World War I. The second, a period of

Reprinted by permission of the American Farm Economic Association, from Journal of Farm Economics, *Vol. XLIII No. 5, December* 1961, *pp.* 1103–1108.

unbalanced growth both in terms of output and of income, covered for the most part, the interwar period of Japan's overseas expansion. During, and immediately after, World War II, there was a transition period in agriculture with abnormalities caused by the war, during which time the relative income position of farmers had been much improved under conditions of a food supply deficit. After normal conditions came again, around 1950–53, the third period began, and problems of balanced growth again arose. I would like to set the problem in this long-term perspective, with particular reference to the several factors mentioned above.

Land Reform and Changes in Human Factor

Through the first and second periods, a long-inherited landlordism constituted the basic institutional framework of agriculture. Tenanted land was almost half of the total arable acreage. High rent, paid mostly in kind, reached almost half of the yield. During the first period, landowners played a leading role in raising agricultural output and productivity as they were rural "enterprisers," but toward the start of the second period they turned out to be merely interested in their absentee ownership. Thus the land system before World War II survived as an important factor limiting the improvement of agriculture.

Immediately after World War II, the government, in cooperation with Occupation Authorities, carried out a drastic land reform program, transferring most of the tenanted lands to the tenants. Less than 10 percent remained as tenanted land. Absentee ownership was completely abolished, the upper limit of ownership being set at less than one hectare for noncultivators. Rent in kind was replaced by a controlled low cash payment. The compensation fee fixed at a more or less reasonable amount turned out to be an extremely low rate as a result of the galloping inflation that followed the land reform. Thus postwar agriculture started from a completely new owner-cultivator system without any burden of compensation debts.

A great change in the human factor was created by the land reform, associated with a fresh atmosphere of the democratization of political, social and economic life in postwar Japan. Farmers' ability and initiative were emancipated, their desire for expansion and progress was awakened, and their response to incentives was strengthened. Thus a fresh enterprising mentality has newly infused work in improving agriculture.

Worsened Man-Land Ratio

The working population in agriculture immediately after World War II increased to 16.6 million from the 13.9 million in 1940, and until 1953 it did not decrease materially. The number of farm households also increased to 6 million from the prewar level of 5.5 million. This increase was caused by the repatriated people from overseas and by retardation in the absorptive power of the labor force in urban industries.

Throughout our first and second periods the number of working population and that of farm households had been almost unchanged, so that the net increase of labor force in agriculture had been almost completely absorbed by the nonagricultural sectors. Viewed historically, therefore, the increased postwar population pressure in agriculture deserves particular attention. The average size of farms nationally dropped to 0.86 hectare in 1955 from the 1940 level of 1.12 hectares.

The program of land consolidation was not successfully carried out by the land reform scheme, so that the long-inherited tiny portions of land remained scattered here and there. In addition, the scheme legally limited farm size, 3 hectare (12 hectare in Hokkaido) being set as the upper limit, and land transfer was put under strict control, so that the possibility of enlarging farm size was placed in an unfavorable situation. In comparing all farms in 1955 with those in 1940, farms less than one hectare increased from 66 to 71 percent, while those of one to two hectares decreased from 25 to 23 percent and those of more than two hectares decreased from 9 to 6 percent. This aggravation of the farms of tiny size is now a serious limiting factor in improving agriculture, particularly since the human element has been much improved.

Technical Progress and Mechanization

In spite of the worsened man-land ratio, postwar agriculture has made remarkale progress both in biological technology and in mechanization. One type of technical progress concerns the greater use of fertilizers, chemicals for insecticides and disease control, associated with the introduction of improved seeds, and with increased possibilities of moving planting seasons. This type of progress was pushed mainly in conventional cereal cultivation, especially in the case of rice. Another type of technical progress concerns diversification. The best example is a surprisingly rapid progress in dairy farming. The population of milk cows jumped to 750,000 in 1960 from the prewar level of less than 100,000. Farmers became much more aware of livestock farming and introduction of fodder cultivation into their traditional simple systems of crop rotation.

Mechanization of the Japanese type started before World War II, when fewer than 100,000 electric motors were used on farms and combustion engines numbered only 200,000. Now the former have increased to more than a million and the latter to 1.5 million. The agricultural censuses reveal that farm households which used electric motors or combustion engines increased from 57.7 percent in 1950 to 88.4 percent in 1960, that the tractors numbered 517,000 in 1960, an increase of eight times from 1950, and that motor sprayers numbered 400,000 in 1960, an increase of six times from 1950. These increases may be enough to show the extremely rapid tempo of mechanization of agriculture in the postwar period. Of course the smallness of farm-size is a great limitation to mechanization both technically and economically. Even machines of small size are too costly for most Japanese farms. Farms that used a motor cultivator or a tractor constituted 35 percent of the total in 1960, but only 30 percent used their own machines, most of the remaining hiring machines from other persons.

Rapid Increases in Output and Productivity

The agricultural production index showed an increase of output from 45.4 in 1945 to an average of 79.1 in 1951–53, taking 1955 as a base. This implies an abnormal tempo, caused by postwar rehabilitation, but even after normalization the average annual rate of increase in agricultural production was 3.9 percent for the years 1951–60. The real national income produced in agriculture also increased rapidly, though at a slower rate than that of the production index, as meanwhile the ratio of cost (expenditures for intermediate goods and services and depreciation) to gross output increased. The cost ratio rose from 26.2 percent in 1951 to 35.7 percent in 1958. For 1946–52 the annual average rate of increase in agricultural income was 4.2 percent and for 1952–59, 2.7 percent. The rate of increase in income per head in agriculture was 5.3 percent for the former period, 3.2 percent for the latter. The comparison of these figures after normalization with those of prewar periods suggests that postwar agriculture made a second spurt in accelerating its rate of growth. During the first period, before World War I, Japanese agriculture made its first spurt, with a growth rate of net income producing around 2–3 percent. During the second period, however, it decelerated to an average of 1–2 percent. The postwar spurt therefore deserves particular attention from the long-term perspective. What factors or what combination of factors were responsible

203

for the second spurt? It is difficult to answer this question quantitatively. It can be said with confidence, however, that land reform and the renewed human factor did contribute to it basically. More directly, the technical progress backed up by the increase in both working capital and equipment investment was certainly responsible for increases in ouput and productivity in agriculture. Several analysis revealed that the technical progress of biological nature directly effected output increases, but that the mechanization had rather indirect effects, in saving the labor input which in turn was transferred to intensifying the cultivation of other crops.

The Government played a great role in implementing big scale projects of reclamation, irrigation, drainage, etc., either directly or through public cooperations. Conventional measures of supporting prices, giving various subsidies, enlarging extension services, and the like also must be counted among the factors accelerating output increases.

Lastly, the favorable terms of trade to agriculture, which were basically caused by the postwar over-demand situation in the food economy, was a good incentive for farmers. After normalization, rapid progress in diversifying food demand, mainly due to the rapid increase in real income per head, was an additional incentive. In this respect, the rapid rate of growth of the nonagricultural sector contributed much in making better conditions for improving agriculture.

Unbalanced Place of Agriculture

With these improvements, farmers enjoyed a better income position than they had in prewar days, and this favored their increasing both consumption and investment. As the process of normalization was completed, however, problems of unbalanced income of farmers again gradually came into issue, because the rate of increase in income per head in the nonagricultural sector continued to be larger than that of agriculture. The income per head of farm-households (non-farm income included) in 1951 was 94 percent of that of the urban worker's household; it decreased to 70 percent in 1958.

The relative position of agriculture in the national economy changed greatly in the postwar period. Immediately after the war, the agricultural income in the domestic net national product at factor cost rose to 31 percent, which was as high as that of the 1920's. Since then it has decreased sharply year by year to the present level of 13 percent. On the other hand, the working population in agriculture decreased from 49.9 percent in 1947 to 37.7 percent in 1955, though it was still very large. Hence relative income per capita of working population in agriculture decreased rapidly to the recent level of 34 percent from 58 percent in 1947, taking the nationwide averages as base. During the same period farmhouseholds which have off-farm jobs increased also rapidly. It rose from 44.6 percent in 1947 to 65.8 percent in 1960. The proportion of nonfarm income to the total of farm-household income increased from 28.9 percent in 1950 to 44.5 percent in 1959. This shows a significant increase in the relative position of nonagricultural income in the farm economy, though some allowance should be made for an upward bias due to the revision of survey methods. Thus problems of the "unbalanced growth" of agriculture, which existed in the second period, again became an issue in the process of rapid growth of the Japanese economy. This is the core of the agricultural problem in the *third* period.

Outlook for the Coming Decade

Two factors are prominently influential in forecasting the future trend of Japanese agriculture: (1) A change in the composition of demand for food, and (2) a decrease in the working population in agriculture. Both factors have recently shown noticeable effects on the economy and are expected to continue to do so for the decade to come, as the growth rate of the Japanese economy can be expected to continue to be rapid. The former relates to balanced growth in the supply of and demand for agricultural output, the latter concerns the balanced growth of farmers' income.

The Government has inaugurated a "Doubling Income Plan" (1961–1960) and the maintenance of balanced growth of agriculture is one of its major targets. The annual growth rate of agricultural output is projected to be 2.9 percent, implying changes in output composition as follows—the output proportion of livestock farming will rise from the present 14 percent to 30 percent, while that of the conventional farming will decrease from the present 86 percent to 70 percent in the target year. The working population in agriculture is expected to diminish by an annual rate of 2.9 percent, so that the rate of increase in income per head produced in agriculture is projected to be about 5.8 percent, a rate almost equal to that of the nonagricultural sector.

Whether these targets can be fulfilled will depend basically upon the capability of overcoming the "diseconomy of small scale" which has widely prevailed in the Japanese farming up to the present time. Cereal production now tends to be in over supply, but the desirable diversification needs both investments and cost-reducing innovations. A rapid income rise also requires productivity increases dependent upon enlarging farm size. Analytical reasoning which follows is based on the retabulated data of the Farm Economy Survey. A basic relationship that labor productivity (net output per unit of labor input) tends to increase as the land intensity (land area per unit of labor input) and the capital intensity increases is discernible in Japanese farming, but it is particularly to be noted that there is a *turning point* in this relationship. From the middle income class, whose size of land holding is 1.2 to 1.5 hectares, to the upper income classes, the above relationship is strongly positive and the elasticity seems to be greater than unity, but towards the lower income classes there is no positive (in the case of land) and even a negative (in the case of capital) relationship.   As will be expected, the capital-output-ratio tends to decrease sharply from the small size to the middle size, and still decreases moderately towards larger sized farm. This suggests a basic fact that diseconomies of small scale definitely exist and that in particular a diseconomy in the employment of capital is significant.

If the excess-employment of labor is lessened by the expected decrease of the labor force in agriculture, and if the program of consolidation toward a larger size farm than the size of the middle class farm mentioned above is effectively encouraged by various measures on the part of the government, then we would possibly expect a balanced growth in the coming decade.

FOOD CONSUMPTION

PATTERN

Study of food consumption requires two kinds of approach: one from the aspect of nourishment intake and the other from the aspect of economic behavior. Food policy aims at improvement of both the level and composition of nourishment intake but it can be implemented only through the economic behavior of the individuals. For analysis of food consumption, therefore, data are required for both kinds of approach.

Nourishment Intake

An overall statistical tabulation of changes in Japanese nourishment intake is presented as Table 1.[1]

[1]   Cited from Saburo Yamada, *Long-term Changes in the Level and Structure of Food Consumption* (mimeographed in Japanese), *Nogyo Sogo Kenkyusho* (Institute of Agricultural Research, Ministry of Agriculture and Forestry), Tokyo, 1969. I would like to express my deep gratitude to Mr. Saburo Yamada who has generously allowed me the use of his materials. In our knowledge, this is the most reliable data for a long-term analysis, though some under-estimation may remain un-adjusted for the very early years. The food consumption is estimated at the level of primary production, mostly depending upon Mataji Umemura *et al*. *Agriculture and Forestry*, Vol. 9 of *The Estimates of Long-term Economic Statistics of Japan Since* 1868, edited by K. Ohkawa, M. Shinohara and M. Umemura, Toyo Keizai Shimposha, Tokyo, 1966 for prewar years and Ministry of Agriculture and Forestry, *Tables of Food Balances* (in Japanese) for the postwar years. The calorie content is from the standard table, the third revision, compiled by the Agency of Science and Technology, 1963.

Reprinted by permission of the Asian Productivity Organization and thanks to the generosity of Mr. Nobukiyo Takamatsu, my collaborator, from a part of the Report of the Survey on Japanese Experiences of Changes in Food Habits in Relation to Production Pattern,

Table 1.   Per Capita Calorie Intake Per Day by Major Food Groups, 1878–1965

| | Plant source | | | | Animal source | | | |
	Starchy staples*	Veget-ables, Fruits	Sugar	Sum	Live-stock products	Marine pro-ducts**	Sum	Total
1878–82	1669	59	19	1747	3	45	48	1795
83–87	1732	69	26	1827	5	48	53	1880
88–92	1861	76	38	1975	7	51	58	2033
93–97	1873	79	48	2000	9	51	60	2060
98–1902	1907	78	69	2054	11	49	60	2104
1903–07	1975	90	59	2124	12	36	48	2172
08–12	2021	95	58	2174	14	37	51	2225
13–17	2031	95	63	2189	16	58	74	2263
18–22	2087	96	98	2281	20	74	94	2375
23–27	1987	92	125	2204	25	91	116	2320
28–32	1822	93	138	2053	29	94	123	2176
33–37	1821	94	135	2050	34	108	142	2192
38–42	1854	90	141	2085	29	116	145	2230
1951–53	1715	67	110	1892	33	64	97	1989
54–56	1791	73	136	2000	53	73	126	2126
57–59	1865	89	150	2103	76	96	172	2276
60–62	1824	120	171	2115	118	95	213	2328
63–65	1815	148	187	2150	164	97	261	2411

APO Project *No. SUV-III-70, March*, 1971.   *Slight revisions are made regarding some of the statistical data.*

The level of calorie intake during the early years of modern economic growth in Japan has been a controversial issue in relation to the estimates of agricultural production.   On this issue, see Yujiro Hayami and Saburo Yamada, "Agricultural Productivity at the Beginning of Industrialization" in *Agriculture and Economic Growth: Japan's Experience* edited by K. Ohkawa, B.F. Johnston and H. Kaneda, University of Tokyo Press and Princeton University Press, 1969.   In this paper, the authors give evidence for the validity of agricultural products estimates contained in the above-cited volume in terms of international comparisons of calorie intake.   Yamada's data cited here are endorsed by this work.

The calorie intake data contained in Seiki Nakayama, "Long-term Trend of Food Consumption in Japan, 1878–1955" (in Japanese) in *Nogyo Sogo Kenkyu*, October, 1958, had often been used before the Yamada data became available.   Since the basic estimates of agricultural products, on which Nakayama depended, have since been revised, we cannot rely upon his data.

Percentage distribution

	Plants source				Animal source			
	Starchy staples*	Veget- ables, Fruits	Sugar	Sum	Live- stock products	Marine pro- ducts**	Sum	Total
								(%)
1878–82	93.0	3.2	1.0	97.3	0.2	2.5	2.7	100.0
83–87	92.1	3.6	1.4	97.2	0.3	2.5	2.8	100.0
88–92	91.5	3.8	1.9	97.2	0.3	2.5	2.8	100.0
93–97	90.9	3.9	2.4	97.1	0.4	2.5	2.9	100.0
98–1902	90.6	3.7	3.3	97.6	0.5	1.9	2.4	100.0
1903–07	90.9	4.1	2.7	97.8	0.6	1.7	2.2	100.0
08–12	90.8	4.3	2.6	97.7	0.7	1.7	2.3	100.0
13–17	89.8	4.2	2.8	96.8	0.8	2.5	3.2	100.0
18–22	87.9	4.1	4.1	96.1	1.1	3.1	3.9	100.0
23–27	85.7	3.9	5.4	95.0	1.3	3.9	5.0	100.0
28–32	83.8	4.2	6.3	94.4	1.5	4.3	5.6	100.0
33–37	83.1	4.3	6.2	93.5	1.3	4.9	6.5	100.0
38–42	83.1	4.0	6.4	93.5	1.3	5.2	6.5	100.0
1951–53	86.2	3.4	5.5	95.1	1.7	3.2	4.9	100.0
54–56	84.2	3.4	6.4	94.1	2.5	3.4	5.9	100.0
57–69	82.0	3.9	6.6	92.5	3.3	4.2	7.5	100.0
60–62	78.4	5.2	7.3	90.9	5.1	4.1	9.1	100.0
63–65	75.3	6.1	7.8	89.2	6.8	4.0	10.8	100.0

Remarks: * Plant oils such as sesame, rapeseed and the like are included because of their small amount.

** Fish oils are included in the livestock products for the postwar data because of the lack of breakdown data.

From the table we note the following:

1) Daily per-capita calorie intake was around 1,800 for the earliest years of the period under review. After that time, a trend of sustained increase is evident and an early peak of 2,375 is reached in 1918–22, a period immediately after World War I. This is followed by a slight decrease mostly occurring during the 1930s. For the years during and immediately after World War II reliable data are lacking. However, even in 1951–53, the level was lower

than that of 1883–87. In 1963–65 for the first time calorie intake became higher than the peak.

2) The interruption of a trend of increase in the calorie intake corresponds to the factors related to the main food. The calorie intake by this item, starchy staples from plant sources, decreased during the 1920s while all other items continued to increase (except for a slight decrease in calorie intake in vegetables and fruits).

3) Chronological change in the percentage distribution, shown in the table, is a crude indicator of improvement of the quality of foods. The share of livestock and marine products was extremely small during the early period of modern economic growth. Its rate of increase is modest throughout the prewar period, but its postwar performance is impressive.

Quality improvement of nourishment intake over the years is further indicated by changes in protein intake. In Table 2[2] the basic data are given in a form comparable to Table 1. We note the following:

1) Daily per capita protein intake was around 54 grams for the earliest years of Japan's modern economic growth. It shows a tendency to increase which was interrupted during the 1930s. During the years immediately after World War II it must have dropped sharply although reliable data are not available. Even at the beginning of the 1950s, the level of protein intake is recorded as low as 58 grams. In keeping with Japan's rapid economic growth since then, it has increased at a very rapid pace, recovering wartime and postwar losses.

2) A small share of animal proteins (or a large share of plant proteins) characterizes the composition of protein intake. Until the time of World War I the ratio of animal proteins to the total protein intake shows a tendency to decrease. Even allowing

[2] Table 2 is based on the same data as Table 1 so that footnotes to the latter also apply to the former.

FOOD CONSUMPTION PATTERN

Table 2.   Per Capita Proteins Intake Per Day by Major Food Groups, 1878–1965   (Unit: Grams)

	Plant source			Animal source			
	Starchy staples	Others	Sum	Livestock products	Marine prodoucts	Sum	Total
1878–82	43.2	2.9	46.1	0.4	7.4	7.8	53.9
83–87	44.7	3.3	48.0	0.7	7.9	8.6	56.6
88–92	48.9	3.5	52.4	0.9	8.4	9.3	61.7
93–97	49.0	3.8	52.8	1.1	8.4	9.5	62.3
98–1902	50.5	3.7	54.2	1.4	8.1	9.5	63.7
1903–07	51.8	4.2	56.0	1.5	5.9	7.4	63.4
08–12	52.8	4.4,	57.2	1.7	6.1	7.8	65.0
13–17	50.3	4.4	54.7	1.8	9.6	11.4	66.1
18–22	51.7	4.6	56.3	2.3	12.2	14.5	70.8
23–27	51.1	4.3	55.4	2.8	15.0	17.8	73.2
28–32	46.4	4.3	50.7	3.1	15.5	18.6	69.3
33–37	44.4	4.3	48.7	3.6	17.8	21.4	70.1
38–42	45.9	4.1	50.0	3.1	19.1	22.2	72.2
1951–53	4.17	3.2	44.9	2.5	10.5	13.0	57.9
54–56	45.2	3.1	48.3	3.5	11.5	15.0	63.3
57–59	46.0	3.6	49.6	4.6	13.9	18.5	68.1
60–62	47.2	6.5	53.7	6.3	15.1	21.4	75.1
63–65	47.3	7.6	54.9	9.4	14.4	23.8	78.7
Percentage distribution (%)							
1878–82	80.1	5.4	85.5	0.7	13.7	14.5	100.0
83–87	79.0	5.8	84.8	1.2	14.0	15.2	100.0
88–92	79.3	5.7	84.9	1.5	13.6	15.1	100.0
93–97	78.7	6.1	84.8	1.8	13.5	1.52	100.0
98–1902	79.3	5.8	85.1	2.2	12.7	14.9	100.0
1903–07	81.7	6.6	88.3	2.4	9.3	11.7	100.0
08–12	81.2	6.8	88.0	2.6	9.4	12.0	100.0
13–17	76.1	6.7	82.8	2.7	14.5	17.2	100.0
18–22	73.0	6.5	79.5	3.2	17.2	20.5	100.0
23–27	69.8	5.9	75.7	3.8	20.5	24.3	100.0
28–32	67.0	6.2	73.2	4.5	22.4	26.8	100.0
33–37	63.3	6.1	69.5	5.1	25.4	30.5	100.0
38–42	63.6	5.7	69.3	4.3	26.4	30.7	100.0
1951–43	72.0	5.5	77.5	4.3	18.1	22.5	100.0
54–56	71.4	4.9	76.3	5.5	18.2	23.7	100.0
57–59	67.5	5.3	72.8	6.8	20.4	27.2	100.0
60–62	62.8	8.7	71.5	8.4	20.1	28.5	100.0
63–65	60.1	9.7	69.8	11.9	18.3	30.2	100.0

Remarks: the same as for Table 1.

for the crudeness of statistical estimates, it would be safe to say that the percentage did not increase. Since then, the prevalent trend changed to an increasing one but it is to be noted that the highest recorded value is only 30 per cent. This corresponds to the percentage distribution of the major food groups shown in Table 1. As is widely known, marine products play a major role in supplying protein sources in Japan and the statistics in the table reflect this fact. Also the extremely minor role in Japanese agriculture played by livestock products is reflected in Japan's poor performance with regard to animal protein intake. An appreciable increase in the animal protein intake from non-marine sources is only a recent phenomenon.

3) In this regard, the importance of plant proteins in particular attracts attention. The amount of plant protein intake shows neither a tendency to increase nor a tendency to decrease in the table. The major source is of course rice—the most important product of Japanese agriculture. But it is to be noted that pulses, particularly soy-bean, also play a considerable role in this respect. For example, according to the estimation carried out for 1934–38, the percentage distribution of the major items in the plant protein intake is as follows (on the average): rice 54.4, pluses 23.5, barley and wheat 14.3 and others 7.8.[3]

Japan's long-term conditions described above are summarized in Chart 1. The relationship between calorie intake, which is an indicator of quantitative progress, and protein intake, which is a qualitative indicator, is shown. The break caused by World War II was enormous so that a prewar curve and a postwar curve are drawn separately. Prewar performance is not so uniform, but postwar curve appears to pass through more or less the midpoints of the prewar curve, showing the process of recovering to the prewar levels.

[3] Kazushi Ohkawa, *Theory and Measurement of Food Economy* (in Japanese), Hyoron-sha, Tokyo, 1945, p. 345.

Chart 1.   Historical Relations Between Calorie and Protein Intake
(Per capita, per day)

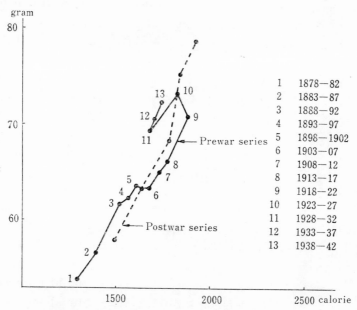

1	1878—82
2	1883—87
3	1888—92
4	1893—97
5	1898—1902
6	1903—07
7	1908—12
8	1913—17
9	1918—22
10	1923—27
11	1928—32
12	1933—37
13	1938—42

The two, taken together, represent a broad schema of Japan's
historical experience.   There was quantitative progress accompanied by qualitative improvement, the relationship between the
two being represented by a slight curvature favorable to the latter.
For simplicity, if we take as the initial year 1880, the mid-year
of the first period, and as the final year 1964, the mid-year of the
last period covered by the tables, and compute the compound
annual rates of increase between the two, we find the rates to be
0.45 per cent for protein intake and 0.35 per cent for calorie intake.

Food Consumption Expenditure

Let us turn to the second approach to the study of food consumption, as an economic behavior.   In order to give a broad

Table 3. Food Expenditures in Relation to Total Consumption Expenditures, 1878–1968 (Per capita, per year)

unit: prewar yen, postwar 1,000 yen

	In current prices			In constant prices			Other ratios	
	Food (1)	Total consump. (2)	Ratio (1)÷(2)	Food (3)	Total consump. (4)	Ratio (3)÷(4)	(1)÷(3)	(2)÷(4)
1878–82	13.8 yen	20.8 yen	66.4%	59.0 yen	91.0	64.8%	22.9%	23.4%
83–87	12.2	19.0	64.2	61.6	93.6	65.8	20.3	19.8
88–92	15.2	32.6	64.4	67.2	106.4	63.2	22.2	22.6
93–97	21.0	33.0	63.6	71.6	116.4	61.5	28.4	29.3
98–1902	30.8	48.8	63.1	75.4	125.0	60.3	39.0	40.9
1903–07	35.2	55.2	63.8	69.2	117.4	58.9	47.0	50.9
08–12	45.4	71.6	63.4	77.8	129.0	60.3	55.5	58.4
13–17	50.0	82.6	60.5	82.4	134.4	61.3	61.5	60.7
18–22	118.8	198.7	59.8	90.6	163.0	55.6	122.0	131.1
23–27	124.4	215.2	57.8	101.6	178.8	56.8	120.4	122.4
1928–32	94.2	177.6	53.0	97.2	179.2	54.2	96.9	96.9
33–37	96.0	192.6	49.8	96.0	191.2	50.2	100.0	100.0
38–40	127.7	261.0	48.8	94.0	194.3	48.4	135.9	135.9
1954–56	32.0	58.7	54.5	44.7	89.3	50.1	71.6	65.7
57–59	37.0	76.7	48.2	51.4	106.8	48.1	72.0	71.8
60–62	45.2	106.8	42.3	57.6	134.0	43.0	78.5	79.7
63–65	62.9	160.7	39.1	66.7	169.8	39.3	94.3	89.6
66–68	85.0	228.7	37.2	77.8	208.3	37.4	109.3	109.8

Source: Miyohei Shinohara, *Personal Consumption Expenditures*, Vol. 6 of *The Estimates of Long-term Economic Statistics of Japan Since 1868*, edited by K. Ohkawa, M. Shinohara and M. Umemura, Toyo Keizai Shimposha, Tokyo, 1967, is the most comprehensive, reliable data of personal expenditures for the prewar years. We depend upon solely on his data. Yamada's data previously cited are consistent with Shinohara's data. For the postwar years, the source is *Annual Report on National Income Statistics*, Economic Planning Agency, Government of Japan, 1970. Prewar and postwar series are comparable except that the prewar year value includes a small amount of non-household expenditures.

As for the total population, for the prewar period the series of per capita consumption Shinohara's estimation is used as such, and for the postwar period, the data estimated at October 1, are used. Bureau of Statistics, Prime Minister's Office, *The Monthly Statistics of Japan*, No. 27–No. 95.

216

historical picture of Japan's experience, data at the level of personal expenditures will be used.

First, reference should be made to Table 3, where it may be seen the relation between the food expenditures and the total personal consumption expenditures on both per capita, per year bases, valued at both current prices and constant prices (1934–36 for prewar and 1965 for postwar years). As will naturally be expected from the previous discussion, the real expenditure for food show a long-term trend of increase, interrupted during the 1930s and with the abnormal conditions caused by World War II. This is a historical performance of the real cost, personally paid, for improving food consumption, as mentioned previously. The ability to achieve improvement was given by the trend of sustained increase in the total personal consumption expenditure, which in turn was made possible by a sustained growth of real national income. What is shown in Table 3 is a general phenomenon to be seen in all cases of modern economic growth. As a general trend the percentage of food expenditures to the total personal consumption expenditures tends to decline rather slowly from 65–66 per cent in the earliest years to 48–49 per cent in the last prewar years. Its tempo of decrease has been accelerated during the postwar years due to the processes of economic recovery and accelerated economic growth. It is to be noted that the changes in food prices relative to the consumers' prices in general had been minor in the prewar long-term trend, although we see some deviation for the postwar years.

Changes in the composition of food consumption in terms of expenditures are shown inTable 4 by major food groups valued at 1934–36 constant prices. The table is self-explanatory.

As for the postwar years, no comparable data are available in aggregate terms, so that data of family budget surveys are arranged so as to be approximately comparable to the prewar series.

Tables 4 and 5 follow the conventional way of classifying the

217

Table 4. Composition Change in Food Expenditures by Major Groups, 1882–1940 (%)

	A	B	C	D	D	F	Total
1882–91	41.8	8.1	12.1	7.6	28.3	2.2	100.0
92–1091	40.1	8.2	10.9	7.8	30.3	2.7	100.0
1902–11	43.8	9.6	9.7	7.8	26.2	2.9	100.0
12–21	42.1	9.6	11.6	7.6	25.1	4.0	100.0
22–31	41.0	7.7	14.4	7.6	24.2	5.1	100.0
31–40	42.6	7.6	17.5	8.0	19.3	5.0	100.0

Remarks: A-Rice, barley, wheat flour and other cereals, and products processed from them are included.
B-Vegetables and fruits.
C-Livestock products, marine products, and products processed from them are included.
D-Seasonings.
E-Tea, beverages and other miscellaneous food included.
F-Tobacco, cigarattes.
This is a simplified presentation of the table given in p. 17 in M. Shinohara's work cited above in footnote to Table 3.

Table 5. Composition Changes in Food Expenditures by Major Groups, 1954–1968 (%)

A: Urban households

	A	B	C	D	E	F	Total
1954–56	41.1	10.7	27.3	7.2	10.5	3.2	100.0
1957–59	37.2	11.0	29.3	6.4	13.1	3.0	100.0
1960–62	31.3	12.2	32.4	6.1	15.4	2.6	100.0
1963–65	29.0	12.5	33.8	6.1	16.0	2.7	100.0
1966–68	25.0	13.1	35.6	5.2	17.6	2.5	100.0

B: Farm households

	A	B	C	D	E	F	Total
1954–56	54.6	7.4	10.8	9.5	13.7	4.1	100.0
1957–59	51.3	6.8	13.1	8.2	16.3	4.3	100.0
1960–62	45.2	7.7	15.8	7.9	19.3	4.1	100.0
1963–65	40.5	.73	18.1	7.3	22.7	4.0	100.0
1966–67	37.5	7.4	19.5	6.4	25.1	4.1	100.0

Source: For urban households, 1953–62: Bureau of Statistics, Prime Minister's Office, *General Report on the Family Income and Expenditure Survey*, 1946–62, 1964, Table 1–1, pp. 2–5, and 1963–68: the same series cited from the *Annual Report*, 1968. Table 11, pp. 170–3. For farm households, *The Economic Survey of Farm Households*, Ministry of Agriculture and Forestry.
Remarks: Classification is the same as in Table 4, but in B it is slightly different.

major groups. However, there is some inconvenience in that they are not directly comparable to Tables 1 and 2. A computation of the unit price of calorie intake is a means to effect a direct link between the nourishment approach and the expenditure approach. To do so, it is desirable to distinguish between the primary production (or input) level and the final expenditure (or demand) level. Between the two levels are various activities such as processing, transportation and distribution. Viewed from this standpoint, two kinds of unit price of calorie intake are needed: one at the primary production level and the other at the final expenditure level.

The data given in Table 6 are estimated for this specific purpose. Regarding the details of procedures see footnote[4]. We note the following:

1) The unit price of calorie intake valued at the final expenditure level shows a distinct tendency to increase and this can be a rough indicator of quality improvement of food consumption valued at the price system of the base year. However, strictly speaking, the indicator must be the unit price of calorie intake valued at constant farm prices at the level of primary production. This shows no tendency to increase until the years before World War I and only since then has shown a moderate increase, corresponding to the performance of animal protein intake previously observed.

[4] The estimates of food expenditures at the primary production level have been made by ourselves. The principle is to evaluate food and food materials at the farm price or their approximates. Imported foodstuffs are also valued at domestic farm prices of corresponding products. An alternative is to use the imports prices as such and in this case the total food expenditures thus estimated should be said to be at the "primary input level" rather than primary production level. The actual difference between the two may be small in Japan's case.

Incidentally, with respect to this kind of approach, see Simon Kuznets, "The Share and Structure of Consumption," VII, Quantitative Aspects of the Economic Growth of Nations, *Economic Development and Cultural Change*, Vol. X, No. 2., Part II, January 1962.

Table 6. Unit Prices of Calorie Intake and the Two Components of Food Expenditures: Primary and Intermediate, 1878–1968

	Unit price of calorie			Food expense ratios to total personal expense		
	Final exp. level (A)	Prmiary prod. level	Difference (C=A−B)	Ratio C×A	Primary (B′)	Interme-diate (C′)
1878–82	9.00 sen	5.41 sen	3.59 sen	39.9%	38.9%	25.9%
83–87	8.98	5.38	3.60	40.1	39.5	26.3
88–92	9.06	5.36	3.70	40.8	37.3	25.9
93–97	9.52	5.35	4.17	43.8	34.6	26.9
98–1902	9.81	5.40	4.41	44.9	33.2	27.1
1903–07	8.73	5.04	3.69	42.3	33.9	25.0
08–12	9.58	5.44	4.14	43.2	34.4	25.0
13–17	9.98	5.63	4.35	4.36	34.6	26.7
18–22	11.10	57.8	5.32	47.9	28.7	26.9
23–27	12.00	6.09	5.91	49.2	28.9	27.9
28–32	12.24	6.40	5.84	47.7	28.3	25.9
33–38	12.00	6.37	5.63	47.0	27.2	23.0
1954–56	58.3 yen	27.7 yen	30.6 yen	52.5%	23.8%	26.3%
57–59	62.3	27.3	35.0	56.1	21.2	26.9
60–62	67.3	29.7	37.6	55.9	18.9	24.1
63–65	76.3	31.0	45.3	59.3	17.0	22.3
66–68	85.6	31.5	54.0	63.1	13.9	23.6

Remarks: Sen is 1/100 yen. Prewar years are at 1934–36 prices and postwar years are at 1965 prices.

B′ stands for the ratio of food expenditures at the primary production level to the total personal expenditure and C′ the ratio of intermediate expenditure of food.

2) The difference between the two, C in the table, is of special significance. It is the price paid by the consumers for the inter-mediate activity related to food and occurring between the pri-mary production and the final demand level. It is generally expected that this "intermediate part" tends to increase over time as modern economic growth proceeds, primarily because of the urbanization process. In fact, its ratio to the final expendi-ture prices, shown by C/A in the table, shows a long-term tendency

to increase: from a ratio of 40 per cent in the early period to 60 per cent in the recent period.

3) The two components of food expenditures, one for primary and the other for intermediate activities, can easily be determined by use of the prices ratio (C/A in the table) and the total food expenditures given in Table 3. In this table they are given in terms of their ratios to the total consumption expenditures (B' for the primary and C' for the intermediate). As a long-term historical trend B' tends to decrease faster than C' and this resulted in a conspicuous contrast in recent years: the former becomes as low as 14 per cent while the latter still stays at 23–24 per cent, a ratio not much different from the early years.

Measurement of Income Elasticities

The historical performance of food consumption as described in the preceding section can be analyzed by use of the conventional concept of income elasticity (η), if regularities are more or less found between the food consumption and income changes. We will use this concept in a crude way in the following analysis. It is crude because we will not treat factors other than income, which must affect food consumption changes over time. To mention a few, they are relative prices of food, taste or wants, composition of population, working conditions, industrial structure and income distribution—historical changes in all these factors should not be ignored. Mostly because of technical limitations in their statistical treatment, they cannot be adequately treated here.

The "income" in such an approach is not necessarily clear. Viewed from the order of indirect relation with food consumption, we have to distinguish at least four: national income, personal income distributed, personal disposable income and personal expenditure. The income (or expenditure) elasticity will be different

221

according to the selection one may make out of these terms. As will be explained in later pages, there have been some confusion in this respect with regard to interpreting the measured income elasticities of food demand in Japan. In principle, personal expenditure or preferably personal disposable income is adequate because of its direct relationship with food consumption behavior. However, national income per capita has often been used. This is partly because of the limitation of available data and partly because of its practical convenience.

Let us begin with the nourishment approach. S. Yamada made a comprehensive measurement of η with respect ot the calorie intake and proteins intake respectively in terms of national income per capita, using the basic series of his data, on which Tables 1 and 2 are based. He divided the entire period into three: from 1878–82 to 1918–22 (Period I), from 1918–22 to 1938–42 (Period II) and from 1951–53 to 1963–65 (Period III) and furthermore the last period was divided into two sub-periods, taking 1957–59 as the dividing point. The figures given in Table 7 are cited from his work for the major food groups.[5]

As a preliminary comment it should be mentioned that knowledge we have gained in the preceding section that the Japan's historical experience seems to have some peculiarity in food consumption performance, first for the 1920s and 1930s and second, for early postwar years. Viewed from this point, Yamada's demarcation of periods seems good, broadly speaking. We note the following:

1) First of all, η of calorie intake from the total food consumption is mostly explained by that of calorie intake from plant sources, the two moving almost in parallel for the entire period.

---

[5] S. Yamada, *Long-term Changes...*, *op. cit.* For all items log $F = a + b$ log Y, where F is food consumption per capita in terms of calorie intake or proteins and Y is national income per capita. Income elasticity η is thus measured by b as constant.

FOOD CONSUMPTION PATTERN

Table 7. Income Elasticities of Food Intake by Major Groups:
S. Yamada's Measurement

		Period I	Period II	Period III	Sub-period 1	Sub-period 2
Calorie intake						
Total food	a	6.843	8.044	6.514	5.648	7.168
	b	0.183	−0.062	2.208	0.353	0.094
	R^2	0.918	0.237	0.888	0.930	0.893
Plant source	a	6.864	8.249	6.777	5.883	6.513
	b	0.171	−0.111	0.143	0.301	0.023
	R^2	0.884	0.453	0.768	0.905	0.398
Animal source	a	1.990	−0.025	−1.239	−2.336	0.224
	b	0.480	0.912	1.061	1.254	0.824
	R^2	0.564	0.851	0.976	0.989	0.920
Protein intake						
Total food	a	3.282	3.830	2.124	1.654	2.512
	b	0.184	0.077	0.352	0.436	0.347
	R^2	0.903	0.334	0.955	0.955	0.857
Plant source	a	3.386	4.936	2.504	2.126	2.255
	b	0.125	−0.179	0.237	0.307	0.276
	R^2	0.690	0.610	0.880	0.891	0.755
Animal source	a	0.233	−1.934	−1.211	−2.140	−0.218
	b	0.439	0.877	0.687	0.852	0.527
	R^2	0.524	0.861	0.974	0.953	0.947

Remarks: For the period demarcation, see the main text, and for the equation used, see footnote 5. (p. 222)

2) The negative figures for plant and animal sources for Period II reflect the decline in the 1930s we already noted in referring to Table 1. A negative value of η for the plant sources is understandable, but it is peculiar to see also a negative value of η for the total food because it is still positive even for the postwar sub-period 2. Considering also the weakness of correlation in these two series, we hesitate to give a substantive interpretation on this point. It is to be explored further whether this is a fact or merely a statistical illusion.

3) For the postwar figures, this interpretation can be reasonable: because of the process of economic recovery, between the two sub-periods changes in η appear great both for total food and plant sources. A greater value of η as computed for the entire postwar period in comparison with that of Period I cannot accordingly represent the long-term normal performance.

4) As for η of protein intake from both total food and plant resources, the peculiarity is similarly noted for Period II as before and the effect of economic recovery is also witnessed.

5) The values of η of animal sources both for calorie and protein intake are far bigger than those for plant sources. They appear to show first a tendency to increase which then reverses, after allowances are made for the effect of economic recovery.

Now, we examine here the relation between calorie intake and personal consumption expenditure. An overall picture is shown as Chart 2. Both the peculiarity during the 1920s and 1930s and the postwar recovery process can be distinctly seen in the chart. For period II demarcated above it is almost impossible to find regularity. For the period similar to Period I above η is 0.437 and for the postwar period, 1953–68, η is 0.181, applying the same equation as before. As a normal long-term performance of income elasticity (strictly speaking, expenditure elasticity) of this kind, it may be safe to say that we can assume a distinct tendency to decline. It is to be noted that the elasticity of this category should in principle exceed the elasticity in terms of national income discussed above, because as a trend, apart from swings and cycles, the rate of growth of national income has been greater than that of personal consumption expenditures in Japan's economic history.

In proceeding to the expenditure approach, let us first review a pertinent controversy. T. Noda did pioneering work in this field and his findings show that income elasticity of agricultural food products was very high for the early years before around World War I but it turned out to decrease drastically to a very low level.

Thus Noda and others believed that a drastic change had taken place in Japan's income elasticity of food demand during the prewar period, although a satisfactory interpretation of the reasons for it remained to be given.[6]   Recently, H. Kaneda has done new research in this field, using new data which had not been previously available.   He concluded that the income elasticity for food is estimated to be 0.3–0.4 for the entire prewar period, and asserted that the drastic change in the food consumption alleged to have occurred around World War I may be an illusion.[7]

According to our view, the controversial issue was partly solved but hence also partly unsolved.   For the early years before World War I, which roughly corresponds to Yamada's Period I, Kaneda estimates η as to be 0.2 to 0.4 for the agricultural food products, basing upon the following estimates: the average annual rate of total population increase 1.0 per cent; that of national income produced, 3.2 to 3.8 per cent and that of agricultural food products available for consumption, 1.4 to 2.1 per cent.   These are the newly revised data which were not available to Noda, so that it is clear that Kaneda's estimate is more reliable and acceptable as far as this procedure is concerned.   We are inclined to adopt a value close to 0.4 rather than to 0.2, which was based on a too-conservative estimate of agricultural production.

---

[6]   Noda's first estimation was 0.63 for 1878–1921 and 0.23 for 1922–1937. See Tsutomu Noda, "Long-term Changes in Demand for Agricultural Products and Income Elasticities" (in Japanese), *Nogyo Sogo Kenkyu*, October 1956.   His second revised estimation was 0.59 for 1878–1917 and 0.18 for 1915–1937. See Tsutomu Noda, "Long-term Changes in Demand and International Trade" (in Japanese), in *A Growth Analysis of Japanese Agriculture*, edited by K. Ohkawa, Taimeido, Tokyo, 1963.

[7]   Hiromitsu Kaneda, "Long-term Changes in Food Consumption Patterns in Japan" in *Agriculture and Economic Growth: Japan's Experience*, edited by K. Ohkawa, B.F. Johnston and H. Kaneda, University of Tokyo Press and Princeton University Press, 1969.   Kaneda uses a familiar relationship expressed as follows:

$$\dot{F} = \dot{N} + \eta \ (\dot{Y} - \dot{N}),$$

where N denotes population, the others being the same as before.   The dot stands for a rate of change.   This is essentially the same as Noda's case and ours stated above.

Chart 2. Relation of Calorie Intake and Consumption Expenditure
(Both, per capita)

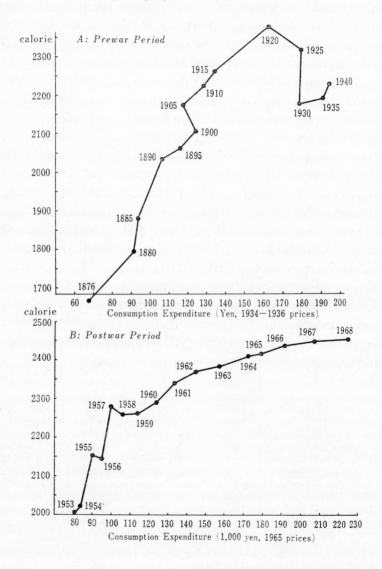

As for the period which roughly corresponds to Yamada's Period II, Kaneda derives 0.3 or 0.4 for income elasticity of food demand, based on Shinohara's data, the nature of which is different from the previous data.   His approximation is as follows. Over the period of 25 years between 1911–15 and 1936–40, total private consumption expenditure (per capita in 1934–36 prices) increased at the annual rate of some 1.6 per cent while per capita food expenditures rose at 0.6 per capita per year.   Moreover, the latter category increased at about 0.4 per cent when measured from 1921–25, whereas per capita real expenditures increased at the rate of approximately 1.0 per cent per year.

The data are the same as for Table 3.   There are two problems: one concerns the questions we raised previously with respect to the peculiar performance for the 1920s and 1930s and the other concerns η measurement of different levels.   In solving the former problem, he roughly measured η with average trends of the relevant terms and this is a matter of one's judgment.   Kaneda was aware of the second problem, but Shinohara's data for Period I was not then available to him.   At any rate, his estimates for the two periods cannot be directly compared.

An attempt has been made by use of Shinohara's data for the entire prewar period, hoping to solve the problem.   A rate of change in both series in 1934–1936 prices (food expenditure and personal consumption expenditure, both per capita) is examined on an annual basis.   (Refer to the scatter diagram shown in Chart 3).   Very broadly speaking, a regular relation is seen between the two.   Dividing the time span into two periods, however, the relationship is closer during the former period whereas it appears less intense during the latter period as will be expected from our previous observation.   As a demarcating year, 1902 is taken, and η is computed as follows: 1.07 for 1875–1902, and 1.06 for 1902–1938.   The formula of deriving η is the same as for the previous cases. With respect to the detail of this computation see footnotes.[8]

We note the following in interpreting the results of computations:

1) η appears to be surprisingly high, being near unity for both periods, and one may doubt its reliability particularly in comparison with the previous estimations mentioned above. We share a view that Shinohara's estimate of food consumption may have some upward bias, particularly for the former periods. Even allowing this possibility, however, we are inclined to say that η may not be much less than unity for the early phase of Japan's modern economic growth. For the later phase, particularly for the 1920s, the regularity is much less and we judge that η tended to decline slightly, being influenced by factors other than income-expenditures.

2) The constant term has a negative value for both periods, the absolute number being bigger for the latter period. Although the statistical significance is not satisfactory enough, this may suggest that other factors' influence tended to reduce the rate of of increase in food exenditures. Among the other factors, the urbanization effect can be mentioned in particular.

3) Between Kaneda's estimates and ours no great inconsistency may exist. Since no reliably revised data on national income are available as yet for the early years, we have no direct means to check the relation between the two. However, if the elasticity of personal consumption expenditure with respect to national income is something like 0.3–0.4, then the two estimates can be consistent and this may not be improbable.

[8]　For 1875—1902　　$\dot{F}=-0.235+1.065\dot{C}$, $R^2=0.879$, $S=1.813$
　　　　　　　　　　　　(0.362) (0.076)

　　　For 1902—1938　　$\dot{F}=-0.788+1.055\dot{C}$, $R^2=;.706$, $S=2.348$,
　　　　　　　　　　　　(0.413) (0.035)

where, $\dot{F}$ and $\dot{C}$ denote annual rate of changes in food expenditure and personal consumption expenditure per capita respectively.

228

Chart 3.   Relation between Food Expenditure and Total Consumption Expenditure

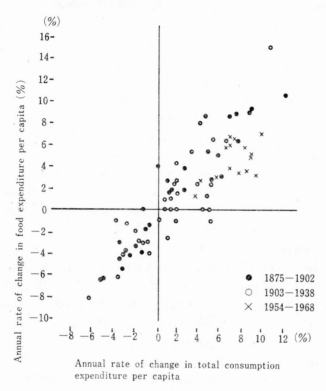

4)   The preceding nourishment approach suggests that some changes took place in the food consumption pattern in the prewar latter phase.   Paying due consideration to this, we share a view that no drastic change took place between the former and the latter phases with respect to Japan's food consumption pattern.

In Chart 3 the postwar data are plotted and this study cannot be completed without discussing the postwar experience.   The regularity appears rather weak against our expectation. η is 0.52–0.75 for the postwar period, when the same formula is applied, as before.[9] It is clear, we believe, that η is definitely smaller as compared with prewar values. We conclude that the income (expenditure) elasticity of food consumption has a long-term tendency to decline throughout the entire period of Japan's modern economic growth and that in this respect Japan's experience presents no peculiarities by international standards. In addition to this broad remark, the following can be said. During the latter phase of prewar period, a strange event took place: the rate of decline of η slowed and the factor other than income-expenditures appeared to be stronger, the interpretation of which remains to be given.

In order to provide some statistical background for what we said above a simple estimate of η by use of quinquennial averages of the original series, which correspond to the periodization of Tables 1 and 2, is presented in Table 8.

The following are to be noted:

1) Elasticities of food consumption expenditures, $(4) \div (1)$, shows a trend of decrease from 0.8 in Period I to 0.6 in Period III. The prewar values are lower than the previous ones calculated by equations. This is understandable as here the negative constant terms are ignored. In particular, an exclusion of most of the irregularity in the 1930s affects the value of Period II.

2) Its breakdown into two parts, (one is an elasticity at the primary production level and the other an elasticity for the intermediate expenditures for food), gives us interesting facts.

---

[9] For 1954−1968 we obtain $\dot{F}=0.968+0.515\dot{C}$, $R^2=0.284$, $S=1.464$.
$$(1.779) \quad (0.244)$$
As this is too weak, the following is obtained tentatively by excluding a few exceptional years.

$$\dot{F}=0.124+0.75\dot{C}, \quad R^2=0.552, \quad S=1.312$$

The data are from Economic Plannig Agency, *Annual Report on National Income . . . op, cit.*, both series being valued at 1965 prices. In principle the postwar data must be more reliable than the prewar data, so that the irregularity observed needs further scrutiny. We believe that the rehabilitation effects described in the preceding discussion may not be its cause.

Table 8. Expenditure Elasticities of Food Demand by Quinquennial Averages, 1878–1968

Average annual rate of growth[b]	1878–82→ 1898–1902 (I)	1898–1902→ 1928–32 (II)	1954–56→ 1966–68[a] (III)
Personal consumption expenditure (1)	1.62	1.21	7.65
Food consumption at primary production level (2)	0.82	0.62	2.45
Intermediate expenditures (3)	1.59	1.25	6.40
Total food expenditures (4)	1.11	0.84	4.69
Crude expenditure elasticities			
(2)÷(1)	0.51	0.50	0.32
(3)÷(1)	0.98	1.02	0.83
(4)÷(1)	0.80	0.71	0.61
(Weighted elasticities)[c]			
(2)÷(1)	0.32	0.26	0.13
(3)÷(1)	0.44	0.45	0.48

Remarks: a) For the postwar years, a three year-average.
b) Average annual rate of growth is calculated by bridging the mid-years of two periods.
c) The average of two periods bridged is taken. The data are from Table 6. The basic data are the same as for Table 6.

The elasticity at the primary production level, $(2) \div (1)$, is small and tended to decrease from 0.5 to 0.3 whereas the elasticity with respect to the intermediate expenditures, $(3) \div (1)$, is great and shows a much less distinct decline. The conventional notion of income (expenditure) elasticity of food demand is composed of these two elasticities.[10] The weighted values of the two, shown in the last lines of the table, deserve particular attention. With respect to the change in income (or consumption expenditures), the rate of response is much less at the primary level of production (or input) than for the intermediate activities.

[10] In the table, the sum of weighted elasticities do not exactly coincide with the values of $(4) \div (1)$. This is because of an approximation.

PART IV

AGRICULTURAL DEVELOPMENT AND TECHNOLOGICAL PROGRESS

BALANCED GROWTH

AND

THE PROBLEM OF AGRICULTURE*

Introduction: The problem

The recent literature of economic growth pays particular attention to the problem of "balanced growth". Two different aspects of the problem are taken up, though they are interrelated with each other. One is a purely theoretical approach and its problem is to examine the existence and stability of balanced growth paths in a general equilibrium system under certain assumptions. The other concerns practical strategy for economic development as its objective, though in most cases it is given some sort of theoretical basis. There are two types among the second group,—"balanced growth doctrine" of the Nurkse-Rodan type[1] and that of the A. Lewis type[2]. The former advocates a plan

* I have benefited from the discussions with my colleagues at Hitotsubashi University and the group of agricultural economists in Tokyo. I would like to thank all of them.

[1] P.N. Rosenstein-Rodan, "Problems of Industrialization of Eastern and South-eastern Europe," *The Economic Journal, June-September*, 1943. Ragnar Nurkse, *Problems of Capital Formation in Underdeveloped Countries* (Oxford, 1953).

[2] Arthur Lewis, *The Theory of Economic Growth* (London, 1955). Albert O. Hirschman criticised this version of the balanced growth concept and said this is "essentially an exercise in retrospective comparative statics" in Chapter 4 of his book "*The Strategy of Economic Development*" (New Haven, 1959). In my impression, he seems to disregard

A revised and condensed version of a paper with the same title in Hitotsubashi Journal of Economics, *Vol. 2 No. 1 September* 1961, *pp.* 13–25.

of simultaneous investment for industrialization and mainly concerns the investment criterion *within* the modern sector, while the latter deals with balanced growth between various sectors of the economy, in particular, between industry and agriculture. I want to deal with the problem of agriculture in a general framework of balanced growth equilibrium, so that this paper concerns both theoretical and empirical aspects of the problem, although the main interest lies in the practical problem of the latter type.

H.T. Oshima recently stressed the strategic importance of agricultural development as against industrialization-minded theories and policies with special reference to Asian economic development problems.[3] Similar assertions can be found in the literature of agricultureal economics,[4] but very few in the circle of general economists. A remarkable exception is Kaldor's paper, as far as I know.[5] I myself share with these opinions. The place and significance of the peasant economy, however, seems to remain not fully clarified in the general framework of economic development possibilities. The purpose of this paper is to give further clarification along this line.

It can best be fulfilled by the common approach of a two-sector model, composed of capitalist sector and self-employed sector, because the process of economic development is that of enlarging the former and contracting the latter. Theoretical strictness will be sacrificed to some extent in order to weigh the practical considerations in meeting the real circumstances. I

entirely the problem of backward sectors, where almost no automatic incentives can be expected in the balancing adaptation process of the economy.

[3] Harry T. Oshima, "*A Strategy for Asian Development*", 1961, an unpublished paper. (Later, published in *Economic Development And Cultural Change*, Vol. X, No. 3, April, 1962).

[4] As a best example, we can quote William H. Nicholls' paper "*The place of Agriculture in Economic Development*", presented to the Gamagori Conference of I.E.A. in 1960. (Later, published in Kenneth Berrill ed., *Economic Development With Special Reference To East Asia*, Macmillan, London, 1964).

[5] Nicholas Kaldor, Characteristics of Economic Development, in "*Essays on Economic Stability and Growth*" (London, 1960).

shall stress the importance of output balance, in particular that of food, the main output of the self-employed sector assuming a closed system. Hence the discussion that follow depend upon the key assumption that food can be supplied only by the self-employed sector to meet the demand from both sectors. In my knowledge, this assumption is appropriate to most countries in Asia, and without placing this fact at the center of theoretical formulation, no attempt can be successful in analyzing the problem of economic development. Thus we arrived at a different conclusion from other authors' approaches. A. Lewis rightly treated this point, but did not elaborate it in connection with his general thesis of "unlimited supply of labor". The concept of unlimited supply of labor would be more useful both in theoretical and practical application to the problem of initial economic growth, if they are backed up with food supply possibilities.

A Static Equilibrium of a Two-Sector Economy

The economy is assumed to be composed of two sectors as mentioned above. Hereafter we call the former "sector I", and the latter "sector II".[6] In the following suffix 1 stands for the capitalist sector, and 2 for the self-employed sector. The basic assumption is that each sector is producing different goods. Sector I produces both capital goods and consumption goods other than food while sector II produces food only. Of course this is a great simplification. In reality the latter sector produces many kinds of consumption goods of the traditional type and

---

[6] I tried a two-sector model of the capitalist sector and the non-capitalist sector in my earlier paper "Fukinto seicho to teii koyo" (Unequal growth and underemployment), in "*Nihonkeizai no bunseki*" (An Analysis of the Japanese Economy) Vol. II Edited by S. Tsuru and K. Ohkawa, Tokyo, 1955. The non-capitalist sector does include landlords as its essential element. Here we prefer the *self-employed* sector, which roughly corresponeds to the "subsistence sector" in Lewis' terminology. But I prefer "self-employed" rather than "subsistence" because this sector is not self-sufficient but has trades with the capitalist sector.

even some capital goods, and some goods are supplied competitively by both sectors. Our assumption of no substitution of supplying food between the two sectors, however, may be a reasonable one in order to analyze the core of the problem. In fact, where the land value is too high because of excessive demand for it by peasants as a means of self-employment, the capitalist does not like to enter the production of basic food. We ignore the landlords and assume all the agricultural land is directly cultivated by self-employed tillers. In reality, the role played by the landlords in economic development deserves particular attention in most Asian countries, but it would be difficult to take this fact into consideration in our model, without altering its basic nature. This would better be discussed in a separate treatment.

We assume that the output of sector I (Y_1) and that of sector II (Y_2) can be measured by a common unit of one sort or another and we will treat them in constant price terms. We assume that the existence of capital stock (K) in sector I, and that of land stock available to food production (L) in sector II, in other words, that there is no land in the former, no capital in the latter. The unit of measuring capital stock is simply assumed to be common to that of output, mentioned above, and no differential quality or location of land is assumed, so that we can avoid the difficulties of measuring capital and land stock. There are a certain number of labor force population in sector I (N_1) and in sector II (N_2) in terms of man-year labor of homogeneous quality and we assume no technical difficulty in transferring labor force between the two sectors. The number of consumption population is assumed to correspond to these numbers N_1 and N_2.

Two production functions are given in a general form as $Y_1 = F_1(K, N_1)$ and $Y_2 = F_2(L, N_2)$, where a decreasing return being assumed for both functions. As for distribution and expenditure of income, the followings are assumed for the sake

238

of simplicity. Y_1 is distributed among capitalists and workers in sector I while in sector II all the income produced is attributed to peasant proprietors. All the personal income distributed to the workers in sector I and to the self-employees in sector II will be consumed with no saving, and the capitalists will save all the profits they gain. Thus we have $Y_1 - S = wN_1$, a definitional equation, where S and w stand for the amount of savings and wage rates, and $wN_1 + Y_2$ is aggregate expenditure for consumption. All these quantities are measured in annual units to be consistent with the definition of labor unit. In these treatments, we have to ignore all the intermediate goods in order to avoid complexity. It may be, therefore, helpful to assume a constant ratio of net product to the gross product at least in the case of treating food production and agricultural income. Particular attention is paid for the ratio of food expenditure to the total consumption expenditure, which is denoted by f. This ratio is assumed constant for a certain range of per head income and is also assumed to have no difference between workers and self-employees. We do not intend to deny the well-known Engel's law, but merely want to represent the elastic demand for food with regards to the change in per head income of low levels (income elasticity $= 1.0$), a fact which was revealed by several surveys about underdeveloped economies in Southeast Asia. We know that there is sometimes a significant difference of this ratio between urban workers and rural self-employees, but disregarding this difference may not be a serious misgiving for the purpose of this article.

Under these assumptions, we consider the conditions of equilibrium or balance as follows. First, in order to maintain a certain amount of capital stock (K), the capitalist is assumed to invest all the savings and the period of replacement (r) is assumed to be given by a relationship $K/r = S$. This is a greatest simplification of both the investment behavior and the saving-

239

investment equilibrium. Second, "total employment" is assumed, so that we have $N_1+N_2=N$, where N is the total number of labor force. We disregard differentials of both the wage rate (w) within sector I and average productivity of labor or per head income in sector II (Y_2/N_2). Therefore, total employment means also no differentials of income in each sector. If there occurs some shortage of employment demand in sector I, the residual labor force is assumed to be able to find jobs in sector II without causing differentials of their income within this sector. Third, in the equilibrium state the wage in sector I is equal to the average productivity in sector II, that is $w=Y_2/Y_2$. This is a condition of fulfiling "income parity" in real terms. It goes without saying that this condition can permit us in giving certain allowances for the "differentials" of equilibrium income due to various other factors, which operate differently between rural and urban lives. Fourth, it is of course necessary to balance demand for and supply of food, which balance is simply expressed as (wN_1+N_2) $f=Y_2$. Lastly, an equation $\partial Y/\partial N=w$ is introduced as the condition of maximizing profit of capitalist in sector I.

We define the economy to be at a static state of balanced equilibrium when all the conditions above mentioned are fufilled and there is no endogenous movement to change this routine path. In order to check the possibility of reaching such a state, we build a simple model as follows:

Model I:

$$1) \quad Y_1=F_1(K,\ N_1)$$
$$2) \quad Y_2=F_2(L,\ N_2)$$
$$3) \quad K/r=S$$
$$4) \quad Y_1-S=wN_1$$
$$5) \quad N_1+N_2=N$$
$$6) \quad w=Y_2/N_2$$
$$7) \quad Y_2=f(wN_1+N_2)$$

$$8) \quad \partial Y_1/\partial N_1 = w$$

The number of variables in this model is eleven (Y_1, Y_2, N_1, N_2, N, K, L, r, S, w, f). If we assume that the stock of land, the number of labor force and the ratio of food expenditure given as constants ($L=\bar{L}$, $N=\bar{N}$, $f=\bar{f}$,) this model will be consistently solved and we will be able to obtain an equilibrium distribution of labor force between the two sectors (N_1, N_2), that of output (Y_1, Y_2), and wage rate (w), savings (S), capital stock (K) and its period of replacement (r) in sector I. As a matter of fact, the assumption of a fixed stock of land available to agriculture is close to reality for most countries with already densely populated areas, and that of fixed ratio of food consumption expenditure may be permitted within a certain range of low income level as already touched upon. These are substantial assumptions, but the constant number of population is nothing but an artificial assumption for the sake of simplicity. The economic meaning of its mechanism can best be explained as follows.

Let us start with a certain amount of capital stock (K^*), an arbitrary choice, under the condition of a prevailing equilibrium wage rate w (hereafter, no star notations will stand for equilibrium values). From production function 1) and the profit maximizing condition 8), the amount of employment (N_1^*) and the output (Y_1^*) of sector I will be determined. The saving amount (S^*) and the replacement period (r^*) are to be fixed respectively from equation 4) and equation 3). On the other hand, the number of self-employees (N_2^*) will be obtained from equation 5), and the amount of food output (Y_2^*) is determined accordingly by production function 2). There remain two equations 6) and 7) still unused. We can obtain the amount of food demand from 7), using N_1^*, Y_2^* and K^* and w which we assumed at the very start. This amount of food demand is denoted by Y_2'. There must be no balance between Y_2' and Y_2^*. Let us assume $Y_2'>Y_2^*$ or a state of excess-demand. It is of course possible and desirable to consider an adjustment process toward an equilibrium by assuming an increase in the relative price of food, but this is not the process we would like to follow. We want to treat the problem in constant price terms, for the sake of simplicity and assume that the state of demand will be adjusted by eliminating the real cause, that is the excess-existence of capital stock and in fact, this is proved as follows.

If K^* were larger than K, it follows $Y_1^* > N_1$. According to the assumed condition of decreasing return, $N_1^* > N_1$ is necessary by a larger degree than the above inequality. As for sector II, $Y_1^* < Y_2$ is derived from $N_2^* < N_2$. Equation 7) thus leads to $Y_2' > Y_2^*$. This may be almost self-evident. We can say that the excess-investment (this is corresponding to the excess-existence of capital stock) will cause an increased demand for food on one hand and lead to a decreased supply of food on the other, thus resulting a disequilibrium of food balance. The reverse assumption will certainly lead us to a state of oversupply of food. Therefore between them there must be a certain amount of capital stock, which can exactly correspond to a state of supply-demand balance of food. In other words, this reveals a mechanism, where the food supply is a limiting factor to capital accumulation.

This is not the end of our story of the stationary state. There remains equation 6), the mechanism of which is to be explained. Contrary to the former case of starting from arbitrary capital stock, let us assume first an arbitrary level of prevailing wage (w^+), under the state of capital stock of an equilibrium value (K). If the chosen wage rate is higher than the equilibrium one, namely $w^+ > w$, the production function tells us that N_1^+ will be smaller than the equilibrium number and this will lead to an inequality $N_2^+ > N_2$ for sector II, according to the assumption of total employment. The overemployment in this sector will cause a lower average productivity, thus making a differential between the wage rate in sector I and the per head income in sector II. The existence of "cheaper" labor in the self-employed sector will give capitalist an incentive to expand his business and there will occur more "job opportunities" in sector I and some of the self-employed will be hired in sector I. This will cause a falling level of wages, which will continue to the point where the income differentials between the two sectors completely disappear, reaching equilibrium wage rates. In the reverse case of $w^+ < w$, there is no difficulty of giving another explanation of a process towards equilibrium.

Thus we can give a fairly general explanation of the mechanism of our model although it describes a very simplified case. Of course, these two mechanisms caused by equations 6) and 7) should be understood simultaneously, affecting each other. The above explanations are obliged to be partial in order to avoid complexity. It is to be noted at least that a simple equation $f = N/\bar{N}$ is derived as a combination of equations 6) and 7) at the factor equilibrium of $w = Y_2/N_2$.

A Path of Balanced Growth

Starting from the static state of Model I, I would like to give a simple growth model. Both technical progress and increase in population are taken into consideration, and the income elasticity of food demand (η) is introduced. All the other variables are given time element (t) and are denoted like $N(t) = N(O)e\lambda$, where λ stands for the rate of increase of labor force population. The production functions F_1 and F_2 are given shift variables of neutral nature α_1 and α_2 respectively. I am aware of an increased importance of the capital and investment in agriculture in discussing a growth model, particularly in relation to the technical progress in this sector. For the sake of simplicity, however, the non-capital assumption is still kept for this sector.

Model II:

1) $Y_1(t) = F_1[(Kt), N_1(t)] + \alpha_1(t)$

2) $Y_2(t) = F_2[L(t), N_2(t)] + \alpha_2(t)$

3) $S(t) = dK/dt$

4) $w(t)N_1(t) = Y_1(t) - S(t)$

5) $N_1(t) + N_2(t) = N(t)$

6) $w(t) = Y_2(t)/N_2(t)$

7) $G_2 = \eta\omega + \lambda$

8) $\dfrac{\partial Y_1}{\partial N_1}(t) = \omega(t),$

where $G_2 = \dfrac{dY^2}{dt} \cdot \dfrac{1}{Y_2(t)}$ and $\omega = \dfrac{dw}{dt} \cdot \dfrac{1}{w(t)}$.

The variables are Y_1, Y_2, N_1, N_2, K, L, ω, S, η, λ, α_1, α_2, totaling 12. In order to arrive at a consistent solution of this model, we have to give four more relationships or variables from outside. It may be most natural and practical to assume a constant stock of land $(L = \bar{L})$, a constant rate of population increase $(\bar{\lambda})$ and a constant income elasticity of food demand $(\bar{\eta})$. In addition to these three, if we introduce another exogenous factor with regard to one of the technical shift variables, then we can solve this system. The five equilibrium conditions—3), 5), 6), 7), 8) will be fulfilled continuoulsy in the course of growth. This can be a path of balanced growth at least in a formal sense.[7]

A special attention, however, is required to the shift variables of production functions in both sectors. The technical progress or the flow of technical knowledge has usually been considered to be given from outside the economic system. In our case, however, one of the two shift variables is to be determined within

[7] Mitsuharu Inage's model is an excellent suggestion for us in this respect, though his conclusion is not the same as mine. See his paper "Keizai Seicho to Nogyo" (Economic Growth and Agriculture), *Keizai Kenkyu* (*The Economic Review*) Vol. 12, No. 1, January 1961.

the system, if a balanced growth has to be maintained. Of course we have no empirical evidence for determining which is exogenous or endogenous of the two shift variables. As far as the spontaneous nature of technical innovations is concerned, it may be natural to assume that the shift variable of the capitalist sector (α_1) is responsible. If this is taken for granted, a balanced growth can and should be explored when α_1 is given. In this case the point is that whether α_2 can be adjusted or not to meet the conditions of balanced growth.

In this respect a few words on a possibility of maintaining balanced growth paths will be needed from the veiwpoint of agricultural policy. In most advanced countries, the government plays an important role in encouraging technical progress of agriculture. In the developing countries where peasant economy is dominant in agriculture, this is of strategic importance for economic development. Suppose that the shift variable of production function in sector I is given or projected. The government's policy can be expected to lead the rate of technical progress in sector II in order to make approximation to a balanced growth. Such an interpretation, however, will change the nature of our model and we should call it a *policy* model in this context. But it is to be noted that the policy model of this kind is backed up with the analytical content of a balanced growth.[8]

The nature of technical progress thus required under the condition of constant stock of land available to agriculture must be land-saving. If the number of labor force in agriculture

[8] Particular attention is drawn to the existence of the two conflicting forces which are necessarily caused by the progress of agricultural techniques. The productivity growth will certainly contribute to both increasing food supply. and raising the income level of peasant in sector II. It has twofold effects-one is the "output effect" and the other the "income effect". From the standpoint of capitalist, it has sometimes been argued, the former is favorable but the latter unfavorable because a higher equilibrium wage, caused by a level-up of the peasant income, will operate as a brake to capital accumulation. As A. Lewis points out, the latter may discourage the rate of shift of production function in sector II, depending upon the capitalists' influence on the policy-making of the government.

is assumed to be kept unchanged throughout the growth process as in Japan's historical experience, it should be also labor-saving. If that number is to be decreased in order to accelerate the supply of labor to the capitalistic sector, the improvement of agricultural technique should be more labor-saving than in the former case. Suppose that $\alpha_2{}^*$ represents such a required rate of technical progress under the condition of constant labor force in sector II, then from equation 2) we have a simple relationship $G_2 = \alpha_2{}^*$, and from equation 7) we can obtain another simple equation $\alpha_2{}^* = \lambda(1 - \eta)$, considering $\omega = G_2$, the condition of maintainng "income parity."

This simple case is described as a sort of standard. If the actual rate of technical progress tends to be smaller than $\alpha_2{}^*$, we have an inequality $G_2 > \alpha_2$. In order to meet G_2, the labor force in agriculture should increase, resulting a disparity between the wage income in sector I and the average productivity in sector II, and/or food supply will face deficit, calling for food imports. In either case, there may be no automatic mechanism which would restore again a balanced path of growth where $\alpha_2{}^*$ works. In this sense, the important implication of our model is that the central core of the development strategy concerns the problem of technical progress in agriculture.

In this respect, the thesis of disguised unemployment with regards to development policies cannot be justified. This thesis depends, as is widely known, upon an assumption that the marginal productivity of labor in sector II is zero or nearly zero. Nurkse's formulation may be a typical one in asserting that there can be a possible increase of labor availability for economic development, without reducing the food supply. I have doubt on its empirical validity so that in our model the reduction of labor force in agriculture is assumed to reduce food production so long as the production method and organization remain unchanged. Our thesis is that without an increase of food supply there can be no increase of labor availability. And in order to increase food output, a shift of production function in agriculture is indispensable because without technical progress one cannot expect an increase of food supply, avoiding the opertaion of decreasing return tendency. The thesis of unlimited supplies of labor seems not necessarily depends on the unrealistic proposition that the marginal productivity of labor is zero. A. Lewis' formulation of this thesis is causious in this respect. However, if one want to apply this thesis to the development strategy, irrespective of the possible equilibrium of demand for and supply of food, it would be unrealistic. In Model II, as a result of accelerating the rate of capital accumlation in sector I, there would be an increase in the demand for labor force. Without having an upward shift of production function correspondingly in sector II, no labor force can be released from this sector. In this sense, our model reveals that the possible supply of labor from sector II to sector I is "limited" by the food production conditions.

Having stressed the strategic importance of technical progress in agriculture. it is worthwhile to elaborate the nature of the agricultural production function. In our Models I and II we discussed the production functions in quite a general form throughout the whole process. During long-run economic growth, however, the agricultural production function may have significant changes due to the improvement of the farmer's management ability as well as the type of technology. During the initial stage of economic development, because of the low level of these qualifications, a decrease of labor in agriculture would cause a decrease of total output, labor productivity being kept almost unchanged. In other words, we cannot expect an economies of scale at such a stage. By economies of scale I mean here that a larger land per labor brings forth a higher productivity through introducing technical improvement. This possibility will be given at the later stage when the labor force can be reduced by the expansion of sector I. For the developing economy whose labor force is obliged to increase in sector II, therefore, the rate of productivity increase in this sector tends to be limited. This observation makes more urgent the policy implication of Model II.

For the sake of illustrating the analytical implication of Model II and of clarifying the possible performance of the economy at the later stage, let us discuss further the effect of scale economies with respect to the land(L). In so doing, the total area is assumed unchanged($\bar{L}$). It is convenient to take up a particular form of production function (productivity function, P,) as follows:

$$\frac{Y_2}{N_2}=P_2\left(\frac{\bar{L}}{N_2}\right),\ \frac{Y_1}{N_1}=P_1\left(\frac{K}{N_1}\right).$$

Chart 1 may serve to illustrate the nature of this form of productivity function of agriculture in relation to its counterpart in the capitalist sector.

Chart 1. Productivity Functions

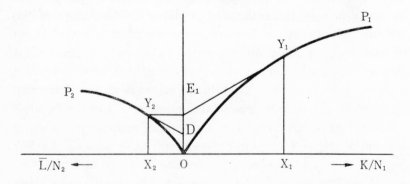

On the horizontal axis from the origin K/N_1 is measured to the right and $\bar{L}/N_2$ to the left. Suppose that at a certain period, K/N_1 is at X_1 and $\tilde{L}/N_2$ at X_2. On the vertical axis the productivity is measured. Suppose that the average productivity in

248

sector I is X_1Y_1, and that of sector II, X_2Y_2. A straight line tangential to P_1 at Y_1 determines a point E_1 and OE_1 gives the marginal productivity of labor in sector I. Likewise we get OD for sector II. We see $X_1Y_1>X_2Y_2$ and $OE_1>OD$ because of the basic assumption of our two-sector model.

The condition of maximizing profit will be satified when OE_1 is equal to the prevailing wage. The condition of income parity equilibrium will be satisfied if X_2Y_2 (or OE_1) is equal to the prevailing wage. We can suppose that an equilibrium wage determined by Model II satisfies these conditions at the same time.

Next, Chart 2 gives an illustration of a growth path with shifts of productivity functions, from P_1 to P_1' and from P_2 to P_2'. Let us first suppose a change in K/N_1 combined with an increase of N_1 in sector I as a result of labor force shift from sector II. This is shown by a shift from X_1 to X_i' on the horizontal axis. In this case the change in the marginal productivity of labor is gven by $OE_1 \rightarrow OE_1'$ and the demand wage rate will increase accordingly. But if the productivity function in sector II remains unchanged, two unbalances will occur. One is the disparity of income, and the other the unbalance of demand for and supply of food.

Chart 2. Shifts of Productivity Functions

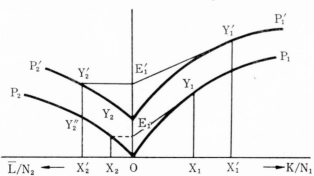

249

The average productivity can increase from X_2Y_2 to $X_2'Y_2''$ as a result of reducing the number of labor force, but not enough to be equal to OE_1', so that a shift from P_2 to P_2' is needed in order to reach $X_2'Y_2'=OE_1'$. The shift of agricultural production function of this kind was the case in the previous discussion of the policy model. We cannot be sure that such a specific shift as illustrated here will meet the food balance condition. This balance is to be given by the whole system of Model II. What we can say by this illustration is that at this stage the food supply can be increased concurrently with a reduction of labor force in agriculture.

By way of conclusion, the following remarks are stated.

1) The balanced growth in terms of equilibrium of both the demand=supply of food and the income parity can be conceived analytically but cannot automatically be obtained between the capitalist sector and self-employed sector.

2) The strategy for encouraging the rate of technical progress in agriculture, therefore, is the core of the developing policies.

3) This is the more important in light of the fact that the possibility of productivity growth in agriculture is heavily limited by the current situation of aggravating man-land ratio in most of the developing countries in Asia.

ASIAN AGRICULTURAL

DEVELOPMENT

[A] Problems and Proposition

Introduction

This paper is intended to provide a sketch of my views and observations on the selected topics which are, I believe, most important in discussing the problems of Asian agricultural development. The scope is far from comprehensive, and description is not undertaken in rigorously defined terms.

First, let us begin by setting our problem broadly as follows: acceleration of the current rate of output growth of agriculture is required on three major given conditions of resource availability; first, a serious limitation for expanding area of arable land; second, a high rate of increase in the labor force;third, certain limitations on the supply of capital which stem from its competitive uses in industrial expansion.

A revised and combined version of two notes by permission of the Asian Development Bank: [A]—*"On Asian Agricultural Development Problems" submitted to the first meeting of the Consultative Committee, held by the Asian Development Bank, on the Asian Agricultural Survey, July* 1967 *and* [B]—*"Policy Implications of the Asian Agricultural Survey", presented to the Regional Seminar on Agriculture, held by the Asian Development Bank, Sydney, April* 1969.

251

The required rate of acceleration differs from one country to another. However, the general consensus is that the difference or gap estimated between the required rate for the future and the realized rate of output growth in the past is not small but sizeable for almost all countries in the region. In most cases, the magnitude of the gap is so large that it claims the transformation of the traditional agriculture towards modernization: it requires a shift from the old phase towards a new phase, which, beyond an acceleration of output growth within the traditional structure of output-input relationships, implies an unprecedented "magnitude" never experienced in the history of advanced countries.

The required change in the basic structure of output-input relationships, however, can only be realized subject to the three conditions above-mentioned. The degree of limitation of expanding arable land may differ from one country to another, but in general the new phase of agriculture can only be realized with raising yields (land productivity) rather than expanding arable area. It is a well-known fact that the effect of recent population explosion is assumed to last at least for several decades to come. A 2–3% rate of annual increase in the labor force is so high as to present a different order of magnitude as seen from the historical experience of the developed countries. With the most optimistic perspective for the future increase in labor employment in the non-agricultural sector, an increase in the labor employment in agriculture is unavoidable.

The concurrent growth of agriculture with industry is a particular requirement for countries of economic backwardness. Agricultural development is not a pre-condition for industrialization, unlike the case of advanced nations. Both sectors are required to grow side by side; the sectoral inter-dependence, therefore, is a problem which concerns us specifically, although the Survey[1] is planned to cover only the industries which are directly related to agriculture. A well-known problem of competitive use of limited resources, especially capital between agriculture and industry is a serious problem in view of a general situation of the deficits of domestic supply of capital (in terms of both money and goods). As has often been pointed out, the transformation of the traditional agriculture technologically requires an enormous amount of capital formation in building up infrastructures. From economic point of view, however, the capital allocation for developing agriculture will considerably be limited for several decades to come.

With these given conditions, towards which direction can we draw appropriately the required changes in the traditional relationship of output-input? It is my proposition that the strategy of agricultural development can best be designed in promoting a fuller utilization of land as well as labor. This is a hypothetical proposition, the plausibility of which needs detailed examinations. In the sections that follow the examination will be developed mostly in terms of the farmers' behaviors and the pattern of technological progress.

Phases of Agricultural Development

A phase is a distinct time segment of a secular growth, the unique characteristics of which can be identified empirically by certain indicators. Certain criteria are needed to select these indicators, and they can be adopted in one way or another depending upon the purpose of the analysis one has in mind. The major criterion here is the pattern of output-input relationships in agriculture. It can sometimes be approximated by a representative indicator (for example, the ratio of irrigated area to the total arable land area) but basically it should represent

[1] The Asian Agricultural Survey. Hereafter the same.

over-all pattern or structure of agricultural growth. The aim of this section is first to describe roughly the characteristics of the present situation of Asian agriculture in terms of our setting, and secondly, to consider the problems of the new phase along the line of the hypothetical proposition.

Let us begin with the discussions on the pattern of agricultural development in the past which led to the current situation of Asian agriculture. According to the two papers (one by Dr. Hsieh and the other by Dr. Hsieh and Professor Ruttan)[2], both in the Philippines and Thailand the cultivated area of rice had expanded considerably while rice production per land unit (land productivity) had not grown appreciably. The average annual rate of area increase was 2.72% during 1900–1960 in the Philippines and 2.98% during 1910–1960 in Thailand. These are a surprisingly high record of area expansion. If the historical statistics are reliable enough and we can assume a similar pattern for other developing countries in this region, then we can say that the output growth has been mostly achieved by area expansion—a performance which manifest itself in a sharp contrast to the pattern of Taiwan and Japan, where yield increase has undoubtedly been the major factor of output growth. Let us call these Group I and Group II, the former with an *extensive* pattern and the latter with an *intensive* pattern.

The Chart given in Hsieh's paper illustrates another fact that the cultivated area per farm is on the average much bigger in Group I than in Group II. The ratio of paddy field to the total arable land differs from one country to another. This difference as well as the difference of family size should be taken into consideration in appraising the above-mentioned average difference

---

[2] S.C. Hsieh, "Some Problems of Improving Agricultural Productivity (mimeographed), 1966. S.C. Hsieh and V.W. Ruttan, "Techological, Institutional and Environmental Factors in the Growth of Rice Production: Philippines, Thailand and Taiwan" (mimeographed), (Later published in *Food Research Institute Studies*, Vol. 7, No. 3, 1967).

of the cultivated area per farm. Here, let us assume for the time-being that this phenomenon can be understood as another indicator for distinguishing the extensive pattern and the intensive pattern which currently characterizes Groups I and II. The last indicator of the three is given by yield, and farely reliable data are available for individual crops, especially in the case of rice, as is shown in Hsieh's paper. It is more difficult to compare the total farm output per unit of land and further surveys are needed to obtain reliable data. However, we can assume broadly that the difference of crop yields or farm output per unit of land is enormous between Group I and Group II (for example, on average Japan's rice yield is more than 4.0 times of that of the Philippines).

The pattern of output increase, the land size per farm, and the yield or farm output per unit of land—these indicators, taken together, suggest that between these two Groups, i.e., the extensive and the intensive types, the difference in farming systems is great enough to be distinguished in connection with the concept of phases. With respect to the inputs to agriculture, the available data are very limited, especially for their historical trend, so that the irrigation ratio can roughly be used as a representative indicator. To be comprehensive, we need further survey on the performance of other various inputs. However, we can safely assume that the above-mentioned output indicators imply a distinct difference in the amount of inputs also between the two groups and that the output-input relationship can be distinguished between the two groups. On this assumption, we can proceed to the next problem.

The shape of the new phase will differ according to the strategy taken by the country at issue. In terms of the hypothetical proposition previously made, however, we may expect that this may simply lead to a growth path from the state of Group I to that of Group II: it is implied that the currently witnessed differences of farming system can be narrowed if countries of Group I follow the pattern of historical growth path of Group II at a faster pace of growth. This idea seems plausible so far as the crop yields or farm output per area will have a trend of increase without expanding the area of cultivated land. It can furthermore be speculated that it should be accompanied by a trend of increasing inputs to agriculture with a similar pattern witnessed in the historical path of Group II countries.

However, the problem is not so simple, and it is extremely difficult to be comprehensive in this respect. For example, the record of agricultural development in Japan since the 1870's had no trend of decreasing the size o˝ arable land per farm, whereas, the growth path from the state of Group I to that of Group II clearly suggests that a trend of that pattern is inevitable. Because of an unprecedentedly high rate of increase in the labor force the fuller utilization of labor and land has previously been proposed. It is true that this coincides with the hypothetical trend of decreasing the size of arable land per farm from Group I to Group II. The coincidence, however, does not provide us with a solution of the problem, because there are other important factors to be considered. An example can rightly be presented: the initial condition for agricultural development in Japan was different from those of Group I countries, particularly in terms of the irrigation ratio; the infrastructures built up during the pre-modern epoch was an important backlog for the subsequent growth, whereas, a path from the state of Group I to that of Group II needs much more capital formation than in Japan's path of agriculture in modern economic growth. Another example can be raised about the level of technological knowledge. This is an advantage of Group I countries instead of disadvantage as suggested by the former example. Technological potential is now quite higher than in the old days but this needs a separate treatment in the next section.

These examples lead to some idea of the characteristics of the coming phase envisaged along a line of our hypothetical proposition. It is really a new phase: it is not only a shift from the old phase but also has no exact counterpart phase in economic history. Although the pattern of output growth will be similar to that of the historical path of Group II countries, the pattern of input (and production organization) appears to be substantially different in several important respects. In the discussions that follow let us speculate the direction and pattern of the possible change in the output-input relationship during the new phase. Although the available data are poor for knowing the input side, some suggestions can be drawn.

Our hypothesis about the output-input relationships during the new phase is that between most of various inputs to agriculture a technical complementarity, instead of substitutability, will be sustained in a broad sense. Particularly viewed from the direction towards fuller utilization of labor and land, this hypothesis can roughly be stated as follows. First, the increase in labor input per unit of land together with an increase in the non-labor inputs, technically required, will raise crop yields. Secondly, if the price-cost relationship is maintained favorable to this change, it is possible to envisage a growth path which is characterized by a trend of increases in both the labor input and the non-labor input per unit of land. It goes without saying that this path meets the requirement of our proposition. Much has been discussed with the importance of technical complementarity with regard to the experience of Japanese agriculture. It is widely accepted that between improved varieties and fertilizer input, technical complementarity exists: in a broader sense the same can be assumed also between the non-labor input and the infrastructures. The particular point here is that it can further be assumed between the labor input and the non-labor input.

In the light of Japanese experience, the last point is not necessarily confirmed. Instead, in the case of rice cultivation the labor input per land has shown a trend of decrease, instead of increase, since around the 1910's. Since the number of gainful workers on the farm had only slightly decreased during the prewar period, the total labor input on the farm might be kept more or less unchanged although the data are not available continuously. Taiwan's experience, however, demonstrates a possible increase in the labor input on the farm. Therefore, a simultaneous increase in the labor input with that of the non-labor input has a possibility but cannot be taken for granted: it requires further scrutiny particularly on a possible rate of substitution of fixed capital for labor. For the time being, let us observe this problem simply in two ways. First, in comparison with Group II countries, Group I countries seem to show a much smaller labor input per farm: the order of difference is as sizeable as 2:1. Second, in comparison among regions and countries within Group I, a positive association seems to exist between the rice yield and the labor-input per unit of land; partial data of farm economy surveys suggest further that a larger labor input is generally accompanied by a greater non-labor input and a higher yield.[3] These require statistical confirmation by the planned Survey. If such phenomena are confirmed, our hypothetical proposition will be plausible empirically in terms of farmers' behavior.

Borrowed Technology and Capital Requirement

If the nature of the new phase previously proposed is broadly accepted, strategy for selecting the type of technology must be

---

[3] Mostly depends upon Professor Shigeru Ishikawa "Supplies of Farm Labor During Economic Development" (In Japanese), in *Keizai Kenkyu* (*The Economic Review*), Janaury 1965. (Later, contained in *Economic Development in Asian Perspective*, Kinokuniya-Shoten Tokyo, 1967, Chapter 3).

the next subject. This will first be discussed in terms of the well-known thesis of borrowed technology.

It is a widely-accepted view that the greatest advantage for the growth of countries of economic backwardness lies in the possibility of borrowing the technologies which were developed by advanced countries. This implies that the cost of developing new technologies are paid by the enterprises or governments in advanced countries and that the developed backlog of techno- logical knowledge can be purchased cheaply and utilized without much difficulty by follower countries. In reality, "without much difficulty" needs further comment. Because of the difference of given conditions concerned, the follower countries have to make considerable efforts for succeeding in borrowing the techno- logical knowledges in order to modify them for their own economic circumstances. In most cases of manufacturing industries, it has been said that these difficulties are not decisive.

How about agriculture? One may have the impression that the situation is quite different in agriculture; the difficulty appears to be enormous. Various basic factors such as natural endow- ments (climate, soil, etc.), social and institutional set-ups, scale and organization of existing farming, limited facilities of infra- structures,—differences of all these which exist between advanced and backward countries seem to be decisive in preventing the successful utilization of this possible advantage. Furthermore, one may say it is still more difficult because of the "location specific" nature of agricultural technology. We would say, however, the advantage of borrowed technology is the key factor for accelerating the rate of growth of all industries in follower countries; agriculture cannot be an exception of this general thesis. Most of the difficulties mentioned above do not prevent, they only modify, the process of borrowing advanced technology. What is most important is first to identify the peculiar nature of agri- culture and second, to find the right direction and appropriate type of modifications which might be required to fit the advanced technology into the desirable pattern of agricultural development in follower countries. A complexity of many problems is involved in this process; I cannot enter into detailed discussions on them. From the viewpoint of economic observations, however, I would like to point out the followings.

First, the flexible nature of agricultural production in terms of factor-proportions and input divisibility can be counted as a favorable element for borrowing advanced tecnhology in agriculture as compared with manufacturing industries. In manufacture, technological requirements often operate as a decisive factor (the rigid factor-proportion) in borrowing advanced technology of the capital-using type in changing the scale and organization of production which sometimes is out of keeping with the economic situation of follower countries where labor supplies are very flexible. But in the case of agriculture, the inputs which embody directly biological-chemical technology such as seeds, fertilizers and insecticides are all highly divisible and they can be used with different scales of farms without causing efficiency differences. The direction toward borrowing advanced technology of this type will face no resistance which stems from the problem of factor price differences; rather, it fits well into the situation of factor prices of the follower countries. The alternative direction is towards mechanization of agriculture with enlarging farm sizes. The international backlog of technological knowledge along this line is now also rich. Relative price of machines is far lower than in the past. It may be possible to develop farm mechanization to a certain extent. But from the strategic point of view of guiding toward fuller utilization of labor and land, policies to encourage this direction is not appropriate for the present situation of Asian agriculture, so far as its essential function is to substitute capital for labor and to introduce economies of scale. Postwar Japanese experience shows that small-size machines can effectively be used even on a very small size farm. But be aware of the fact that this was introduced mostly because of the labor shortage in agriculture.

Second, it is not possible to borrow ready-made technologies of foreign origin particularly in the case of agriculture. Special efforts and a certain time interval are required before foreign inventions can be effectively used to establish their own system of agricultural technologies in follower countries. To establish a new firm system of technologies on farm level (not an individual technique separately) is not an easy task: it is a process of trial and error and requires accumulation of empirical knowledge. Scientific investigations in various fields of agriculture seem to show a promising prospect in this regard. The production of improved varieties of seeds has recently been promoted for the particular purpose of applying their achievements to developing countries in this region. This will certainly back up strongly the effectiveness of the borrowed technology. However, if we ignore the importance of invention and diffusion of indigenous technology in follower countries, our view may be criticized as being biased. Even the traditional technology can sometimes be improved appreciably. A too-sharp distinction cannot be made between the traditional and the modern technologies (and accordingly inputs) in this regard. It goes without saying that if the advantage of borrowed technology is combined with these indigenous achievements, it would contribute much to establish one country's own system of improved technologies for developing agriculture.

Now, another aspect of the criteria of selecting the type of a system of agricultural technologies concerns the amount of capital requirement. What is preliminarily required in discussing this aspect of the problem is to make a distinction among various decision-making units. Aside from the economies of central planning, a great number of inividual farmers and/or land-owners are the decision-makers in the market economy. To a different extent the public authorities, central and local, are also the decision-makers in making and implementing plans or programs of developing agriculture in most countries of this region. There are various kinds of intermediaries between the two which we will not discuss here. At any rate the fact that the farmer's decision is the most important cannot be exaggerated. The farmer's behavior has often been said irrational, but we believe it is rational. Even the extensive type of agricultural development previously discussed can be recognized as a rational path under the given conditions of the past. Public decision needs its own footing and criteria, and with respect to developing agriculture, it is admitted, the strategy cannot be appropriate without being based on the macro-economic criteria, but its policy implementation cannot be successful without being closely tied with the economic behavior at the farm level.

Now, in the process of transforming traditional agriculture towards the new phase, farmers require a certain amount of capital both working and fixed, in order to raise yields because of the complementary demand for the non-labor inputs. To create a breakthrough towards raising yields, the credit and/or subsidies for providing these capitals and the overhead invest-ment for constructing infrastructures are particularly required. But if the effect of these outside impacts is once-and-for-all and fails to lead to a self-generating process, the transformation cannot be achieved. The self-generating process of growth can only be achieved when the capital investment is carried out for realizing appropriate type of technology. The problem of capital requirement must be considered from this point of view. Aside from lumpy public investment to be discussed later, the needed annual amount of investment for the farmer must be moderate. Introduction of improved varieties, fertilizers together with small improved implements is comparatively well suited for this requirement. If price relationship between output-input can be kept favorable to these inputs, these must provide good incentives for implementing these inputs to farming. This may be called a "non-big-push" thesis. It may not be out of place to recall the relatively neglected fact that even during the "industrial revolution" in advanced countries an accumulation of a number of small, interrelated inventions played an important role: a moderate amount of investment enabled their realization.

A trend towards increasing labor input per unit of land is an important part of our proposition. Capital formation is required to implement it. An increase in the labor input must be pursued in terms of farmer's behavior in relation to their capital formation (including the case of using labor directly for capital formation). If incentives are favorable this will be realized. It was a widely accepted fact in prewar Japan that in the case of farm-households of smaller cultivated area much more effort was paid toward fuller utilization of land than in the case of farm-households of larger cultivated area: the labor input per land as well as the non-labor input per unit of land was appreciably higher in the former than in the latter. A similar fact seem to exist in some regions in other Asian countries. This deserves particular attention because farmers' behavior toward intensive farming is identified under the present circumstance. However, this is only a half of the story. The other half is the fact that the output per labor input (labor productivity) is distinctly lower in smaller size farms as compared with that of larger size farms. If a trend towards fuller utilization of labor and land resulted in lowering labor productivity, farmers would have no intention to increase labor inputs. A shift of the "production function" is therefore necessary without losing their motivation toward intensive farming. The Nurksian thesis

263

had once been believed widely to be a good strategy with respect to utilizing disguised unemployment for capital formation. In retrospect, the missing point was that it neglected entirely the effect of technological progress and its dynamic effects on people's behavior. To introduce a process of chain-reaction between increased inputs, particularly capital formation, and technological progress is thus a basic thought for the strategy of developing agriculture.

The construction of infrastructures is of course an indispensable part of the simultaneously required increase in the input or capital formation. The investment for this purpose varies widely in its size, its type and its decision-making. Where rice cultivation is developed on a big river delta region, it is entirely open to the "unstable river" and has to adapt itself to natural conditions. A transformation toward the new phase needs "normalization of nature" in Professor S. Tohata's concept,[4] as a prerequisite, which requires a tremendous amount of investment and high level of technology. The construction of this sort is far beyond the farmers' level: program and decision-making here entirely belongs to the public authorities or international organizations. If decisions can be made for an enormous investment of this kind, it would be a wonderful thing for transforming agriculture to the new phase. Foreign aid has a good objective here too. I am not concerned here with such big projects carried out without relying upon farmer's expenditures or tax payments. If farmer's expenditures are partially involved in these, the cost-benefit calculation is a problem to that extent. In the light of postwar Japanese experience, although the project for irrigation facilities were of much more moderate size, the cost-benefit relation did not always have favorable results for farmers. Here again the type and degree of technological progress expected as

---

[4] Seiichi Tohata and Kazushi Ohkawa, *Chosen Beikoku Keizairon* (A Treatise on Rice Economy in Korea), Nihon Gakujutsu Shinkokai, Tokyo, 1935.

a result of such a lumpy investment seems a problem to be considered carefully.

On the other hand, there are a number of regions where various kinds of small-scale construction of irrigation facilities are required: these are not entirely beyond the hands of farmers, landowners and/or their communities. The cost-benefit relation appears favorable in many cases. From the viewpoint of building up and sustaining a growth path of chain reactions, this type of construction investment deserves particular attention. The construction of this type can gradually be expanded, repaired and improved by farmers or their organizations once a change towards increasing yields is firmly attained. It certainly contributes to leading agriculture towards the fuller use of labor and land.

Lastly, by way of conclusion, let us say a few words on the problem of selecting priorities for development strategy. In view of a broad technical complementarity of increasing various inputs which are required for the new phase of Asian agriculture, it is difficult to give a general list of priorities: the situation may differ from one country to another and from one region to another within a country. For example, in the situation of the Philippines, which is vividly described in Dr. Hsieh's paper cited above, undoubtedly the priority must be the supply oɪ irrigation facilities because a system of new technologies in introducing new varieties of rice appears to be already established. However, there may be a number of regions where introduction of improved varieties with increasing inputs must be the priority. Therefore, what I can say in brief is as follows: The priority for developing strategy is first to be found in terms of limiting factor or factors of technological requirements: the "limiting factor" is intended to mean that its incremental increase in input will contribute to raising yields to the largest extent. Second, economic appraisal of these technical priorities should not be ignored. Not only the required amount of capital formation for supplying these limiting factors, but also the criteria for guiding Asian agriculture towards the appropriate path of growth, in my view, a path towards fuller utilization of land and labor, is to be taken into consideration. Third, these priorities are preferably to be tested at the farm level in the light of the farmer's behavior and motivations. It must be the major objective of the planned Survey to identify and appraise these strategic priorities which cannot be assumed *a priori* to be the same through all regions and countries.

[B]   Policy Implications

Policy implications extending over a wide range of issues are covered in the two volumes of the *Asian Agricultural Survey* (hereafter *AAS*)[5]. A brief personal note such as this cannot attempt to make a comprehensive review of these implications, but is intended to highlight certain points in order to provide discussion material for the participants.

For this purpose, I have selected the five specific topics that follow which, I believe, are of primary importance in view of the present circumstances of this region. However, other important policy problems such as terms of trade and other intersectoral relations between agriculture and the rest of the economy are not touched on here.

Economic Growth and the People's Welfare

The Report of the Consultative Committee (RCC) clearly presents the main objective of the ADB. It "must surely be through economic growth to raise the standard of living of the mass of the people in this region..." (pp. 5–6, *AAS*). The additional statement that "the material welfare of the masses in

[5]   The Asian Development Bank (ADB), *Asian Agricultural Survey*, published jointly by University of Tokyo Press and Univeristy of Washington Press, 1969.

terms of income is a cardinal part of the development objective" certainly underscores the welfare objective which takes on particular relevance in view of the fact that the mass of the people are at present engaged in subsistence agriculture in this region. In my view, it will perhaps be helpful to think of the RCC statement on objectives as implying two basic points: first, economic growth is the general setting through which the main objective is to be realized and second, in formulating developmental policies, the participation of the mass of the people in the development process should be taken into consideration.

The main objective stated above is based on the notion that the welfare of the mass of the people can and should be raised *through economic growth*. In a broad, long-run sense this should be acceptable as the setting of any economic policy of the member countries. However, this does not necessarily warrant that any kind of developmental policy can automatically satisfy the welfare objective in its immediate results. This in turn raises certain complex problems inherent in the basic mechanism of economic growth. The dynamic process of economic development requires an initial breakthrough towards sustained increases in productivity for realizing profitable investment. This does not necessarily warrant an even distribution of the benefits of growth to the mass of the people. Recognition of this problem, however, does not imply the alternative notion that the main objective can better be fulfilled by not implementing growth policies. For example, income transfer policies can make for a better income distribution, but without economic growth no resource can be increased continuously to satisfy the welfare objective.

Significance of Agricultural Development

The RCC assumes that accelerating agricultural development is an urgent problem in most of the member countries. On two

267

points I would like to make comments regarding this basic setting:

First, this does not necessarily imply that agricultural development is the pre-condition for industrialization—a notion of historical stage theory which held that first would come agricultural development and then industrialization. Instead, the basic thought is that agricultural development is urgent as an integral part of an overall economic growth whose dynamics require a balanced development of various sectors of the economy. The *concurrent* growth of agriculture and industry must be the aim of developmental efforts. This is particularly to be noted in view of the follower countries' circumstances which are historically different from advanced countries. Second, the importance of agricultural development in the present situation of most of the member countries in this region is of course widely recognized in terms of the need of increasing farm product—food and export goods. Particularly, import substitution policy is urgent for food. However, our concern cannot merely be limited to output growth. Agricultural development basically concerns itself with a sustained increase in income of the mass of the people on the farm. This goes without saying in view of the fact that in this region agriculture is the dominant sector in terms of the sectoral distribution of labor force employment.

We must, however, emphasize here that need does not warrant possibility. As is pointed out in the RCC (p. 7, *AAS*), there is a widely held view that "agriculture in the region is not a good investment in terms of what the additional productive capacity from such investment can contribute to the economic growth of these countries". We do not oppose this view so far as traditional agriculture is concerned. However, we must not overlook the possibility of making breakthrough via traditional agriculture towards modernization which can be more promising for investment for essentially two reasons: first, the marked advance which has recently been made in technological knowledge

to be used in the agriculture of this region and second, the pro-
liferation in most countries of this region of various constraints
on the agricultural sector which depress the economic incentives
of farmers to adopt efficiently these advances in technological
knowledge. It is possible that these constraints can be minimized
by developmental efforts, particularly in relation to the new circumstances created by the technological advances mentioned above.

There is a difference of opinion as to the effectiveness of the
two factors mentioned above for formulating strategy of achieving the breakthrough towards dynamic growth. For example,
some assert that institutional improvements, such as land reform,
are pre-requisite while others hold the view that the impact of
technological progress must be the element making for the real
breakthrough. As a matter of fact, the inter-action between
technological advance and institutional-organizational reform
is a problem quite complex in nature. Nobody can deny the
necessity of both in transforming the traditional agriculture.
However, in the light of present state of affairs of agriculture in
most countries of this region, the recent extraordinary advances
in technological knowledge should be considered, in my view,
as the primary factor for making policy decisions.

Pattern of Technological Progress[6]

Certainly most relevant here is the thesis of borrowed technology. It is a widely-accepted view that the greatest advantage
for economic growth which accrues to follower countries lies
in the possibility of "borrowing" the technological knowledge
developed by the advanced countries. This implies that the
cost of developing new technological knowledge is paid by the
governments, non-profit institutions or private enterprises in
advanced countries and that the developed backlog of techno-

[6] Made short the original text to avoid duplication with the content of [A] (pp.
258–261)

logical knowledge can be purchased cheaply and utilized without much difficulty by follower countries. In reality, "without much difficulty" needs further comment. Because of the differences in the given conditions involved, the follower countries have to make considerable efforts to borrow the technological knowledge in a form modified to suit their own economic circumstances. In fact, it seems widely believed that in the case of agriculture the thesis of borrowed technology is least applicable. I do not share this view and would emphasize that the advantage of borrowed technology is the key factor for accelerating the rate of growth of agriculture in follower countries. Most of the difficulties in the international transfer of technological knowledge of agriculture do not prevent, but only modify, the process of implementing the strategy of borrowing advanced technologies.

At present, we must note the rich international backlog of technological knowledge which is becoming more favorable to farming in this region. The advances in agricultural science and research techniques provide the basis for the rapid technical progress which has made possible the increasing yields and productivity of recent years, particularly for the major crops— rice, wheat and maize. The international backlog of technical knowledge is also of great importance in ensuring the availability at low cost of the key complementary inputs—chemical fertilizers and pesticides. Technical innovations that are continuing to reduce the real cost of nitrogen fertilizers are particularly significant because this item is likely to bulk large as intensification leads to increased use of purchased inputs. This has sometimes been called the "green" or "seed-fertilizer" revolution.[7]

The process of technological progress in follower countries does not necessarily imply a "reproduction" of the process followed by the advanced countries. As suggested above, the

---

[7] Bruce F. Johnston and John Cownie, "The Seed-Fertilizer Revolution and Labor Force Absorption," *American Economic Review*, Vol. LIX, No. 4, September 1969.

implementation of new technologies also requires inventions on the part of follower countries. In traditional farming the system of practices of crop cultivation has historically been established as a sort of routine in which the seed-fertilizer revolution will require drastic changes. Locally it requires great efforts in order to establish a new system of crop cultivation practices which can utilize efficiently the possibility of increasing productivity using the newly introduced technologies. In this sense, local research and extension services are of great importance. This is, I believe, widely recognized. What is particularly noticeable here is the fact that the process of changes seems to be incomparably drastic in terms of the historical experience of the advanced countries. For example, the rice yield difference between IR 8 and the traditional varieties is so enormous and the tempo of diffusion of the former is so speedy in certain districts that almost no comparable experience can be found in the process of development of rice cultivation in advanced countries. This tends to raise many problems which call for the attention of the policy-makers in developing advanced technologies in agriculture in most countries of this region—problems which had never been so serious in advanced countries.

Institutional-Organizational Constraints

As has been mentioned before, improvements towards minimizing various constraints which have long existed in rural society, in our view, will contribute much to accelerating agricultural development. It has often been asserted that this is especially important from the viewpoint of the welfare of the mass of the people when the constraints are of an organizational and/or institutional nature. This view also implies that organizational and institutional reforms are a pre-condition of the agricultural transformation and that without these reforms it cannot be car-

ried out. Without accompanying technological progress, however, these reforms, whether organizational or institutional,
would not appear capable of achieving the agricultural transformation envisaged by this view. Instead the real pre-condition
seems to be the possibility of utilizing advanced technologies.
As mentioned above, this possibility is now at hand so that the
problem for us is to consider an appropriate time sequence to
carry out the appropriate reforms. In my view, these must be
an important element of the dynamism which is *first introduced*
by technological progress. The following is not intended to be
a comprehensive treatment but is presented to illustrate possible
incentives to facilitate the implementation of these reforms.

1) Where group instead of individual decision making is called for (as in the case of spraying and intensifying irrigation
etc.), rural organization problem becomes increasingly important.
Without solving these, further progress in increasing yield may
not possible. The point is that possibility of obtaining benefit
from using the new technologies may make it easier to treat
these organizational problems.

2) Farmers in most countries of this region had shown little
interest in credit system and organization reforms. But as they
need increasing purchased inputs such as chemical fertilizers and
pesticides, the situation has begun to change. They are now
more interested in being helped by the establishment of the
credit system and organization, as well as the improvement of
marketing system.

3) They will become more cognizant of the benefits which
will accrue from improvements in tenancy contracts and land
reforms, if tenant farmers can really recognize the possible gains
which can be obtained by introducing advanced practices of
crop cultivation.

On the other hand, however, we cannot be too optimistic
concerning the technology impact. These incentives as illustrated

above may not be enough to overcome the difficulties of mini-mizing the constraints. When and where this is the case, policy measures to promote these improvements and reforms are neces-sary in order to be successful in sustaining the process of agri-cultural transformation. In the Report of the Consultative Committee we emphasized the importance of these measures to be considered by policy makers, referring to the individual reports of the *AAS*.

The inter-action between the type of technological progress and the organizational-institutional changes presents a most intricate problem and further comments are needed in this respect. As has been suggested before, agricultural technology centered about the seed-fertilizer revolution can by its nature assume incentives for its general application for all farmers ir-respective of farm-scale if the necessary conditions for its diffusion are more or less speedily fulfilled. In practice, however, these conditions may not necessarily be arranged satisfactorily. If this is the case, differentials in incentives will emerge between rich and poor farmers and small and large-size farms. As compared with the historical experience of advanced countries where the diffusion of such a technology could go on more slowly and continuously, most of the member countires of this region have more possibilities of facing such a case because the process of transforming agriculture is much more drastic and discon-tinuous.

Thus when these differentials appear so distinct and sustaining, technological advance will contribute to bringing forth a new agrarian structure—a differential structure in agriculture as well as in rural society where progress is biased towards rich farmer leaving many other farmers far behind in the process of transformation. This danger is by no means hypothetical. In reality, it may take place, if the seed-fertilizer revolution is carried out by higher class farmers via the introduction of modern mechanization techniques. This requires serious consideration because mechanization of the modern type, unlike the technology of biological-chemical type, is biased *vis a vis* the scale of farming; namely it is more advantageous to large-size farming. The required rate of output growth of agriculture may be obtained through such a differential progress, but the mass of the people cannot participate in the transformation. Where and when signs of movement towards this type of development appear, policy decisions concerning institutional and organizational constraints would require serious consideration.

Rates of Return on Capital Investment

It is to be noted that an increase in the capital formation proportion (and savings ratio as well) is a self-generating phenomenon of economic growth. Once the breakthrough has been made, then the development promotes capital formation and the capital formation in turn brings forth development—a chain reaction process will form a sustained growth. In transforming traditional agriculture, farmers require a certain amount of capital both working and fixed. To create a breakthrough towards raising yields, however, the credit for providing them and overhead investment for constructing minimum infrastructures are particularly required. But if the effects of these outside impact are once-and-for-all and fail to lead to a self-generating process, the transformation cannot be achieved. The problem of capital allocation policy for introducing new technology to agriculture must be considered from this point of view. The needed amount of investment for the farmer must be moderate. Introduction of improved varieties and other complementary inputs is relatively well suited for this requirement. If price relationship between output-input can be kept favorable to agriculture, these must provide good incentives for implementing

274

these inputs to farming. This may be called a "non-big 'push'" thesis.

As capital is a relatively scarce resource at present in most countries of this region, capital investment in agriculture requires in principle a rate of return competitive with investment in other industries. This principle, however, requires the following qualification for making policy decisions because of the characteristics of agricultural production.

First, the rate of return on investment, often referred to in the RCC, does not necessarily mean the private profit rate. Investment in agriculture, like in some other industries, should also aim at the prospective social rates of return they are likely to earn, although it is not easy to arrive at exact estimates of this kind. This does not mean, however, that investment resources should be directed to a less productive use rather than a more productive use in private accounting. When such an allocation of resources is thought desirable on social grounds, it is a problem of transfer of income and/or wealth and should be distinguished from the standpoint of economic policies.

Second, in view of the importance of the mass participation of the farmers in agricultural transformation, investment in this sector needs consideration of the possibility of raising also the level of returns on other production factors than capital. Fuller utilization of land and labor is an important requirement and for this reason capital-using type of technology may not be suitable because it does not necessarily warrant appropriate rates of return on other factors. Fortunately, the biological-chemical technologies do not seem to be of the capital-using type. In most cases a competitive rate of capital return can be expected together with promising rates of return on fuller utilization of land and labor. When the rate of investment is discussed in the RCC, this is, in my view, implicitly assumed.

Third, even within the category of economic policies, there are certain cases which warrant capital investment with some subsidies (soft loan) because of the nature of agricultural production. For example, the output effect of investment can fully be realized after passing through a long period. In such a case current investment appears to be unrewarding at least in the short run. In the long run, however, a greater rate of return can be expected and investment with some subsidies can be justified for a certain period.

AGRICULTURAL TECHNOLOGY

AND

AGRARIAN STRUCTURE*

Introduction

One of the characteristics of the so-called "Japanese Model" is that the bulk of the nation's farmers have been involved in increases in agricultural productivity associated with the use of improved varieties, fertilizers, implements and other complementary inputs within the almost unchanged organizational framework of the existing small-scale farming system. This type of technological progress is called biological-chemical (BC for short).

The "Green Revolution" which emerged in south and southeast Asia is in essense of the same type of technological progress as it is often called a seeds-fertilizer revolution. Nevertheless, the organizational framework of the existing farming system appears

* I would like to acknowledge the great benefit I received from the intensive discussion with Professor Shigeru Ishikawa, which we had in writing our joint paper on a similar subject as this, "Significance of Japan's Experience—Technological Changes in Agricultural Production and Changes in Agrarian Structure", presented to the Conference on Agriculture and Economic Development, sponsored by the Economic Research Japan Center, Tokyo, September, 1971.

This is written based on our notes, "Nogyo Gijutsu no Keizaiteki Taipu to Nogyokozo", *No. 1, 1970 and No. 2, 1971 (mimeographed).* *I would like to express my gratitute to Mr. Nobukiyo Takamatsu, my collaborator, who has allowed me the use of these notes as the materials.*

277

to have undergone some changes. According to S. Ishikawa the pattern of response to the new high-yield varieties is not uniform to all strata of the agricultural community: the innovators have emerged from only the upper strata; capitalist-type tenant farmers have newly appeared as the innovators; the non-cultivating landlords have become cultivators, at least partly, if not fully, engaging in direct farming operations or they have been leading their tenants to adopt the new technology. It is too early to say definitely which will be the dominant pattern among these at present as the Green Revolution is still going on. It is also to be noted that there is a case where the response has emerged from almost all strata of the agricultural community. However, a question can be posed—why is the Green Revolution appears to produce such organizational changes in other Asian countries whereas in Japan the organizational framework remained virtually unchanged?

Being motivated by this question, we have been interested in comparative survey of Japan's experience and what has been brought about by the Green Revolution. This empirical survey leads me to an analytical problem—some kind of relationship should be searched for between the type of agricultural technology and the pattern of agrarian structure. By agrarian structure I mean a combined distributive composition of the owner-tenureship of land and the size of farming operation. The problem is too big and too broad to be treated in such a small paper and here I will confine myself to the specific aspects of the problem which, I believe, are relevant to the question posed above. They are:

(1) Is it possible to identify the factors which are common to both Japan and other Asian countries with respect to the stabilized (a sort of equilibrium) relationship between the existing technology and the agrarian structure?

(2) Is it possible to understand in a systematic way the impacts of technological changes on the direction of changes in agrarian structure?

(3) What are the major factors which are responsible for the difference between Japan and other Asian countries in the response to the emergence of new technologies in agriculture?

A Simple Model

A most simplified but useful model for approaching the aspect of the problem (1) mentioned above is, I believe, a production function of the Cobb-Douglas type with specified behavior of producers regarding the self-evaluation of labor and land.

A number of cross-section measurements of an agricultural production function of this type give a fairly firm empirical basis, showing common features: first, the output elasticity of land is bigger than the output elasticities of labor and capital, approximating to the average relative income shares of production factors; and second, constant returns to scale is broadly revealed.[1] The point here is that with the existing agrarian structure the pattern of agricultural production of the community as a whole can be described homogeneously by such simple relationships.

I would like to draw your attention to two major features of productivity distribution which widely prevail in agricultural

---

[1] For example, my own measurements of rice cultivation in prewar eastern Japan give the following elasticities:

	Labor	Land	Capital	Sum
1937	.237(.017)	.555(.024)	.205(.017)	.997
1938	.280(.021)	.510(.024)	.155(.018)	.945
1939	.185(.017)	.622(.020)	.190(.014)	.997

K. Ohkawa, *Shokuryo Keizai no Riron to Keisoku* (Theory and Measurement of Food Economy), Nihon Hyoron-sha, 1945, pp. 145–164. Several measurements about Indian agriculture give more or less the same pattern. See A.M. Khusro, "Structural Change in Indian Agriculture", a paper presented to the Conference on Agriculture & Economic Development, Tokyo, September 1971, sponsored by the Japan Economic Research Center.

Table 1.   Productivity by Size of Farm, 1964, Japan.

Unit		Thousand yen per ha	Yen per hour	Thousand yen per worker	Thousand yen per ha	Labor hour per 0.1 ha
Size	(ha)	Y/B	Y/B	K/L	K/B	L/B
(1)	Under 0.5	510	75	235	100.0	679
(2)	0.5–1.0	479	96	301	85.3	495
(3)	1.0–1.5	421	110	336	70.2	381
(4)	1.5–2.0	378	124	360	59.1	306
(5)	2.0–2.5	344	143	341	46.0	241
(6)	2.5–3.0	343	158	348	41.9	217
(7)	Over 3.0	345	200	372	34.5	163
(8)	Average	402	115	326	63.9	350

Source: *Farm-households Economy Survey*, Ministry of Agriculture and Forestry, 1964, Vol. 7, published in 1966, which classifies farm-households into several types.   The source is for *Sengyo*, the farm-households excluding part-time farming.   The tabulation excludes Hokkaido.

Remarks: Y=net product, B=area of cultivated land, K=fixed capital stock and L=working hour, or number of workers.

production both in Japan and other countries in Asia under the operation of the functional pattern above described.   First, with regard to average labor productivity, its level tends to vary with the size of farm-operation in terms of land-holding: the bigger the size the higher the level.   Second, with regard to the average land productivity also we see a relationship to the farm-operation size, but the relationship is reverse.   As an example, Table 1 is presented.

Regarding Y/L, average labor productivity, a remarkable difference by farm-size is seen with regular association mentioned above, whereas for Y/B, average land productivity we see a narrower range of difference.   (To other terms, K/B and L/B we shall return later).   The prewar data, though lacking data for K show similar tendencies: taking the size group of 0.5–1.0 ha as 100, Y/L is 120–140, Y/B is 65–80 for the size group of over 2.0 ha for the 1922–40 period.   It is to be noted that a range of Y/B difference was much wider in prewar than in postwar years.

I believe such a size-associated distribution of productivity variation is important. In order to interpret it, two inter-related assumptions are introduced: one is that the smaller the size of farms the lower the self-evaluation of labor; and the other the smaller the size of farms the higher the self-evaluation of land. These assumptions about the subjective behavior of peasants can be positively treated in terms of marginal products of labor and land. Let α, β, and γ stand for the output elasticity of labor, land and capital respectively, and suffix 1 for larger farm-size and 2 for smaller farm-size. Assuming equal output elasticities, we have

$$\frac{\partial Y_1}{\partial L_1} = \alpha \frac{Y_1}{L_1}, \quad \frac{\partial Y_2}{\partial L_2} = \alpha \frac{Y_1}{L_1} \text{ and } \frac{\partial Y_1}{\partial L_1} > \frac{\partial Y_2}{\partial L_2} \qquad (1)$$

$$\frac{\partial Y_1}{\partial B_1} = \beta \frac{Y_1}{B_1}, \quad \frac{\partial Y_2}{\partial B_2} = \beta \frac{Y_2}{B_2} \text{ and } \frac{\partial Y_1}{\partial B_1} < \frac{\partial Y_2}{\partial B_2}. \qquad (2)$$

A state of equilibrium implies (1) and (2), namely that the marginal product of labor is bigger in farm 1 than in farm 2, whereas the reverse is true for the marginal product of land. If our assumptions are all valid, this confirms that the agrarian structure contains the differentials of marginal productivities with respect to labor and land at a state of equilibrium in the sense mentioned above. This is a kind of differential structure.

Under the operation of a single production function of the above mentioned type, we have

$$\frac{Y}{L} = A\left(\frac{B}{L}\right)^{\beta}\left(\frac{K}{L}\right)^{\gamma} \qquad (3)$$

$$\frac{Y}{B} = A\left(\frac{L}{B}\right)^{\alpha}\left(\frac{K}{B}\right)^{\gamma}. \qquad (4)$$

These present the relations between average productivities and factor intensities. By use of (3) and (4), it is intended to discuss the relation between what has been said and the role of capital. According to our assumption about the peasants' behavior,

B/L must be larger in farm 1 than in farm 2 and actually an empirical endorsement is given in Table 1 in terms of L/B—the fact that a much greater labor input per unit land area prevails in farm 2. With equation (3) this can explain a lower level of average labor productivity of farm 2 even if the capital intensity, K/L, is equal between farms 1 and 2. With equation (4) likewise, the higher level of L/B of farm 2 can explain its higher level of Y/B even if the capital-land ratio, K/B, is the same as between the two farms.

In a very backward condition of agricultural produtcion, the above simple interpretation may not be far from reality as the role of capital may be minor. As technological progress goes on its role becomes increasingly significant and productivities of both labor and land will be influenced by the inequality of both K/L and K/B as between various farm sizes. Under the assumed production function, however, the self-evaluation behavior of labor and land, with market prices of capital, will be responsible for determining K/L and K/B. If K/L is bigger in farm 1 than in farm 2, Y/L will be higher to that extent in the former. If K/B is bigger in farm 2 than in farm 1, Y/B will be higher to that extent in the former. In Table 1 we see a moderate increase of K/L as the farm-size becomes bigger whereas a sharp reverse tendency is seen with respect to K/B.

So far we have described a very simple model which can link the differential level of productivity with the structure of size distribution of farm holdings. The point is that the linked relationship is possible at a state of equilibrium, which can be identified under the operation of constant returns to scale. It seems to me that there has been some confusion in this respect. The well-known controversies with regard to possible polarization in agriculture have been majorly discussed in terms of productivity. Those in favor of polarization assert the higher labor productivity of larger farms while those against the polarization thesis assert the advantage of, higher land productivity of smaller farms. It is my view that if there exist differentials of evaluating labor and land in the agricultural community (and I believe these do exist in Asian countries), the productivity differentials need not necessarily be a dynamic factor and that, they can be a static phenomeon in a sort of equilibrium relationship with the existing agrarian structure.

Another aspect of agrarian structure concerns the owner-tenureships of land. Institutional factors are no doubt decisive in this respect. However, to a certain extent, this aspect can also be clarified by functional economic analysis. Here I will take up a specific problem of criteria involved in the decision making of a landlord who faced with selecting alternatives between two cases: whether to be an owner-cultivator or to be a rentier who simply receives rent without engaging in farm-operation.

Again assuming production function of the same type, the owner-cultivators' income, Y^*, is given by

$$Y^* = Y - L\frac{\partial Y}{\partial L} = B\frac{\partial Y}{\partial B} + K\frac{\partial Y}{\partial K}$$ or the income per unit area

of land is

$$\frac{Y^*}{B} = \frac{\partial Y}{\partial B} + \frac{K}{B}\frac{\partial Y}{\partial K}, \tag{5}$$

assuming that the owner cultivator pays wage rates which are equal to the labor's marginal product. He is a capitalist-farmer in this respect but he is not purely so as his income contains rent. The rent income is the income he would receive as a rentier, $Y^{\ddagger}$, which is

$$Y^{\ddagger} = B\frac{\partial Y}{\partial B}$$ or per unit area $\frac{Y^{\ddagger}}{B} = \frac{\partial Y}{\partial B}. \tag{6}$$

A comparison of (5) and (6) gives $K\frac{\partial Y}{\partial K}$ or per unit area

$\frac{K}{B}\frac{\partial Y}{\partial K}$.

If there is no difference in productivity between the two cases, it is clear that the case of owner-cultivator is advantageous. The point here is that Y/B tends to be higher for tenant-farmers than for large-scale owner-cultivators as we previously discussed with respect to farms 1 and 2. If the difference of Y/B is equal to the income to be imputed to capital, then we have a sort of indifference point between the alternatives. If the output elasticities are again given as equal to farms 1 and 2, we can have

$$\frac{Y_2}{B_2}\beta \gtreqless \frac{Y_1}{B_1}(1-\alpha) \text{ or}$$

$$\frac{Y_2}{B_2}\Big/\frac{Y_1}{B_2} \gtreqless 1+\frac{\gamma}{\beta}. \tag{7}[2]$$

This equation describes the criteria for the choice of alternatives by a simple relation between the ratio of land productivity on the one hand and the ratio between output elasticities of capital and land on the other. The numerical example is .338 for γ/β if the average of the values of three years is taken from the measurement of prewar Japan's case previously mention.

I believe what has been described above is something more than an illustrative exercise. Of course the reality of landlordism is far more complex and many other factors, both economic and non-economic, are involved in the criteria. Nevertheless, it is significant to note that the existence of a degree of land productivity of smaller size farms is the indispensable basis for the maintenance of rentier-tenant structure and that the co-existence of large and small size cultivators requires that there be little or no differential of land productivity between them. In this sense, the degree of land productivity is a crucial factor in identifying the relationship

[2] This is derived simply as follows. The difference of rent income per unit area is, according to (6) above, $\dfrac{\partial Y_2}{\partial B_2}-\dfrac{\partial Y_1}{\partial B_1}$, which is $\beta\left(\dfrac{Y_2}{B_2}-\dfrac{Y_1}{B_1}\right)$. On the other hand, $\dfrac{K_1}{B_1}\cdot\dfrac{\partial Y_1}{\partial K_1}=\dfrac{K_1}{B_1}\cdot\dfrac{Y_1}{K_1}\gamma=\dfrac{Y_1}{B_1}\gamma$, so that the difference of the two is $\beta\left(\dfrac{Y_2}{B_2}-\dfrac{Y_1}{B_1}\right)-\dfrac{Y_1}{B_1}\gamma=\beta\left(\dfrac{Y_2}{B_2}\right)-(\beta+\gamma)\left(\dfrac{Y_1}{B_2}\right)$.

which exists between agricultural technology and the agrarian structure—i,e. landowner-cultivator-tenant composition.

Impact of Technological Changes

Having described a static equilibrium relationship between technology and structure, let us discuss the impact of technological changes—a dynamic process.

Since the man-land ratio is the basic factor which determines the pattern of agrarian structure, the industrialization, particularly its capacity for absorbing rural labor force cannot be ignored. Rather we can discuss industrialization as the major dynamic factor but this would need a separate treatment. In the following this will be discussed only implicitly so far as is reflected in changes in our terms used in the preceding section.

To begin with the impact on the size distribution of farm operation units, first, two types of agricultural technologies are to be distinguished: the BC type, mentioned in the Introduction and the other mechanical or engineering type (M for short). The former is neutral with respect to scale while the latter has economies of scale. These two, however, cannot function separately. Every agricultural technology is a combination of the two and accordingly it would be better to speak of the BC element and the M element. The technology which has BC elements as its core is neutral with respect to scale whereas the technology of which the core is M elements has scale economies. The nature of BC elements is clear enough but that of M elements needs clarification as their function varies. At least two different functions are to be distinguished: one is substitution for labor and the other complementary with labor. These are not necessarily always separable, but in essense the former is the case for the technology of which the core is M elements and the latter is the case for the technology of which the core is BC elements. With these qualifications, for simplicity I will use the terms BC and M technology.

The state described in the preceding section is of course characterized by BC technology and the impact of its progress should first be discussed within this framework. It goes without saying that the observable indicator of the progress is yield or output per unit area, Y/B. From the viewpoint of the characteristics of BC technology, an increase in Y/B can take place in all strata of farm-size, without discrimination. In reality, however, we cannot necessarily expect such a homogeneous case. Larger scale farmers will first be the innovators. Using notations, Y_1/B_1 increases in comparison with Y_2/B_2—as a result of an increase in K_1/B_1 as mentioned previously. Such changes can take place within the existing agrarian structure to a certain extent. The eventual impact will be found in two different cases. First, if farm 2 could follow farm 1 in implementing the new technology sooner or later, there will be no change in the agrarian structure. Second, if the increase in Y_1/B_1 could not be followed by an increase in Y_2/B_2 a change will take place in the initial framework. For example if Y_1/B_1 becomes equal to Y_2/B_2 and this relation is stabilized, the assumed properties of the original state cannot be maintained.

In the former case we can assume that the output elasticities of production factors are eventually not altered by the impact of introducing improved varieties. If we look at the process of its diffusion, it may appear to bring forth some changes in the output elasticities. But this should be understood afterall as a temporary phenomenon. What kind of changes will take place in the latter case? Answer cannot be given in general but can be illustrated by the example of the competitive relation between owner-cultivator and rentier discussed in the preceding section. If the value of the ratio of Y_2/B_2 to Y_1/B_1, the left hand side of equation (7), becomes smaller than the value of the right hand side, to be a rentier is disadvantageous to the land-owners. There will be an incentive to be owner-cultivators and the agrarian structure will change.

From the viewpoint of the production function approach, it is not possible to say definitely what kind of change will correspond to the state illustrated above. It would be possible, however, to say that the output elasticities of production factors will eventually be altered but the production structure still retain the property of constant returns to scale. This can be conceived by assuming a situation where farm 1 and farm 2 have different output elasticities. It can be simply expressed by $\beta_1 < \beta_2$ as we should still retain the assumption that the self-evaluation of land is higher in farm 2: we have $\dfrac{\partial Y_1}{\partial B_1} < \dfrac{\partial Y_2}{\partial B_2}$ for a special case of $\dfrac{Y_1}{B_1} = \dfrac{Y_2}{B_2}$. Because of the lack of empirical studies[3], we cannot tell the actual contents of the elasticity difference by farm-size in general. I believe, however, it is meaningful to consider this case. The point is to answer the question why different technologies (defined in terms of different elasticities) can exist concurrently? Analytically this should be a state of equilibrium and the differentials of peasants' behavior, regarding not only self-evaluation

---

[3] Comparisons of the output elasticities mentioned p. 279 and those measured by Shintani for 1888–1900 ($\alpha = 0.215$, $\beta = 0.631$ and $\gamma = 0.154$) suggest a decrease of β and increases in α and β though slight. Masahiko Shintani, "Quantitative Analysis of Rice Production in the Middle-Meiji-Era," (in Japanese), *Nogyo Keizai Kenkyu* (Journal of Rural Economics), Vol. 42, No. 3, December 1970. Several measurements of postwar output elasticities show a distinct change—a decrease in β and increases in α and γ. For example, Kaneda's figures are $\alpha = 0.523$, $\beta = 0.315$ and $\gamma = 0.407$ for Japan 1952–1961. Hiromitsu Kaneda, "The Sources and Rates of Productivity Gains in Japanese Agriculture, as Compared with the U.S. Experience", *Theory and Measurement of Gains in Agricultural Productivity* 1967.

It is to be noted that the ratio γ/β in equation (7) had a historical tendency to increase first rather moderately during prewar years and then distinctly during the postwar years. To that extent, a force acted in favor of owner-cultivators. But this was not influential during the prewar period whereas the land reform changed the situation after the war. Based on these measurements, however, it is possible to think of the co-existence of different output elasticities analytically as mentioned in the main text.

of production factors but also elasticity of substitution etc. may be involved. In the following an answer will be given from rather an empirical point of view.

Given the pattern of agrarian structure, there are various factors which are responsible for differentials among farmers with respect to their capability of responding to new technology. These I would like to call *"differentiating factors"*. A higher level of BC technology needs an increase in complementary inputs like fertilizers, insectisides as well as for irrigation facilities etc. It goes without saying that there is great variation of financial capability to providing these supplies. Personal capabiities are also different with respect to implementing farm technology as well as commanding technological knowledge. These cannot be discussed comprehensively, but two points are particularly relevant to our discussion here.

First, the institutional aspect of the differentiating factors and second, the degree of gap between the level of new technology and the farmers' capabilities—these two inter-related aspects, characterize the patterns of impact. To begin with the former, let us take up, for example, a case where the lack of adequate credit organization is the major differentiating factor. So long as this is not reformed, the development of new technology will be limited only to the upper strata of the rural community, and no follow-up can be expected for the innovation. Such institutional *restraints* are sometimes influential and sometimes not according to the level and pattern of the initial conditions. In my view, as far as the BC technology is concerned, the major differentiating factors are restraints of this type. Japan's experience may be cited as an example of the case where such institutional restraints were not influential whereas in most of south and southeast Asia such restraints are influential. Coming back to the question posed before, my answer is that the co-existence of different technologies is possible if the institutional restraints continue to exist with the impact of new BC technology.

The degree of gap between the level of new technology and the farmers' capability involves various factors, all of which cannot be discussed here. What I would like to draw particular attention to is the thesis of borrowed technology in the contex of economic backwardness. When technology is introduced from advanced countries exogenously to an economically backward country, its level is high relative to the general capabilities of the poeple. This is true also in agriculture. Where the pattern of agrarian structure is differential in that the level of capability has a wide range of varience, naturally the differentiating factor will operate much more strongly.

This is most relevant to the present process of Green Revolution in south and southeast Asia, whereas in Japan BC technology has been developed, so to speak "endogenously" and its new level was not far beyond the capability of the mass of peasants.[4]

Now let us proceed to the discussion of M technology. In the Philippines, Pakistan, India and perhaps other countries, large-scale farming with mechanization has recently developed with impacts of new technology of the BC type. In prewar Japan no such phenomenon took place. It goes without saying that what has been said above with regard to the differentiating factors

---

[4] In the Japanese literature on the prewar agrarian structure the following arguments are often found. (1) A tendency of bi-polarization of agrarian structure in terms of operating farm size took place in Meiji Era: *tezukuri-jinushi*, landlords-*cum*-cultivators had expanded. (2) "Pararistic" landlords took the place of land-lords-*cum*-cultivators towards the beginning of this century. (3) Medium-scale farmers increased while both large -scale and small-scale farmers decreased in both their absolute number and relative weights, during the twenties and thirties.

My own view is as follows. The statistical data upon which (1) depends are not reliable enough to confirm the tendency of bi-polarization although the landlords undoubtedly were innovators. (2) and (3) can be explained basically by a tendency of $Y_2/B_2 > Y_1/B_1$ due to the progress of BC technology although the changes in agrarian structure was not so remarkable as has been argued. By international comparison, therefore, we can say broadly that the organizational framework of prewar agriculture had remained almost unchanged in Japan.

should be applied to the case of M technology much more strongly. Distortion of factor prices by government aid policy, it is said, furthermore has been aggravating the operation of the different-iating powers.[5] At any rate we see distinctly a co-existence of different levels of M technology in the agriculturally backward countries.

From the standpoint of strategy of agricultural development, desirability of large scale mechanization is a controversial issue. I have no intention here to join the policy debate. Two points are relevant to the present discussion. One is that mechanization in itself is the most distinct differentiating factor because of its associated economies of scale, and the other is that both in postwar Japan and in other Asian countries a leveling-up of yield or output per unit area appears to be an indispensable condition for mech-anization on the part of larger scale farms.

The first point is almost self-evident. Even in the case of small-scale mechanization which took place widely in postwar Japanese agriculture, measurements of the production function give results which suggest a tendency of increasing returns to scale.[6] I believe that large-scale mechanization in other Asian agriculture undoubtedly has scale economies, together with labor-substituting effects at least in the first instance. How about its impact on the agrarian structure? In answering this question, let us recall its initial pattern which we described in the preceding section—a state of no economies of scale. Surely the agrarian structure will

[5] For example, see Nurul Islam, "Agricultural Growth in Pakistan: Problems and Policies", a paper presented to the Conference on *Agriculture* & *Economic Development*, September 1971, Tokyo, sponsored by the Japan Economic Research Center.

[6] Kaneda's figures cited above (p. 287, footnote) of output elasticities sum up to 1.244. Yuize's measurement, also using a Cobb-Douglas type function gives the sum of output elasticities greater than unity: 1.150 for 1952, 1.200 for 1958, 1.197 for 1960 and 1.206 for 1962. See Yasuhiko Yuize, "*Nogyo ni okeru Kyoshiteki Seisan Kansu no Keisoku*" ("Measurement of Aggregate Production Function of Agriculture") *Nogyo Sogo Kenkyu* Vol. 18, No. 4, October 1964.

change in favor of larger scale farming. The discussion of the second point, mentioned above, will reveal its features more.

The degree of difference of output per unit area between farm 1 and farm 2, to use our terminology, has been described as the crucial indicator in the case of BC technology. This is understandable as it is originally of the land-saving type. An interesting fact is that in comparing prewar and postwar Japanese agriculture, the range of difference has been narrowed to a considerable extent. This took place with the progress of mechanization.[7] According to Khusro's paper cited previously a similar tendency appears to take place in Indian agriculture in the districts where new technologies have recently been introduced rapidly. I am inclined to point out a common factor in these that the progress of BC technology is indispensable in realizing mechanization—a required condition which is specific to Asian agriculture where man-land ratio is unfavorable. In our terms now we can have $Y_1/B_1 = Y_1/B_2$ or even $Y_1/B_1 > Y_2/B_2$ with increasing returns to scale. The self-evaluation of land should be lower in farm 1, so that we have to assume $\beta_1 < \beta_2$. This function leads us to the co-existence of different output elasticities of production.[8]

---

[7] Because of regional difference of climate, fertiles of land etc., national average observation tends often to be misleading in this respect. By use of the same Japanese data as for Table 1, we tested it by regional classification as follows:

Net product of farm-household per unit land by different farm-size is as follows (unit, thousand yen):

Region (ha)	(1) under 0.5	(2) 0.5–1.0	(3) 1.0–1.5	(4) 1.5–2.0	(5) Over 2.0
Tohoku	20.5	28.2	27.7	26.6	25.7
Kanto	41.3	37.3	30.7	28.0	27.4
Kansai	28.8	35.9	32.3	33.4	31.8
Nansei	27.8	26.9	26.7	23.8	23.6

The difference by farm-size in each region seems to be very minor except for Kanto.

[8] This appears to be inconsistent with the previous statement of a single production function with increasing returns to scale. This is in fact not necessarily a contradiction. It is possible to cover a range of varied output elasticities by farm-size by measuring a sigle production function with increasing returns to scale.

How about the eventual result of the impact of technological progress of this type? This is most difficult question to answer at present. However, in a longer-run perspective the following two points can be stated to be most relevant to the answer.

First, the mechanization for the sake of labor-substitution, as distinguished from the complementary use of machines with labor input, will face a certain limit of its expansion sooner or later. It is true that the price of machines at present is much lower as compared with the prewar Japanese case. But on the other hand, in most of the south and southeast Asian regions wage rates will continue to be low. Therefore, the relative factor prices will discourage the labor-replacement requirement—a fact which differs from the postwar Japanese agriculture, whose mechanization has developed for the sake of replacing labor because of the higher wages caused by the rapid industrialization.

Second, the expansion or contraction of large-scale farming based on M technology will depend much on the future performance of land productivity, output per unit area of land, of small-scale farms, which, in turn, will depend heavily upon the possibility of reforms of the existing differentiating factors of institutional-organizational nature. If these reforms will succeed in leveling up of land productivity of small-scale farms by accelerating the diffusion of BC technology, as has been explained earlier, this will discourage the expansion of large-scale farming by mechanization.[9]

---

[9] This statement assumes that the seed-fertilizer technology and mechanization are essentially separable in technical sense. For the validity of this assumption see Radolph Barker, "The Evolutionary Nature of the New Rice Technology", a paper presented to the Conference on *Agriculture and Economic Development*, September, 1971, Tokyo, sponsored by the Japan Economic Research Center.

INDEX OF NAMES

INDEX OF NAMES

INDEX OF SUBJECTS

295

Economic Research Series

THE INSTITUTE OF ECONOMIC RESEARCH
HITOTSUBASHI UNIVERSITY

KINOKUNIYA BOOKSTORE CO., LTD.
Shinjuku, Tokyo, Japan